AF326824

Literary Partnerships and the Marketplace

Literary Partnerships and the Marketplace

WRITERS AND MENTORS IN NINETEENTH-CENTURY AMERICA

David Dowling

LOUISIANA STATE UNIVERSITY PRESS BATON ROUGE

Published by Louisiana State University Press

Manufactured in the United States of America
FIRST PRINTING

DESIGNER: *Amanda McDonald Scallan*
TYPEFACE: *Whitman*
PRINTER: *McNaughton and Gunn, Inc.*
BINDER: *Acme Bookbinding, Inc.*

Grateful acknowledgment is made to the Office of the Vice President for Research at the University of Iowa for support in the publication of this book.

Chapter 3 was first published, in somewhat different form, as "Davis Inc.: The Business of Asylum Reform in the Periodical Press," *American Periodicals* 20.1 (2010): 23–45, and is reprinted by permission. Chapter 6 was first published, in somewhat different form, as "Autobiography as Professional Ethic: Fanny Fern's Vision of Literary Partnership," *a/b: Auto/Biography Studies*, 24.2 (2010): 210–34. Copyright © 2010 by *a/b: Auto/Biography Studies*, reprinted by permission of the editors.

Library of Congress Cataloging-in-Publication Data

Dowling, David Oakey, 1967–
Literary partnerships and the marketplace : writers and mentors in nineteenth-century America / David Dowling.
p. cm.
Includes bibliographical references and index.
ISBN 978-0-8071-3847-2 (cloth : alk. paper) — ISBN 978-0-8071-3848-9 (mobi) — ISBN 978-0-8071-3849-6 (pdf) — ISBN 978-0-8071-3850-2 (epub)
1. American literature—19th century—History and criticism. 2. Authors and publishers—United States—History—19th century. 3. Literature and society—United States—History—19th century. 4. Authorship—Social aspects—United States—History—19th century. 5. Mentoring of authors—United States. I. Title.
PS201.D696 2011
810.9'003—dc22

2011015346

The paper in this book meets the guidelines for permanence and durability of the Committee on Production Guidelines for Book Longevity of the Council on Library Resources. ♾

For Caroline

Contents

Acknowledgments

Instrumental to the production of this book was the insight and wisdom gleaned from fellow panelists and colleagues at a variety of academic conferences. Leon Jackson, with whom I was on the Thoreau society panel on transcendental economies at the 2008 Modern Language Association Meeting, lent valuable advice for the Emerson-Thoreau chapter. Laura Dassow Walls provided excellent feedback on this research in her role as chair of that panel. I owe her my deepest gratitude for including me on that prestigious panel. I also benefited from stimulating responses to my Davis research at the Midwest Modern Language Association Meeting, and Southworth-Bonner work at the American Literature Association (ALA) conference that same year. David Anthony, a fellow panelist at the ALA and scholar of literary commerce, taught me much about the intersection of the sensational public sphere, gender, and professionalism in antebellum America. His work has inspired my own interest in the cultural preoccupation with money in literary texts and the careers of their authors. In 2007, I was privileged to present material from the Fern chapter on a panel with James Machor at the Reception Studies Society meeting. His and Philip Goldstein's support inspired my early commitment to this project. My University of Iowa colleague Loren Glass deserves thanks for providing a valuable fund of knowledge and resources for the study of Ernest Hemingway and Gertrude Stein, whose partnership forms the subject of this book's conclusion. Another Iowa colleague, Linda Bolton, is a fellow LSU Press author and inspiration I have emulated since our first meeting.

My editor John Easterly invested his faith in this book from the beginning. Always supportive and buoyant, he brought life to this project, and its author, in myriad ways. As an author's editor, John's professionalism sets the standard for tact and diplomacy in today's academic publishing world. Finally, I wish to acknowledge my wife, Caroline Tolbert—who is in every best sense of the word a partner—for her roles as consultant, critic, collaborator, and muse on this and many other projects. Her vital warmth nurtured this historical vision of companionship to fruition.

Literary Partnerships and the Marketplace

INTRODUCTION

Care and Commerce in Antebellum Publishing

By the mid-nineteenth century, the delicate interdependence of the author-publisher relationship in America demanded the sort of risk and trust Herman Melville symbolized in the monkey-rope in *Moby-Dick* (1851). Queequeg, tied to Ishmael's rope, dangles above snapping sharks while carefully removing oil from a captured whale, a situation in which "individuality is now merged in a joint stock company of two," as Ishmael muses: "If your banker breaks, you snap."[1] While authors like E. D. E. N. Southworth knew her work for her editor-publisher Robert Bonner was a capital venture in which she played perhaps the most crucial role—for what is a publisher without a writer?—she was nonetheless driven by a curious combination of love and money, since her astute writing, like Ishmael's dexterity with the monkey-rope, was what Bonner relied upon for his livelihood. Author and publisher both held the monkey-rope at opposite ends, and thus enormous responsibility for their combined commercial fates—to be dropped helplessly among the waiting sharks below, or to reap the precious and profitable oil from the whale—as their management of it, like the rope itself, bore the tension of profound consequence. While love is essential to surviving the risks inherent in Ishmael and Queequeg's enterprise, it also shaped the business of the mutually dependent work of literary partnerships, such as Southworth and Bonner's. If, as Thomas Merton has said, "Compassion is the keen awareness of the interdependence of all things," then the mutual compassion of literary partnerships arose from the keen awareness of economic interdependence not only between literary partners, but also encompassing the whale-like mass readership in the ever expanding sea of the literary marketplace, forming a triangle of "reciprocal influence," as William Charvat calls it.[2]

Authorship's evolution from the sedate early system of protected patronage to such perilous "joint-stock" free market ventures coincided with larger industrial and economic developments—from innovations in printing press technology to ever expanding railways—and emergent businesses on the landscape of the nineteenth-century American market. Attendant to this new style of literary business was a series of social relations that supported it, casting into doubt the young nation's myth of self-reliant radical individualism through the exposure of the mutual dependence at its decidedly democratic core. An entire industry cropped up to support authorship's professionalization, as literary intermediaries of all varieties sprouted in the market, from agents, brokers, and collaborators, to mentors, editors, and publishers.[3] Intermediaries, or partners as I call them, were pivotal in the arc of writers' careers. Ralph Waldo Emerson, for example, is remembered now in part for alternately serving as Henry David Thoreau's publicist, editor, promoter, and confidant; he was not only prophet to Thoreau's disciple, but also the more commercially driven master to his apprentice. Their bond was not nearly as lucrative as that forged between the noncanonical popular magazinist Southworth and Bonner, editor of the nation's most profitable weekly, the *New York Ledger.* Bonner would also serve as a surrogate brother of sorts to Fanny Fern, who happily extols his virtues at the expense of her own cold-hearted brother Nathaniel Parker Willis, whose style of patronage she savagely lampoons in *Ruth Hall* (1855), the tale of her rise to literary stardom. Concurrently, Melville's struggles with the Harper Brothers and Evert Duyckinck—epic, fraught, and morally entrenched with fatal urgency—were tantamount to Ahab's wrestling with the whale himself in the final chapters of *Moby-Dick.* The mid-century literary scene did not consist of writers in isolation, but was animated by their headlong immersion into the new support industry of literary intermediaries. This climate gave rise to new business relations rife with the culture's preoccupations and anxieties—especially about the fate of sympathy and humanitarian compassion in the wake of surging capitalism—significant enough to find their way into the pages of the literature itself.

Pressure to survive mounted in the nineteenth century's new market for literature that was just as rapidly rewarding writers like Fern and Southworth with unheard-of profits as it was destroying careers of the artistically ambitious like Melville and Thoreau. Authors sought refuge through the people around them; Melville's older brother Gansevoort was originally his hardest-working and most zealous promoter, who initiated his career by spearheading the publication of his first novel, *Typee* (1846). Gansevoort's sudden death forced Melville to use his editor Duyckinck for the kind of support his brother had provided. Duyckinck subsequently became as close as a brother to the author in a relationship more successful personally than it was professionally; their tumultuous 1852 debacle, however short-lived, was imaginatively immortalized in the pages of *Pierre* (1852) and would prove disastrous for Melville's career. Economic survival is at stake in all of these relationships, some of them professionally contracted, and others informally forged, as in the case of Rebecca Harding and L. Clarke Davis, whose spousal connection enabled literary collaboration of the most loving, socially efficacious, and compassionate sort conceivable.

The formations of these literary networks and partnerships were based on both common artistic visions and commercial objectives, on both literary and economic interests. The new competition in the literary world for financial success in the market encouraged writers to look to each other for support, as they often formed circles of peers and coteries of like minds. Authors knew that "every man works better when he has companions working in the same line," as Henry James observed.[4] Melville clung to the ever-distancing Nathaniel Hawthorne for professional support. Thoreau's career evolved almost entirely under the wing of his literary father figure and mentor Emerson. Fern capitalized on her connections to the newspaper industry to turn herself into a successful author, while also retaining vital relationships among her literary friends, who included her lawyer and financial advisor. Harding married Davis based on his interest in her writing. His position at *Peterson's* ladies' magazine proved instrumental in the publication of Davis's work in this journal, which includes some of her most profitable writings.

Thoreau gravitated toward the Concord transcendentalist literary circle out of a desire to forge a career from his artistic vision. The established circle that published *The Dial* included influential and powerful figures in the literary world such as Emerson and Margaret Fuller, who represented connections vital to the success of a fledgling writer like Thoreau. Fuller and Emerson were not replacements for the traditional patrician patron of the arts in the way they supported Thoreau. Instead of wealthy, leisure-class genteel amateurs, Fuller and Emerson were literary professionals themselves. Their aid to the young Thoreau was not by means of large financial donations. They were instead exemplars of how to attain success in the field, providers of solid personal references, and mentors of the craft. Simply because Thoreau stayed at Emerson's house most evenings while he purportedly was sleeping in his self-made cabin at Walden Pond does not make him the recipient of eighteenth-century-style patronage. It does, however, make him the recipient of a new style of patronage that would guide his ventures into the Philadelphia and New York markets, albeit unsuccessfully, to try to find work as a writer.

I situate such literary partnerships within the historical context of the commercialization of authorship in the nineteenth century precisely to understand how those relationships were transforming at a time when literature itself was becoming entertainment for sale. My research animates the most consequential of those social situations within the context of six of the most pivotal literary partnerships of the American nineteenth century. The "opportunities and obstructions" of the social situations authors confronted indeed shifted over time.[5] The shift from more intimate and personal bonds between authors and publishers in the eighteenth century to the distanced corporate correspondence of the nineteenth century raises questions pertinent to my study: Who, if not the ever-distancing publisher, was in close contact with authors, doing the real work of guiding and nurturing their writing, and negotiating and communicating with them? Were these replacements—first editors, then, by the turn of the twentieth century, agents—somehow in a better position to advise, because of their distance from the larger corporate entity? Thus, were they in a better position to shape the aesthetic choices of writers? Did this alliance create new potential for affinity and warmth in the relationship, and if so, how was it expressed?

Certainly, editors replaced publishers in the book industry as the figures maintaining direct contact with authors before they did so in the magazine industry. This was by nature of the size and frequency of production and the relative returns on each product; a weekly like Bonner's *New York Ledger* had him in the role of both publisher and editor, for example, with a frequency of deadlines that placed him in close personal contact with his writers. This goes far to explain how Fern's and Southworth's relationships with an actual owner-publisher like Bonner could flourish as they did, in comparison to the cold and impersonal tenor of distrust that tinted Melville's relationship with the Harper Brothers. It also explains why Melville's editor Duyckinck, rather than any of his publishers, was the closest literary friendship of his entire career. As competition moved to a larger scale, "trade courtesy," or collusion among publishers regulating the market, eroded, giving way to a more laissez-faire literary market by mid-century. If the publishers were no longer expected to protect each other's interests, but to approach each other as savage competitors, much less "gentlemen," how did they approach their authors?

Publishers tried to maintain gentlemanly ties with their authors despite the growing corporate nature of their positions that naturally alienated them from each other.[6] But there was a substantial difference between magazine editor-publishers (jacks-of-all-trades) and the increasingly specialized big business role of book publishers, especially those in the large markets like Philadelphia and New York City (compared to intellectual niches like the Boston of Ticknor and Fields). Thus, Washington Irving would deal directly with his publisher in 1820, well before corporatization took over, while Melville and Thoreau had, by necessity, someone (politician brother Gansevoort, lawyer brother Allan, and editor Duyckinck for Melville; fellow author Emerson, editor and fellow author Fuller for Thoreau) to represent them as agents. Fern and Southworth had the luxury of close ties with their publisher, who also served as their mentor, editor, friend, and even financial institution (a savings and loan of sorts).[7]

Authorship thus functions in this book as a component of publishing history, which I treat as socially driven, diverse, and dependent on the economies of circulation in the literary market, a perspective that dismantles the myth of the autonomous romantic artist. I engage the pertinent and timely question of how authorial attitudes toward the market have transformed over time through a typology of literary partnerships from 1819 to 1870 as evidence of that historical change. In this sense, I hope to move beyond the confining binary that pits readers for or against self-promoting authors of this study; if anything, my project reveals their attitudes, like those of the other commercially successful writers of this book, to be innovatively integrated into an effective literary marketing campaign given the changing economic terrain of the book trade. I focus not only on how the authors' writing has been shaped by their primary literary intermediaries, but also on how the nature of literary partnership itself evolved over time toward a more fluid and open range of roles that often inverted, and in some cases shattered, conventional codes of behavior, particularly at the intersection of gender and business. Those relationships over time increasingly deployed imaginative methods by which to deconstruct art and commerce as mutually exclusive categories.[8] As they adopted those strategies for success, types of relationships—literary partnerships—emerged that served those strategies. This book's six case studies of literary partnerships expand our knowledge of authors' courtship, whether elegant or awkward, shrewd or naïve, of the proliferating mass readership, authorial methods prompted by each literary partner. The unique idiosyncrasies of those literary partnerships are of particular interest in this book, as they speak to each pair's digression from cultural norms, and their distinct recalibration of inherited business ethics for success at the peculiar, frequently bewildering crossroads of literature and commerce, of art and money, in nineteenth-century America.

Key moments in such relationships that affected the outcomes of literary careers and the content of the literature itself form my subject.[9] Such cultural production becomes apparent in the six case studies of this history of literary partnership featuring some of the most recognizable canonical and popular figures of nineteenth-century American letters. I expand Charvat's rather restrictive definition of professional authorship as providing "a living for the author, like any other job; that it is a main and prolonged, rather than intermittent or sporadic, resource for the writer; that it is produced with the hope of extended sale in the open market, like an article of commerce; and that it is written with reference to buyers' tastes and reading habits."[10] My study examines authorship's nonmonetary economies of exchange, considering writing both as a leisurely source of supplementary income and under production deadlines faced by authors like Fern and Southworth, a class of writers he openly dismissed as hacks. I am interested in all three categories, from the gratuitous champagne gift Duyckinck sent to Melville for his equally gratuitous hosting of him at his country home in the Berkshires, to Irving's exacting handling of his big contract with John Murray, to Southworth's remarkable productivity and seemingly endless string of salary bonuses and gifts publisher-editor Bonner lavished upon her.

Rather than unveiling the capitalistic machinations beneath the ideological cover of autonomous genius, I show how that image was designed to sell in the market, and how it was used, along with other key strategies, to package and promote literary merchandise. The capital companion of the author thus shifted during the early nineteenth century from patron, whose role was limited mainly to financial investor, to a confidant who now became a professional partner in literary enterprise. The shift was patterned after those in the broader market beyond literature, occupying support positions from managers to clerks and helpers in a growing army alternately bright and bothersome, the latter of whom Melville burlesques in "Bartleby, the Scrivener," and whom Hawthorne found insufferable and would artfully mock in "The Custom House." Intermediaries were not always a mitigating abomination, sullying the purity of the author-reader sacred bond. The youthful James saw the midwifery of sentimentality, which he believed should be spontaneous, and not solicited or "for ever tickled and stimulated," for "there is nothing so debasing as to become an agent between the supply and demand of the commodity."[11] Instead, such intermediaries provided authors much needed help: absolute independence was not only an aesthetic impossibility—the derivative, collaborative pastiche of inherited narrative materials ("a tissue of quotations drawn from innumerable centers of culture made up of multiple writings, drawn from many cultures and entering into mutual relations of dialogue, parody, contestation") has been influentially described in Roland Barthes's death knell of authorial autonomy in "The Death of the Author"—it was a commercial necessity.[12] Reliance on agents, friends, and contacts became the new means by which one negotiated with "the publisher." In 1820, Irving dealt directly with his publishers; by 1840, Melville negotiated first through his brother promoter, then always through his editor. Thus authorship was always already a joint-stock venture, even under patronage, but throughout the century grew ever more dependent on professional marketing management of a product and brand name for the mass market.[13]

Despite movement in the field of American authorship toward social history, many critics continue to pursue (perhaps unconsciously) the romantic image of the autonomous author. Fern scholarship is particularly susceptible to this, as her own emphasis on economic independence has deviated attention away from the networks of intermediaries instrumental to her success. Until recently, the same pattern applied to Walt Whitman, who carefully cultivated his poetic voice as a token of his singular autonomous charisma. However irresistible, such an approach obscures the very real social networks in which authors' careers were embedded. Whitman in fact relied heavily on friends for typesetting, print, and editorial work in the crafting of his seemingly self-reliant artisanal editions of *Leaves of Grass*.[14] The social matrix of the authorial condition for Whitman, like that of the authors featured in this book, also consisted of countless other figures of guidance, encouragement, and insulation from real economic harm. Whitman depended heavily on others, as his concern for fame and manipulation of his own publicity reflect how vulnerable, anxious, and needy for public approval he really was.[15] In the 1850s, communities of writers never mattered more, as those connections were indispensible to authors facing reviewers, audiences, and publishing houses. Such approaches have been somewhat rare until recently.[16]

I treat the subject of literary partnerships biographically, looking at how each of the authors was or was not adequately mentored or supported at crucial moments in his or her career. My concern is not so much to look at authors as passive subjects, or as patients to their doctor-like advocates who might be credited with making their careers healthy and powerful, or alternately blamed for their professional deaths. Certainly, the authors of this study received both good and bad advice during their careers; the crucial question is whether they acted upon it and why. Did they directly solicit such advice themselves, or elicit it through their own actions? Throughout the book, I approach authors' careers as developing in relation to their literary partners, not as symbiotic mergers in which individual identities are subsumed, but as members of a team, operating autonomously yet in tandem toward a common aesthetic and commercial goal. I look to the literature to find ways the authors imaginatively processed those pivotal professional interactions, assuming that, as Eudora Welty said of Willa Cather, "The events of a story may have much or little to do with the writer's own life; but the story *pattern* is the nearest thing to a mirror image of his mind and heart."[17]

This book deliberately includes a mix of formal and informal literary intermediaries, friends, spouses, editors, and other authors, precisely because of the range of insights that emerge about the culture as these roles bleed into one another. The central authors of this study similarly reflect the broad array of literary and popular writing from the period.[18] Part 1 treats the more formal employee-employer, author-publisher relationships. Murray, Irving's capital companion, was an actual publisher, while the title of publisher is used honorifically to describe the editor Duyckinck, who was Melville's longest literary partner. I have placed them in this sequence, in part, to show that in Irving's 1819 London, direct dealings between author and publisher were common, and by Melville's mid-century New York, such contact was unusual. These two case studies complicate and expand in the context of romantic and filial love, as discussed in Parts 2 and 3, well beyond that of worker and boss. The formal author-publisher relations in Irving's and Melville's careers were nonetheless anything but conventional, as they were always already freighted with images of the commercially naïve "poor devil author" in Irving to the willfully recalcitrant commercial rebellion of Melville. My concern is with how such attitudes impacted writer-agent power relations to describe a kind of topography of authorial partnerships in the context of nineteenth-century American literary business. Gender is significant in the project, as broader cultural roles determining power shaped these literary partnerships. My findings suggest that the more radically refigured roles generally unleashed greater potential for commercial success if they could maintain particular mainstream qualities, as in Irving's genial drawing room guest (masking his fully engaged capitalist maneuverings) to Murray's welcoming host, and Southworth's and Davis's adoring wives (masking their fully engaged business acumen) to their steadfast male protectors.

Kurt Vonnegut's rather ominous postmodern warning that "we are who we pretend to be, so we must be careful about what we pretend to be" bears a significant relation to my approach.[19] The six authors of my book were exceedingly careful about who they pretended to be, and in fact, made considerable adjustments to those roles to accommodate for capital incentive and the commercialization of the profession of authorship at the time. They adopted the very roles they enjoyed playing the most—from Irving's Murray-inspired genteel aristocrat and Southworth's legal reform crusader sparked by her lawyer husband, to Thoreau's embodiment of Emersonian ideals in his deliberate life at Walden Pond—in tandem with the literary partners who meant the most to them, a process profoundly complicated by the literary market's pressure to suit those roles to commercial interests. Melville was never so careful to avoid pretending to be an author as when he moved to the country and refused to sit for daguerreotypes, while Southworth's ungodly work ethic and attentiveness to her readers' demands were fueled by the larger sense of purpose behind her work to serve the *New York Ledger* and thus the man she loved, Bonner. Careful to preserve her autonomy, hers was no self-sacrificing romantic love for Bonner, but a capital companionship that naturally grew out of their mutual literary business venture. Amid the patchwork of the era's shifting social practices, the literary world retained and recoded (to adapt to the new lexicon and values brought by the market revolution) features of economic safety from the prior era of patronage, especially its intimacy and warmth as a reaction to the savage conditions of free market competition. Sympathy, as Adam Smith had it, was good business; most certainly, such compassion, as my case studies show, was also good literary business.

The emergence of a mass audience in the first half of the nineteenth century supports my characterization of authorship as evolving during this crucial shift in the development of capitalism from 1819 to 1870 toward an increasingly social enterprise, in which authors well attuned to the culture's ideological preoccupations with kinship and sympathy could manage these values to their commercial advantage, as Fern and Davis so masterfully did. Walter Benjamin's foundational theory posits that at this time "the conditions of artistic production underwent a change. This change consisted in the fact that for the first time the form of the commodity imposed itself decisively on the work of art and the form of the masses on its public."[20] Authors responded by assuming the roles of business manager, negotiator, and dealmaker, as potential profit margins grew along with that mass audience. The creative process was not restricted to composition, but extended on a continuum into the business world in which the author was no longer just a writer, but a person enmeshed in a network of the support industry, the middle men and women around the trade. None faced the market alone, because agency was essential to reach that public's increasingly specialized, sophisticated, and diverse tastes, because the market could not be fully accessed in any kind of effective manner alone. James's aforementioned lament about interference between literary supply and demand decries the amalgamation of author into seller—in his view, a profaning of the sacred union of writer and reader—in what is really a lament for the historical shift that necessitated literary partnership, which, contrary to his reactionary depiction, just as often provided authors with a muse, a light in their darkest hours, a creative sounding board, and a capital companion.

With no historical precedent for the new social relationships surrounding the professionalization of authorship, the market was abounding with emergent styles of patronage engaging the free market in ever unique and innovative ways. In this book, I explore how variations in approaches to authorial advocacy by literary intermediaries impacted the careers of six American authors: Washington Irving, Herman Melville, E. D. E. N. Southworth, Rebecca Harding Davis, Fanny Fern, and Henry David Thoreau. My purpose is to discover how literary partnerships—whether formal editor-publishers, or informal collaborator-consultants—reconfigured prevailing business practices in the literary market, and whether such innovations paid dividends. The personal dimension of each of these relationships displays how business dealings echoed social roles predominant in the broader culture at the time. In particular, the function of compassion (and its icy opposite) in these pairings, ranging from author-publisher and author-author to husband-wife, organizes the book into three parts: Irving's and Melville's pivotal and fraught struggles with their publishers; the stunningly efficient compassionate business of Southworth's and Davis's professional and literal marriages; and literary advocates as surrogate siblings and parents in the careers of Fern and Thoreau.

While Part 1 considers author-publisher relations in Melville's and Irving's careers that were alternately menacing and inspiring, marked by mutual finagling between trust, compromise, and radical self-interest, compassion drives the two literary partnerships in Part 2. Southworth and Bonner's successful platonic professional marriage was a business relationship from which love grew; the Davises' love encouraged a literary collaboration that would make history. Both partnerships redefined conventional spousal roles in a business context. Other familial roles are echoed by literary advocates in Part 3 as surrogate siblings in Fern and parents in Thoreau. Did these literary advocates' techniques of guidance and management effectively exploit established economies of circulation at the time? Emerson and, to a lesser extent, Fuller were faced with the delicate business of promoting Thoreau for market consumption despite espousing a radically anti-capitalist transcendental ethos. Was the brutal honesty and cruel kindness of Duyckinck toward Melville a form of tough love reserved only for male authors? Not in light of the abuse that Southworth took at the hands of her first employer, who sent her into the waiting arms of Bonner. Since authors by the mid-nineteenth century were exposed to the scrutiny of reviewers and the mass audience like never before, the work of intermediaries to navigate literary reception took on enormous significance. These intermediaries were the friends, editors, spouses, and fellow writers who "boosted their careers, created contacts with editors, wrote reviews and blurbs for their books, pulled strings and rolled logs, steered appointments, recognition, and book contracts their way."[21]

Thoreau's relationship with Emerson testifies to how the emergence of the mass market for literature complicated such partnerships. As Thoreau's rocky career attests, success did not automatically come to those promising youths endorsed and patronized by such towering figures as Emerson. Increasingly through the 1840s, and firmly by the 1850s, established authors had less power than they had in the 1810s to force their disciples onto publishers because of the proliferation and diversification of the market. Walter Scott figures, who could coerce publishers to sign whomever they chose, were a thing of the past. No longer could one figure dominate the literary market and publishing decisions in the way Scott could for many fledgling writers in Europe. Part 1, "Author-Publisher Struggles," addresses how the commercialization of literature shaped author-publisher relationships in the careers of Irving and Melville. Chapter 1 details how Scott's aid to Irving only partially paved the way to success for the first American international bestselling author whose career anticipated the future of the writer-entrepreneur's methods of self-promotion that would animate the laissez-faire market. The second chapter explores the triumphs and miseries of Melville's relationship with his editor Duyckinck, which yielded an opposite professional fate to that of Irving.

Though not punctuated with such strife, the pairings of Part 2, "Married Interests," also represent such inseparable, devoted literary partnerships that professionally refigure marriage. I examine Davis's collaboration with her husband Clarke to reform lax laws regarding the placement of sane individuals in mental institutions, an alarmingly common practice that victimized women in drastically disproportionate numbers during the nineteenth century. Also enjoying tangible results from their compassionate partnership were Southworth and Bonner. This chapter explores how Southworth's role in the relationship was far more empowered than some critics have led us to believe.

Part 3, "Literary Partner as Parent and Kin," moves from these professional marriages to focus on literary agent as parent and kin. Chapter 5 casts Emerson, with ancillary support from Fuller, in the role of figurative literary parent, engaged in the precarious project of nurturing the wayward career of Thoreau. Chapter 6 examines Fern's career in terms of her search for the ideal brother, a theme she openly pursues at the expense of her real brother in order to extol the virtues of her professional brother, editor Bonner. The chapter focuses on sibling sympathy as a model for social coherence and a call for the reform of models of masculinity. The book concludes with a twentieth-century case study of Gertrude Stein's literary tutelage of Ernest Hemingway. Their relationship—of Stein instructing Hemingway in the spare style he would become famous for—is particularly useful in showcasing the inversions of gender roles I discuss in chapters on the business relationships of the women writers, Southworth, Fern, and Davis. The Stein-Hemingway partnership shows how the humanizing potential of shared ambition brings with it the promise of elevated artistry, of a superior crafted product as in all the pairings of the chapters to which we now turn.

Part 1 ~ Author-Publisher Struggles

1

"THE ROMANCE OF TRADE"

Washington Irving, John Murray, and Genteel Capitalism

HOW WASHINGTON IRVING published *The Sketch Book* in England in 1819—the precise competitive maneuverings that played out his theory of "natural aristocracy"—has taken on a wide variety of significance for almost two centuries. The variance in the record alone is striking: David Pancost has insinuated that Walter Scott may not have even been behind London publisher John Murray's acceptance of *The Sketch Book*, while Stanley T. Williams takes it for granted.[1] Such wildly dissonant readings attest to the competition over placing Irving in history as sycophant to the British, or literary pioneer worthy of the canonization he would earn in 1848. The many retellings of that historical narrative, including Irving's own, reflect its highly contested and unstable status.[2] Each of those narratives assesses his business practice, which set the precedent for American professionalism in the English book market. Irving's monetary success has prompted investigation into his business ethic, with results ranging from Williams's 1935 condemning portrait of financial corruption, to William Cullen Bryant's 1860 flattering picture of commercial perseverance. Irving's economic success, indeed, was no secret, but its method was a mystery to many American authors at the time. James Fenimore Cooper, for example, was baffled by the British book market and asked Irving (despite apparent animosity toward him) to help him market *The Spy* to British publishers. Cooper and others understood that Irving had cracked the code, which they themselves could not decipher, and thus regarded him as a means to advance their own work.[3]

The precise historical account of the sequence of events that led to the publication of *The Sketch Book* in England has remained a mystery, even with the emergence of Andrew Burstein's long overdue 2007 biography. Burstein successfully rescues Irving's memory from the clutches of Williams's belittling 1935 two-volume biography that spawned overwhelmingly negative views of him and a lack of appreciation for his innovations for more than seventy years.[4] In an effort to revive interest in Irving—among the deadest and whitest men from the early national period's "soft focus" circle of authors that included Bryant—Burstein emphasizes the magnitude of that victory Irving won by landing Murray ("John Murray!" he cheers, faithfully echoing the tone of Irving's own account).[5] Murray was the most fashionable and powerful publisher in England at the time; Lord Byron's works bore his imprint after all. But for the specifics of Irving's dealings in England that launched *The Sketch Book*, Burstein draws mainly from Irving's romanticized rendition that prefaces the 1848 edition of *The Sketch Book*. He leaves out many crucial and telling details, settling for the brief, conventional explanation historians and readers have accepted—with one exception—since 1848.

In 1986, Pancost established the definitive account of precisely how *The Sketch Book*'s arrival on London bookshelves differed from the romantic tale Irving sets forth in his 1848 edition, published by the American G. P. Putnam. Pancost's speculation that "maybe [Irving] felt the truth of his business dealings was at odds with the way his readers perceived him" guides this chapter's central concern.[6] I argue that the truth behind those business dealings—particularly with Murray—ran counter to the carefree, dilettantish image of *The Sketch Book*'s narrative persona, Geoffrey Crayon, Gent. Irving embraced mobility and self-interest, but only with tempered restraint from excessive, vulgar ambition, values conveyed through "The Country Church" and "The Legend of Sleepy Hollow" in *The Sketch Book*.[7] The business ethic of genteel capitalism Irving carefully recorded in his journals and stylized in his letters and fiction articulates precisely why he would have wanted to obscure his real negotiations behind *The Sketch Book*'s English publication.

IRVING'S PUBLIC IMAGE

The preface to the 1848 "Author's Revised Edition" of *The Sketch Book* attempts to reclaim Irving's public image from his detractors, who often saw him as a conciliatory Anglophile and slick commercial author. Irving cast himself instead as an accidental capitalist of sorts, ill prepared for the commercially driven world of self-promotion and publicity in the

British book market. To obscure his aggressive efforts to capitalize on his popularity, Irving dramatized his struggle to put out the correct version of his works to his readers. His tale of racing the reprinters (Pancost calls them pirates, but their work was perfectly legal) to publication showcases Irving's mastery of strategic and calculated displays of effort. His tactics exude "the promise of play in classical German aesthetics" predicated upon the ways in which "performance is always tied to a strict economy of when and when not to show them that you're sweating."[8] He thus plays the befuddled neophyte in the British book market, acting more out of modest desperation than calculation in his solicitation of Murray without introduction. Upon Murray's rejection he puts out the work at his own expense with a bookseller who goes bankrupt, leaving the "poor devil author" totally without hope were it not for the generous aid of Scott, who heroically lands Murray for him. Scott thus serves his previously disapproving publisher his just deserts for a satisfying denouement that deftly avoids making Irving appear self-righteous or mercenary.

Misrepresenting Murray—his longtime publisher, friend, and colleague—as an enemy evidently was worth the benefit to Irving of appearing more American before his U.S. audience. In 1848, Irving was in the process of being canonized in America after establishing himself abroad as a celebrated American-born British author of sorts. The placement of his portrait in an honored spot next to Byron's in Murray's drawing room at 50 Albemarle Street attests to his exalted status in England.[9] Irving correctly anticipated the 1848 edition's key role in the initiation of his American canonization. The edition's runaway success for the next decade indeed gave Putman cause to mount an easily won campaign to canonize Irving, as Ezra Greenspan documents, first through a commemorative article in the *Atlantic Monthly.* To immortalize his most famous author who helped build his publishing empire, Putnam then struck a deal with Irving's nephew Pierre for a complete Irving biography in two volumes.[10]

So, with an ideal opportunity in 1848 to reestablish his image with his American audience, and with Murray safely dead since June 1843, Irving could not resist publishing Murray's first letter of rejection, exacting revenge after apparently harboring resentment all those years, as Ben McClary suggests. But there is no evidence in the letters and journals of even the slightest hint of nascent animosity that might account for his tone of "peevish jocularity" in the preface, as McClary calls it.[11] Further,

Irving abhorred the "petulant prefaces" that he had seen in other works.[12] What appeared to be a personal attack on Murray was really a veiled jab at England in hopes of being remembered as an American author. Such a nationalistic appeal was pitched toward the American audience with whom he now took up permanent residence after spending much of his career abroad. Residing at his Sunnyside New York estate with Putnam now as his American publisher, Irving projected his image to fit this defining moment. While eluding claims of conciliatory Anglophilia, Irving was also careful not to portray himself as a scheming capitalist either. Hence the preface emerges as an amusing tale of a romantic writer figure totally without commercial instincts tossed about on the sea of the British book market. Irving was hardly so rudderless: reprinters were never such a pressing issue with Irving, "nor was it so difficult to find publishers as he pretended in 1848, for he certainly knew more than a month before publishing at his own expense that Archibald Constable [Scott's publisher] was willing to publish *The Sketch Book* and share profits with him," as Pancost notes.[13] The slower pace with which Irving really made his decisions speaks to a more calculated plan.

In the English context, Irving's Federalism projected through Geoffrey Crayon played well. His politics were consonant with British distaste for mounting Jacksonian economic values associated with precisely the kind of speculative laissez-faire capitalism Irving himself used to publish *The Sketch Book*. The politics of Crayon, rather than those represented in Irving's business practice, assumed "that it was the personal duty of virtuous republican citizens to maintain [class] order and prevent the disorderly effects of the laissez-faire progressivism favored by democrats," as Walter Sondey notes.[14] Indeed, Herman Melville blasts such politics in his now well-known excoriation of Irving in "Hawthorne and His Mosses." The piece promotes supposedly wholly original native writers like Nathaniel Hawthorne as much as it eviscerates derivative, British sycophants whom he makes Irving, perhaps unjustly, represent. Melville responds to Irving's anti-Jacksonianism and his "imitation of a foreign model, and the studied avoidance of all topics but smooth ones." He laments that there is "no hope for us in these smooth pleasing writers" who do nothing more than "furnish an appendix to Goldsmith and other English authors." Melville's swaggering bravado takes over, as praise for Hawthorne builds into his famous rant against literary flunkeyism to England. He reaches a fever pitch of nationalism in his cultural call to arms against the British necessitating the expulsion from the home front of all imitative "graceful and fragrant" sissies who pretend to represent the United States: "no American writer should write like an Englishman . . . let him write like a man, for then he will be sure to write like an American."[15]

Melville's diatribe is instructive because it showcases a garish, exaggerated Jacksonian spirit at odds with Irving's transformation from social sniper of political phonies in *The History of New York* into an American-born English gentleman. Geoffrey Crayon, in this sense, constitutes Melville's real target. Indeed, Irving's calculated management of the social realities of the market aimed at economic success remained largely hidden from view, as it was isolated mainly to his private correspondence and journals. In fact, Irving privately shared much of Melville's own sentiment, as an 1825 journal entry shows: literature of the old world, he complains, "checks the aspiring vigor of our own country—Our youthful literature should have no ties & bondages—Should be left to run wild and unchecked like a child—but it is councilled & whipped and flogged into tame decency."[16] With such views hidden in his journal, and only Geoffrey Crayon as the face of Irving's successes, other American authors, such as rival Cooper, shared Melville's resentment. Irving raised Cooper's own manly ire against what he, like Melville, assumed was a wholly genteel identity generating the profits. Such profits instead derived from an elaborate economic ethos and careful plan for success blending romance and trade. Cooper refused to credit Irving's rational skill, as he famously groused, "What an instinct that man has for gold!"[17] Cooper's frontier heroes and Melville's "Carolina cousin" from "Hawthorne and His Mosses" personify the Jacksonian independent defiant spirit to lead the cultural fray against the English.[18] While appearing completely Federalist and anti-Jacksonian, ironically enough, economic individualism—however unrugged—was always operating from the beginning of what Burstein notes was "Irving's own long pursuit of financial security and his early comfort with commercial interests in New York."[19] For Irving, drawing room gentility, however leisurely in appearance, was a matter of business; his self-interest was carefully folded in the mantle of deferential respectability.

Like Richard Dana, one of the first reviewers of *The Sketch Book*, most have responded to Crayon and not Irving in this regard. The cultural icon appeared to be the complete identity, reflected in a "feminine, dressy, elegant and languid" prose style and selection of subjects that abandoned a more hairy-chested demeanor of "good bone and muscle." Dana defines his prose style to fit the public image: "his mother English had been sent abroad to be improved," acquiring a "genteel sort of language, cool, less definite and general."[20] The Irving that relished the hunt—its fast-paced aggression and dangers—would emerge fifteen years after *The Sketch Book* charmed the British in his full-voiced celebration of enterprise in *Astoria, or Anecdotes of an Enterprise Beyond the Rocky Mountains* (1836). This account of the fur trade was tellingly commissioned by the era's Donald Trump figure, John Jacob Astor. Thus the Irving who wrote *The Sketch Book* might be best understood not so much as a Jacksonian in Federalist clothes, but as everywhere attempting to intersect the two forces through a "natural aristocracy." The concept defends class mobility as a natural expression of ambition rather than a destructive undermining of social order and cultural achievement. Attainment of social rank functions as proof of one's worthiness to speak on behalf of public virtue and justify the social hierarchy. Irving reflected on his upward mobility in a journal entry that championed the self-made gentleman, as opposed to the gentleman of high birth: "We [middle-class Americans] have no hereditary distinctions [in England], but we enter the classes of society by virtue of our talents, manners, wealth &c. this is a natural aristocracy." Acquiring the title of gentleman through competition "as the trees in the forest" advocates a kind of capitalist, pre-Darwinian struggle for survival.[21]

Peter Antelyes succinctly identifies the central point of contention between Federalists and Jacksonians as "the role that self-interest and mobility should play in the American social order." Unlike the Jacksonians, "The Federalists favored republican values and saw in the self-interest of the marketplace an abandoning of public virtue." Federalists "preferred the preservation of the given hierarchical relations of class, land, and lineage, and saw in mobility an undermining of social order and cultural achievement. The Jacksonians, on the other hand, valued self-interest as a republican virtue in itself, and mobility as a means of a new, more equitable, and more successful order."[22] Irving felt pressed to justify his own mobility, yet was averse to advocating any new social order over established ones, a position well suited to his antiquarian tastes and reverence for the trappings of aristocratic privilege.

The question of how Geoffrey Crayon amassed his wealth is never raised in the 1819 edition of *The Sketch Book*. He possesses capital enough to travel abroad at his leisure but its origins are undisclosed in keeping with the gentleman bachelor's economic, if not ideological, free agency. Irving's public profile would similarly obscure his own ascent as an American author into the English book market. Irving's real professional dealings were overshadowed by Geoffrey Crayon's publicity until the emergence of Irving's own account of *The Sketch Book*'s publication in England in the preface to the 1848 edition. Until then, his public image basked in the spring glow during March and April 1820, when "it became clear that Washington Irving, most often answering to the name of Geoffrey Crayon, was a rising figure in London society."[23] The preface itself, as I discuss later, nonetheless romanticized that tale to keep Irving the rational businessman from public view.

The economic ideology reflected by Irving's public image flew in the face of the social-climbing capitalist ethic. Ichabod Crane's straining, overeager ambition is roundly mocked in "The Legend of Sleepy Hollow" in favor of an agrarian communalism of the sort championed in "Rip Van Winkle." Dame Van Winkle dies in a tense dispute with a merchant, while Rip finds solace in the non-acquisitive life of historical chronicler. As Sondey notes, the "individualistic desire for economic gain" is satirized through Ichabod because of its connection to liberal democratic progressivism.[24] Figures like Brom Bones and Rip Van Winkle remain fixtures in their communities, while Dame Van Winkle and Ichabod are devoured by their own avarice, dying respectively literal and figurative deaths for their economic sins. Most Americans at the time did not heedlessly embrace a capitalist ethos. Instead, they were attracted to such cautionary tales that warn against the dangers of excessive ambition while supporting the comfort and safety of tradition, both features integral to *The Sketch Book*. Americans, however, like Irving himself, were well aware of the economic sea change about them that was rapidly transforming leisure pursuits like sketching, storytelling, and writing into profitable commercial ones. This tacit understanding provided the current of tension underlying *The Sketch Book*'s seemingly blithe, apolitical, financially escapist image.

In the context of political strife and economic opportunity it makes sense that Irving would promote himself with the genteel bearing of one versed in "the studied avoidance of all topics but smooth ones." But was this the whole picture? What we see in Irving repeatedly is a unique accommodation of enterprise within romanticism's otherwise averse relation to economic friction and social advancement. "The romance of trade," the "business of the imagination," and "natural aristocracy" are concepts that typify Irving's capacity to conjoin these usually separate categories.[25] They coalesce in an uncanny approach to the literary market, particularly his competition and alliances, his audience and their sense of fashion. His capacity to wed romantic aestheticism with capitalist progressivism was essential to his success in winning an English market bent against American works and an American one flooded with popular cheap British reprints.

THE ART OF THE DEAL

London publisher Murray was cut from the same cloth as Irving; he was a polished gentleman skilled at cooling hostilities and negotiating deals. McClary notes that he "perfected a smooth reconciliatory technique to use on his authors" irritated with his failure to reply to letters;[26] Richard Ford used the phrase "buttered by Murray" in his letters from the time.[27] Jane Austen saw through his fast-talking, eager-to-please demeanor: "He is a rogue of course," she observed, "but a civil one."[28]

The blueprint of Irving's melodrama of Murray as the villain who might unfairly and arrogantly stop the publication of his best work emerges in his *Notes, 1815–1821*, a document that proves Grantland S. Rice's assertion that "the very composition of *The Sketch Book* was linked explicitly to the demands of the marketplace," reflecting "the asymmetrical desires for financial and intellectual independence."[29] A notation he would later use for his sketch, "Poor Devil Author," in *Tales of a Traveller* is revealing: "I of course thought of the most fashionable bookseller—every author makes for the fashionable bookseller," as he begins his quest innocently enough. With no letter of introduction, "I applied at the door, & was shown into the house I asked for Mr. M——," feeling insecure and socially intimidated enough to adopt a conciliatory manner. "My tone was lofty & peremptory," but of course this would not fool them, as "They supposed me some library Carmudgn & shewed me up stairs." There he found a "fine drawing room surrounded by books and paintings" demarcating a territory steeped in knowledge and culture. Despite such obvious signs of risk, he bravely "advanced to him and offered my work with an air to put to him at once at his ease; I asked 1000 Gs," setting up the deeply wounding rejection: "he looked at me from head to foot and continued writing his letter. I waited for some time, but finding no reply I indignantly walked downstairs." The next line of Irving's notebook is an obvious reference to John Miller, and the risk involved therein: "Publishes book and ruins himself."[30]

The emphasis on social intimidation and a missing letter of introduction in this story largely overshadows the real financial motive behind Murray's rejection. The quantity of writing Irving offered was hardly worth 1,000 guineas. In fact, he presented Murray with a total of only nine sketches in all, less than one-fourth the size of the finished text. Irving was not so much making a naïve blunder based on his inexperience with the English book trade. Quite the contrary, he was offering his work for the highest conceivable price as a buffer against Murray's down-bidding. Irving correctly anticipated Murray's hard bargain. The price of the copyright Murray would finally agree to six months later was 250 guineas, only one-quarter of Irving's original offer.[31] Thus Murray's rejection was not at all unreasonable in strict economic terms.

Murray's letter of rejection implies, however, that more than just the short supply of materials motivated his refusal. He showed distaste not only for the limited quantity of Irving's work, but also for the shallow, or "light," nature of its literary genre. Murray's comment on the lack of "scope in the nature of it" seems to refer to the "sketch" form. A more substantial, less desultory form, Murray said, "would enable me to make those satisfactory accounts between us."[32] Murray's own understanding of the dominant tastes of British readers at the time probably influenced his consideration of the genre. "Sketches" had not been compiled and sold in book form since the eighteenth century. Its earliest application to literature occurs in 1758 in John Armstrong's *Sketches; or, Essays on Various Subjects. The Sketch Book* similarly classified itself as the contents of a miscellany of essays on various general topics. Armstrong, like Irving, isolated one particular issue to each sketch, covering subjects such as language, genius, taste, and wit. Murray knew that the "miscellaneous" form was out of date, yet failed to recognize the market potential of Irving's fictional revision of the bland, yet immensely popular, nonfictional "travel sketch" published widely in magazines of the day. Irving tinted these sober catalogues of standard tourist attractions and historical cites with romance and fantasy. The anachronistic "miscellaneous" form of Irving's work, however, repelled Murray too strongly for him to recognize its application to this popular travel sketch form.[33]

For a man known for his endless chatter, Murray's galling silence—any writer's worst fear—sets up what Irving portrays in his preface as a desperate measure to publish with the upstart Miller. But how desperate was Irving really in his attempt to sign with Miller? Irving had Archibald Constable, Scott's publisher, waiting in the wings. Pancost wonders why Irving refused such an easy way into the British market, especially since he unconvincingly cited imminent reprinting in the periodical presses "as an excuse for rudely ignoring Scott's efforts in his behalf."[34] Constable, rather than Miller, could have easily accomplished what he presents as a pressing need of bringing his sketches "correctly before the public" so as to stop their insertion "occasionally in periodical works, with all the errors of the American edition."[35] Even less convincing was Irving's excuse that he feared *The Sketch Book* would fail to meet Constable's standards, assuming it was "very doubtful whether my work would be of sufficient merit or consequence in Mr. Constable's eyes."[36] Scott's support and encouragement voiced in his letters dated November 17 and December 4, 1820, indicate no such risk existed: "I have very little doubt that Constable would most willingly be your publisher," Scott wrote without qualification. "Constable will be happy to publish for you."[37]

Pancost accurately points out that this situation has largely gone unexplained in *The Sketch Book*'s publishing history: "Why Irving did not follow up is a mystery."[38] Irving's own penchant for economic speculation, I suggest, and high-risk investment schemes offer convincing clues as to why he uncharacteristically rebuffed Scott. Irving was playing the book market the way he had other high-risk ventures, to which he was notoriously susceptible. Moneymaking schemes had the effect of absorbing much of his literary income. In 1820, for example, he began to invest in French navigation companies with his brother Peter and against the advice of his older brothers. The losses of this venture did not deter him from a similarly fruitless 1825 investment gamble in the Bolivar copper mines. Given Irving's penchant for economic speculation and gambler's mentality[39] toward business propositions—after all, he planned to save the family business by *writing* as an American in 1820![40]—he deliberately risked holding out for Murray, the crown prince of English publishers. Within recent years Murray "had made cultural history by paying previously unimagined high prices for copyrights of works by Byron,"[41] as McClary points out. Signing with Scott's Constable would have confined Irving to an ongoing inferior association with the bestselling colossus of the *Waverly* novel franchise. The fledgling Miller was perfect for Irving, precisely because he could provide an immediate outlet for publication, whom he could abandon for more prestigious presses without risk to his reputation and ties in the powerful literary circles.

Irving likely anticipated that publishing with Constable also ran the risk of having readers assume that *The Sketch Book* was really written by Scott, a confusion that actually occurred even under Murray's imprint. Under Scott's publisher, *The Sketch Book* would have appeared to be another production of Scott's, a publicity stunt, and a lark written as Geoffrey Crayon. Certainly *The Sketch Book*'s desultory, breezy prose may have suggested the work was Scott's light-hearted ruse to readers. Lady Lyttleton, eventual governess to Queen Victoria's children, "was made suspicious by acquaintances in the literary world that the collection's real author was Sir Walter Scott," as Burstein notes.[42] Irving indeed felt flattered by such an association after the fact and expressed more gratitude for Scott's friendship: "I cannot help smiling at the idea that any thing I have written is deemed worthy of being attributed to Sir Walter Scott, and that I should be called upon to vindicate my weak pen from the honor of such a parentage . . . he has always been to me a frank, generous, warm-hearted friend, and it is one of my greatest gratifications to call him such."[43] Such instances were clearly happy occasions to show gratitude toward Scott and bask in the success *The Sketch Book* had already established. But Irving likely knew that initiating his marketing campaign of the book under such conditions would have overshadowed Geoffrey Crayon's impact on the public as a singular sensation from which he might draw full credit.

Irving was acutely aware that Murray's quarters possessed prestige far surpassing that of Constable's. Murray's shop attracted such elite and exclusive literary circles that even Scott himself frequented Murray's drawing room, indicating that the *Waverly* novels' popularity was attributable to his own name rather than Constable's. Such an icon of literary fashion as Scott clearly kept Constable in business rather than the reverse. Murray, on the other hand, was a name associated with considerable power in his own right. The benefits of club membership at the House of Murray included exclusive acceptance among the titled literati who convened there. That "invitation only" policy was precisely the one Irving violated as a "poor devil author" on his first offer to Murray: "Murray's drawing room is a great resort of first-rate literary characters; whenever I have a leisure hour I go there, and seldom fail to meet with some interesting personages. The hours of access are from two to five. *It is understood to be a matter of privilege, and that you must have a general invitation from Murray.* Here I frequently meet with such personages as Gifford, Campbell, Foscolo, Hallam (author of a work on the Middle Ages), Southey, Milman, Scott, Belzoni, &c., &c."[44]

Murray was not only more powerful and prestigious than Constable, crucially to Irving, he was more fashionable. Linking power with fashion, Irving compared the two publishers in a journal entry, favoring Murray, "whose shop is more fashionably situated and elegant in its air," over "*Constable, the Booksellers Shop,*" a rather shabby-looking establishment: "a dark, low, dingy shop—I passed it first without noticing it, expecting to find a spacious, striking book shop."[45] Irving aimed his book precisely at those guests of the bookseller's named in his journal. *The Sketch Book*'s success, he was well aware, depended largely on its ability to attract attention, conversation, and favorable approval within such influential circles. Further, Irving's own manners in such fashionable gatherings would dictate his success.

FASHION AND GENTEEL CAPITALISM

Irving concealed the business side of himself in his retelling of *The Sketch Book*'s publication in England to sustain his romantic public image. The private ethos driving that business guile sprung from an understanding of fashion not as mere vanity, but as the barometer of his culture and thus the key to his success. His acute sense of tastes and trends in his culture—as early as 1810 he had taken copious notes on the well-known Scottish clergyman Archibald Alison's essay on *Taste* (1790)—proved useful for cultivating an awareness of the demographic profile of his market and his audience's pattern of consumption.[46] His was not an idle interest in glamour, as his journals focus on the "Dress of some of the Austrian peasants"; the time and place of no less than ten portrait sittings; the tendency of English women "to follow French fashions"; "the edges and corners and angles with which a modern coat is so oddly and formally clipped out at the present day"; and a "fashionable drive on a hill outside of the walls." A meeting with the count to the emperor of Russia is memorable not for the politics discussed, but for the man's elegant deportment: "Count Pushkin—Russian—Aide to Emperor of Russia—tall—genteel figure—thin visage—close firm mouth—light mustache—a double voice."[47]

The code of the English gentleman shaped Irving's sense of the commercial potential of genteel manners. He made particular note of Richard Brathwaite's 1630 and 1631 works republished in 1814.[48] Their titles attest to Irving's interest in the subject: *The English Gentleman: containing sundry excellent rules of exquisite observations, tending to direction of every gentleman . . . how to demean or accommodate himself in the manage of publike or private affaires;* and *The English Gentlewoman, drawne out to the full body: expressing, what habiliments doe best attire her, what ornaments doe best adorene her, what complements doe best accomplish her.* Elsewhere, Irving's 1822 journal contains comments on Lord Chesterfield's long passages on fashionable dicta in *Letters to His Son.* Chesterfield originally wrote the letters in an effort to make this big, clumsy, bastard son into an unlabored, graceful, appealing man of fashion. More important than blood, conduct determined the title of gentleman, according to Chesterfield. This view reinforced Irving's sense of "natural aristocracy," rendering a transnational hybrid of self-interested commercialism and class mobility—Jacksonian capitalism—and Tory politics.[49] If the true gentleman's "stage was society, and occupation was the art of pleasing," according to David Castronovo, that stage was also the site of business in Irving's formulation of authorship.[50] The metaphor worked in the other direction too. A great fan of theater, the sometime amateur actor Irving understood "The Stage," as he wrote in his journal, in terms of "its importance in forming manners."[51] Indeed, some of Irving's deepest philosophical ponderings are devoted to manners, etiquette, "good breeding"—acting in public—and their effect on gaining and maintaining business connections for good "tradesmanship." Commentary on Chesterfield and the necessity of gentlemanly qualities (flatly stating at one point, "If you are not in fashion, you are nobody") sit beside passages from John Locke on the dialectic of truth and appearance.[52]

It was no coincidence that Irving was dubbed "the most fashionable gentleman of the day" when the book catapulted to success in the summer of 1820.[53] Irving epitomized London fashion at the time. A postcolonial American-born English gentleman, he was the zenith of hip and thus a true novelty in the British culture of letters. "Since I have published with Murray, I have had continual opportunities of seeing something of the literary world, and have formed some very agreeable acquaintances," he gushed in a letter to his friend Henry Brevoort.[54] "I am delighted with England," he wrote in a July 5, 1815, letter to Brevoort, glowing with characteristic Anglophilia and designating "The country enchanting" not for its landscape and architecture, but for its social graces: "I have experienced as yet nothing but kindness and civility."[55]

Irving's commercial interests bore the stamp of his genuine affinity for romance.[56] The genial romantic bachelor in love with all things English—from Shakespeare to a simple country church—nonetheless embodied what Byron called "the good old gentlemanly vice of avarice."[57] Capitalism and gentility were quite compatible in Irving's approach to literature. His personal aversion to political strife ("I have a general dislike of politics" and am "averse to political life," he confessed in a letter to Scott) resonated with his efforts to conjoin the forces of fashion and sales.[58] For Irving, writing *The Sketch Book* was an alternative occupation to the government position his brother William obtained for him in the United States. In a December 29, 1817, letter to William, Irving was careful to dissociate his literary venture from the hedonistic world of fashionable letters. He explained that his decision was carefully calculated for commercial success, since "every step I take at present is done with proper consideration. In protracting my stay in Europe I certainly do not contemplate pleasure for I look forward to a life of loneliness and of parsimoniousness and almost painful economy."[59] Irving knew the idle pleasures of the fashionable literary elite dominated the popular image of authorship recognized by outsiders to the book trade like William; the risk and hard work Irving mentions were rarely associated with the occupation. While on the one hand justifying his career choice to his more political and pragmatically employed brother, Irving appeals to the entrepreneurial spirit with which he initiated the project of marketing *The Sketch Book* in England. Ironically, the contemplation of pleasure and the world of fashionable letters necessarily became the terrain upon which Irving would sell his book. In this sense, pleasure was his business.

With fashion as his work and the key to his occupation—his favorite phrase to describe a profitable publisher, indeed his highest compliment, was "fashionable bookseller"—Irving faced unique pitfalls. "An author seldom receives justice from mankind," he complained in an 1810 journal entry, as "his good name is subject to the capricious influences of fashion." Authors must "contend with the captious sneers of the envious, the bickering of the party and personal prejudice, that it is ten to one if he is not defrauded of his dues." Even at this early stage, Irving was well aware of what a literary occupation really entailed. This hardnosed realism disabused him of popular notions of the power of individual genius to transcend market forces. The condition of being "constantly before the public eye and exposed to the full glare of scrutinizing familiarity" had its liabilities. Fame meant being caught in "moments of relaxation of listlessness of vacuity . . . the weakness and follies of other men . . . at times solitary and unsocial—often trifling with the frivolous and not infrequently the dullest among the dull."[60] In addition to the whims and scrutiny of an anonymous mass audience, Irving believed authors must "suffer" the sometimes insufferable celebrities and nobles, great people "distracting his attention and banqueting on his elegant and festive mind [with] the idea that they were patronizing him." He knew this to be a necessary evil of the trade, one involving sacrifice, as "A fine author always sacrifices time, reputation & real enjoyment when he mingles with titled crowds" for the reciprocal consumption that ensues when "the author banquets on the rich man's viands, yet the rich man in return expects to banquet on the author's brains."[61]

Irving entered into such exchanges, socially codified market relationships with real economic consequences, knowing full well the demands and expectations of him as an author to suffer the tedium of fashionable company. Such sentiment even inspired a streak of rural escapism in one entry, as he complained of urbane superficiality: "Society is painful to me. Whenever I am going around I feel neglected. I think there are none at my command. Shallow looks—faint smiles &c but when I get into the country I am another being—the trees look as green to me as in the days of my prosperity—nature never changes."[62] The volatility of public opinion to which authors' reputations are subject clearly was a strain on Irving. But the real worry was not so much the superficiality of marketing oneself in high society. It was his acute awareness of those codes and cues within its social matrix—the "shallow looks" and "faint smiles"—that would indicate polite rejection and further alienation from "the days of my prosperity" prior to the failure of the family business.

SELF-INTEREST AND NOBLE RESTRAINT

If genteel capitalism constituted Irving's authorial occupation as he defined it, replete with the threat of failure in the public eye, the key to his code of manners as a commercial method was the combination of restraint and self-interest. Indeed, if "the only operation we have is by public opinion," as he wrote in his journal, then it follows that some measure of "Secrecy in business but not mystery nor dissimulation" is necessary to maintain that public opinion.[63] Irving justified genteel restraint, not as an end in itself, but as a means to gratifying one's self-interest: "*Good breeding,*" he reasoned in his notebook, is "the result of . . . a little self-denial for the sake of others, and with a view to obtain the same indulgence from them."[64] An 1861 etiquette writer and "Lady of Rank" reveals how self-interest motivates the English gentleman's polite behavior of the period, a point especially relevant to Irving's blend of gentility and capitalism: "Not that you *care* the more for strangers by showing them civility, but you should scrupulously avoid the imputation of being deficient in good breeding; and if you do not choose to be polite for *their* sakes, you ought to be so for your own."[65]

Irving's ultimate goal was to achieve a level of popularity that would gain him financial independence, an alternative to the work-a-day grind he so bluntly rejected based on his distaste for "regular application and local confinement."[66] The sort of fame and admiration that Scott won due in part to his popularization of the code of the British gentleman undoubtedly served as a model for Irving. Scott's status as literary fashion icon is witnessed at the grieving that occurred upon his death. An unprecedented amount of material was published on both sides of the Atlantic to mourn his passing and appreciate his life. The *Richmond Enquirer,* for instance, brought news of his death in 1832 in an issue heavily bordered in black—a courtesy usually reserved for the president.

But to reach for such fame without proper restraint, as "The Country Church" warns in *The Sketch Book,* violates the principle of "natural aristocracy." Irving's ethos of capitalism and gentility surfaces in his analysis of the power structure of a rural community embodied by the church congregation. The sketch functions as a cautionary tale for the upwardly mobile, warning against improper displays of wealth. As a kind of guidebook for those on the brink of joining the ranks of the aristocracy, *The Sketch Book* repeatedly demonstrates that self-assured behavior is essential for acceptance among the elite. Irving-as-Crayon condemns a family at the country church for violating this code, as he chastises their "pedantry of dress which marks a man of questionable pretentions to style" and elite membership.[67]

The original fault of the family is in their dubious source of capital by "purchas[ing] the estate and mansion of a ruined nobleman." The flaw brings about their awkward conflation of financial wealth with class rank. They competitively eye "everyone askance that came near them, as if to measure [their] claims to respectability." They move "artificially," physically revealing their strain for higher status, "for their bodies in compliance with the caprice of the day, had been disciplined into the absence of all ease and freedom." Their fashion fails because of its transparency: "Art had done everything to accomplish them as men of fashion, but nature had denied them the nameless grace." The family's sin lies not in their attempt to signify their status through fashion, for Irving and his readers assume that social climbers should project an image of fashion slightly above their current rank. Instead, their downfall ironically lies in their inability to conceal such "vulgar" ambition. To their shame, their fashion fails to hide that they are indeed "vulgarly shaped, like men formed for the common purposes of life."[68]

Clown-like in his obvious intention to rise in status, Ichabod Crane, the "knight errant" antihero of "The Legend of Sleepy Hollow," is another parody of a shameless social climber. He too is "vulgarly shaped," but because Irving draws him as a caricature, Ichabod's unfashionable appearance is significantly exaggerated. His insatiable hunger as a "huge feeder" bespeaks his materialistic impulse to marry into the wealth signified by the lavish feasts served in the luxurious home of the Van Tassel family. Ichabod's character, like the family in "The Country Church," represents the upwardly mobile gentry who unsuccessfully attempt to join the elite. Ichabod continually reveals the awkward discomfort of moving from a previous position to another. Although he is a grown man, he seems to be literally in the process of growing into his too-large clothes "bagging and fluttering about him," which his disproportionate frame fails to fill out.[69]

Like his clothes, Ichabod's horse is equally unsightly and uncomfortable. Ichabod rides in a crouch "with short stirrups, which brought his knees nearly up to the pommel of his saddle," as if poised to spring into upward flight with "the motion of his arms . . . not unlike the flapping of a pair of wings."[70] Lurching forward, he appears to want to move faster (up the social ladder) and shows the stress of his effort to direct his mobility that the horse resists. When Gunpowder (his horse) does comply with Ichabod's command to flee his nemesis in the final scene, he "dashed forward, snuffling and snorting, but came to a stand just by the bridge with a suddenness that had nearly sent his rider sprawling over his head."[71] In this sense, the uncontrollable steed, like the forces of chance, exposes Ichabod's anxious desire to speed ahead as.the folly of inflated class ambition, by bringing it to an abrupt halt. The horses of the family in "The Country Church" are also beasts whose urges outstrip their station: "The very horses champed their bits, arched their necks, and glanced their eyes more proudly than common horses, either because they had caught a bit of the family feeling or were reined up more tightly than normal." "Straining and scrambling," they "start off almost at a bound," inspiring Crayon to conclude with a remark that could equally apply to Ichabod and also serve as a governing principle of Irving's ethos of genteel capitalism used to both write *The Sketch Book* and publish it in England: "I have no respect for titled rank, unless it be accompanied with true nobility of the soul, but I have remarked in all countries," as Irving's own journals bear out, "where artificial distinctions exist that the very highest classes are always the most courteous and unassuming."[72]

Irving justifies upward mobility through his concept of "a nobility of the soul" and his understanding of manners as the basis for social order. He was not naïve, nor blind to economic friction and political strife; he knew and suffered from the risks of capitalism. That seasoned business identity—not the vulgar, naïve social climbing of Ichabod or the family of "The Country Church," but one based on principled self-interest, mobility, and courage to face financial risk—was nonetheless precisely what romantic authorship demanded he keep from readers. He learned this from his first visit to Murray's shop in a lesson echoed in "Sleepy Hollow" and "The Country Church." The point is not that Irving knew crass materialism was unfashionable. Rather, he refigured genteel codes of behavior to accommodate for a more sophisticated, measured form of ambition than those of Ichabod or the church family. Such a refined business ethos meant that decisions were carefully plotted and planned with an eye toward maximizing long-term profits and maintaining social capital with allies through principled, gracious manners. His method of landing Murray illustrates this. Irving still veiled his business dealings from his readers for they would indeed expose his own careful strategizing within the literary marketplace that might be misread as excessive self-interest. On the prairie in *Astoria*, unfettered capitalism played better, but not in the British-targeted *Sketch Book.*

For Irving, the romance of trade paradoxically grew from his letters and journals that repeatedly express an unromantic, unsentimental view of writing. In the letters and journals, he is fully aware of his limitations in a literary sense and understands his writing as his capital, currency, and "solid credit." Yet he insists on fusing the admirable aspects of the genteel code with business method to civilize capital exchange that in the United States had been increasingly transforming into savagery. He emphasizes in his journal the Smithian virtues of "equity and kindness," of being "open fair and amicable; not trickery ungenerous, & malevolent—Displayed not in deprecating a character of rival, but by striving to surpass him in knowledge and diligence—always put yourself in the place of the person you bargain with & draw our rule of equity and kindness."[73] Ichabod and the family of "The Country Church" are blinded by their self-interest and wholly incapable of such sympathy.

Although its ethos is at work in the sketches, Irving repressed such genteel capitalism from his public image, especially as projected in the preface's romantic self-portrait. Pancost's intriguing proposition that "maybe he felt the truth of his business dealings was at odds with the way his readers perceived him" should now appear less tentative and more resolute.[74] The implications of obscuring the collaborations with a "real" capital companion in order to develop a particular persona both on and off the page point toward the stylized shaping of a public persona for mass consumption that responds to dominant assumptions about economic values, especially business ethics in a capitalist context. The implication for such mask-wearing is that it anticipates how show business would be done in the coming centuries in America, how celebrity personae would be carefully crafted as distinct from behind-the-scenes business dealings. Fanny Fern would master this, as she strategically omitted portions of her own rise to fame in her fictional autobiography, *Ruth Hall,* bringing emphasis to its more salable aspects. Irving should not be dismissed as a hypocrite or a mask-wearer in this regard, but respected as an innovator of the book trade, rearranging outmoded codes of authorial patronage into free market speculation and strategic bidding for publishers—"the romance of trade"—that ushered in the professional era of transnational letters. Such capitalist innovations involved in winning Murray harnessed the cultural potency of civility and the ideal of the English gentleman Scott's *Waverly* novels valorized. For in Irving, here was a new kind of Englishman: an American rising to the heights of English society and the literary market.

2

"DEAR DUYCKINCK"

The Business of Melville's Longest Literary Friendship

STANDING ALONE AT A New York harbor on June 26, 1846, awaiting the packet ship *Prince Albert* carrying the remains of Gansevoort, his devoted brother and prime literary intermediary, Herman Melville pondered his future. Gansevoort had done yeoman's work for him in England to amass support for his first novel, *Typee; or, A Peep at Polynesian Life* (1846), a work that may have never been published without the herculean efforts of his older brother.[1] A well-connected politico in the 1840s and recently appointed secretary of the American legation in London, Gansevoort had aggressively peddled Herman's manuscript, successfully landing it with the powerful publisher John Murray, and subsequently with the American house of George Palmer Putnam. The latter feat he achieved by winning the coveted audience of Washington Irving, and convincing him to peruse the South Sea adventure tale. With momentum for a prosperous literary career established, Herman anticipated a long and fruitful relationship with Gansevoort as his prime advocate, publicist, and promoter. Herman had grown accustomed to trusting Gansevoort, as only a brother could, with his best professional interests.

As Melville brooded over the professional implications of Gansevoort's passing, Evert Duyckinck, the Irvingesque dandy editor of Wiley & Putnam's Library of American Books series that had just accepted *Typee*, entered his life. The meeting richly symbolized the transition from Gansevoort to Duyckinck, from unconditional familial protection and promotion to the conditional compromises of professional patronage of the sort that characterized Irving's and Murray's dealings. Duyckinck did not initially receive him warmly, as Herman observed: "There was a civil scepticism in your manner, My Dear Sir, when we were conversing the other day about 'Typee.'"[2] By contrast, no such skepticism pervaded Gansevoort's natural faith in his brother's word on "the truth of all . . . the narrative."[3] Herman's dealings with the English book market also suffered the loss of his brother's smooth political diplomacy. One business letter to Murray two weeks after his brother's burial attests to Herman's discomfort with communicating his bald intentions on his own rather than through the pen of his trusted intermediary: "The decease of my brother Mr. Gansevoort Melville leaving me without any correspondent in London thro' whom to communicate with you, I waive cerimony & address you at once by letter . . . to inform you of certain matters connected with 'Typee.'"[4]

This unceremonious initiation into the world of literary business forced Herman to negotiate his own deals. He had previously relied on Gansevoort to buffer him from dealing with the myriad intermediaries in the publishing world. It was ironic, therefore, that the figure to replace his own brother was not another family member, but in fact a key player in the literary market. Earning Duyckinck's friendship and faith would be one of the most pivotal accomplishments of Melville's career. Theirs was the most valued and enduring literary relationship of Melville's life, though "adversity drove it underground," as Robert Milder says, amid the fiery reception of *Moby-Dick* (1851) and *Pierre* (1852).[5] It is very easy to pinpoint the cause of adversity that struck in the early 1850s. (Book XVII of *Pierre* speaks to that more eloquently than most critics do.) It is also just as easy to point to the murder of the genteel and prissy Glen Stanley in that novel, or the attack of Irving in "Hawthorne and His Mosses" as evidence of Melville's hatred of fashionable fops like Duyckinck at the controls of the literary market. But most lives, Melville's being no exception, bear a paradoxical complexity that defies organic unity and crisp binaries. Melville may have lashed out at the literary establishment, of which Duyckinck was a conspicuous part, but substantial evidence reveals the quieter truth that he loved him for life.

My chief concern here is to account for the depth of Melville and Duyckinck's relationship that might help answer why, for example, they were not permanently estranged after the upheaval of the early 1850s. (As early as 1856, they resumed their friendship, and by 1860, Melville felt comfortable enough to ask Duyckinck's help in publishing his book of poems, which he eagerly provided.) This bond, I argue, was forged through crucial events—especially the Art Union dinner and Duyckinck's two visits to the Berkshires—that were exalted, shared, transformational experiences. During such experiences they could appreciate and even exchange vital aspects of each other's identities. They emerged with mutually enriched cultural sensibilities and broadened visions of the mid-century American literary scene. They shared a satirical irreverence often identified in Melville, but seldom noticed in Duyckinck. Melville learned from Duyckinck how to be a bibliophile and would forever consider himself a Knickerbocker, albeit a sturdy one, with debts to Irving. Duyckinck ranked his outdoor experience in the Berkshires among the very best days of his life, and praised Melville's work in print more than any other of his contemporaries. Focusing primarily on the documents comprising the history of their relationship, I also consult passages from *Pierre,* which figure into how such seemingly opposite men became steadily more important to each other both personally and professionally in a friendship that oscillated but never ceased.

"A STURDY KNICKERBOCKER"

It matters that Melville never made the "clean break" from Duyckinck and his Knickerbocker roots many critics have assumed since 1975.[6] The connection colored much of Melville's literary palette, tinting his ambitious writings (*Mardi, Moby-Dick,* and at least the first half of *Pierre*) as well as his calculated pitches to the mass audience, like *Redburn* and *White Jacket.* Indeed, the critical commonplace suggests that the Duyckinck circle was Melville's foil, the conservative force repressing his true subversive and grandiose ambition, indeed the very inspiration for the characteristic rebellious, wild spirit in his work. The clubbish all-male strains of chauvinistic narcissism for which modern critics have dismissed the circle obscure the Knickerbocker sensibility—its irreverent political jibes, love of adventure tales narrated by bachelor free-spirits, and warm sentimentality—with which Melville identified.

Melville shared not only Knickerbocker tastes, but also Duyckinck's more serious obsession for establishing high literary standards in America through a cultural agenda that defined itself, often with nationalistic stridency, against England. To this end, members of the Duyckinck circle prided themselves on being well read and conversant on the latest political and cultural issues of the day, their classical educations equipping them to prove wrong Sydney Smith's ringing insult, "In the four quarters of the globe, who reads an American book? Who sees an American play?"[7] Even Edgar Allan Poe, among the most difficult critics to please, praised the strengths of the various group members like Fitz-Greene Halleck, reserving his highest acclaim for Duyckinck as "distinguished for the *bonhommie* of his manner, his simplicity and single-mindedness, his active beneficence, his hatred of wrong done to any enemy, and especially for an almost Quixotic fidelity to his friends." Poe mentioned others who had appeared in *Arcturus*, the first journal Duyckinck edited, which Poe hailed as "decidedly the very best magazine ever published in the United States . . . upon the whole, a little too good to enjoy extensive popularity."[8] His last qualifying clause would also apply directly to Melville's own career, from the metaphysically ambitious and drastically unpopular *Mardi* to *Moby-Dick*, a novel positively "too good to enjoy extensive popularity."

Duyckinck's headstrong defense of his lofty aspirations and idealism was downright Melvillian. Far from a hidebound reactionary, during his brief stint as editor of Wiley and Putnam's *Literary World* in 1847, Duyckinck "gave vent to his convictions by challenging his conservative adversaries and, equally vigorously, broadcasting the nationalists' credos," according to Donald Yanella.[9] Like Melville, Duyckinck suffered career consequences for his high aesthetic standards and moral convictions. John Wiley took exception to the particularly vociferous stridency of Cornelius Mathews in the journal's columns, issuing Duyckinck an ultimatum: if he did not dismiss Mathews, he would be fired. Duyckinck chose the latter, based on the principle of maintaining a journal of important and tasteful distinction that gained momentum under the pens of Henry Wadsworth Longfellow, James Russell Lowell, and Nathaniel Hawthorne. Unlike Robert Bonner's sensationalistic mass market weekly the *New York Ledger*, the *Literary World* reflected the classical readings Duyckinck repeatedly ruminated upon in his diary, including Ovid, Sir Philip Sidney, Voltaire, Samuel Pepys, Shakespeare, Niccolò Machiavelli, Johann Wolfgang von Goethe, James Shirley, the seventeenth-century dramatic poet, as well as writings of his own friends, such as Melville, Poe, William Gilmore Simms, E. A. Fitz-Greene Halleck, and Mathews.

One of Duyckinck's earliest literary impressions of Melville cemented the author's place in the Knickerbocker circle. Duyckinck spotted the influence of Irving, the original Knickerbocker, in Melville's *Typee* in a totally genuine appraisal that appeared in the editor's 1847 diary. "He is cheerful company," he wrote, and apparently "models his writing evidently a great deal on Washington Irving."[10] The compliment not only attests to Irving's commonly overlooked influence on Melville, but also signals Melville's kinship with, and thus membership in, the Knickerbocker circle. Although Melville's pitched diatribe against England appears at Irving's expense in "Hawthorne and His Mosses" (1850), his appreciation for America's first professional author ran far deeper than this famous straw-man attack. Melville's real target in that essay was not so much Irving as it was England (just as his sights in *Pierre* were trained on not just Duyckinck, but also himself, Bentley, and the Harper Brothers, as I argue later).

Indeed, Duyckinck detected Irving's own influence on Melville's writing in the above comment at the very beginning of Melville's career in 1847, a debt that would continue on through the novels, the magazine tales of the 1850s, and even his poetry. William M. Gibson, for example, says the stories are "working in the Washington Irving vein. 'I and My Chimney' (1856) has some of the sunny, easy quaintness of Irving," not to mention an idler husband and industrious, economically driven wife akin to Rip and Dame Van Winkle, "along with 'The Happy Failure,' 'The Fiddler,' and 'Jimmy Rose' (1854–55)." Though their psychological depth exceeds that of the characters of Irving, Gibson accurately notes, "the humor and ease and romantic melancholy, and the backward look are very much the same."[11] Even before the tales, as Hershel Parker shrewdly observes, Melville consciously wrote *Redburn* (1849) with Irving's *The Sketch Book* close at hand. Like Geoffrey Crayon, Melville's roving bachelor narrator is prone to "romantic reveries and to musing about the 'associations' of the names of remote places . . . the sighting of a wreck, an anecdote about a collision at sea, a visit to the reading room of the Liverpool Athenaeum [drawn from 'The Mutability of Literature'], a chapter on the poet Roscoe, sections on rural life in England [based on 'The Country Church'], a dismissal from a library, and even a ringing visionary passage on the future of America."[12]

Duyckinck himself also bore Irving's mark. Like Melville, he was something of a thinking man's Irving, playing the role of lolling idler, for example, after his dismissal from his editor's post at the *Literary World*. In a reflective diary entry, Duyckinck draws on a familiar Irving type who is humble, self-effacing, and admittedly economically useless, "I am an idler and I acknowledge it," yet with a self-consciousness and psychological self-diagnosis that echo Melville: "Albeit this is a calling which to enjoy in perfection one should not be exactly aware of it. But when it comes to watching half the morning on the battery, shouldering the trees and drawing circles on the ground waiting for some such paltry adventure as the arrival of an unmeaning Chinese Junk . . . what is to be made of it?"[13] Such sketches pervade Duyckinck's private writings, suggesting the extent to which Irving had captured his imagination. Duyckinck's highest public praise for Irving would be voiced in his commemoration of the author in his 1860 *Irvingiana: A Memorial.* Melville, Duyckinck, and Irving, perhaps most tellingly, were linked not only as literary kin, but their politics intersected decisively on the Astor Place Riots. They all signed the "Macready Card" supporting James Macready's right to continue performing Shakespeare without crowd interference. The measure came in the wake of a public protest spearheaded by rival actor Edwin Forrest in which Macready was booed off the stage. Macready's supporters included an odd mix of political conservatives and aesthetic radicals such as the decidedly democratic Young America circle of Melville, Duyckinck, and Mathews along with the more Whiggish older Knickerbocker brass of Irving and other elite businessmen such as lawyer and real estate tycoon Samuel Ruggles. In this case, the Astor Place Riots "entangled the traditional urban elites, downtown workers, and the new middle class, the New York City Whig and Democratic machines, the traditional cultural prerogatives of the urban elite and the Jacksonian popular audience as well as the new professional middle-class model of cultural expertise," according to John Evelev's litany of social and political interests at stake in the controversy.[14] The controversy also broke down many of the old binaries dividing Young America from Irving's Knickerbockers, revealing how they shared, as in the case of Melville and Irving, significant political common ground regarding the social and public function of the arts.

The most telling evidence of Melville's enduring debt to Irving and attendant career-long identification with the Knickerbocker circle came on February 13, 1890, one year before Melville's death, when he wrote the touching prose-poetry sketch, "Rip Van Winkle's Lilac" (published with the last collection of Melville's poems in 1924). From Duyckinck's early observation of Irving's influence on Melville, it is clear that "Melville's debts to Irving were real and were to deepen," as Parker mentions in his biography, and indeed span the entirety of his life as a writer from *Typee* to his last poems.[15] In "Rip Van Winkle's Lilac," Melville muses on Irving's profound impact on the course of American literature, counting himself one of many authors to pick up where Irving left off, "who peradventure may be poaching in that literary manner which thou [Irving] left behind . . . thy vision may now be such that it may even reach here where I write, and thy spirit be pleased to behold me inspired by whom but thyself."[16] The poem metaphorically figures Irving's fame in American culture and literature as Rip's lilac, which transforms into a tree during his epic slumber in Irving's original tale. Melville now imagines neighbors planting the flowers, in a wondrous Irvingesque tall-tale flourish, "Till, lo, that region now is dowered / Like the first Paradise embowered, / Thanks to the poor good-for-nothing Rip! / Some think those parts should bear his name; / But no—the blossoms take the fame."[17] This image of Rip is attuned to Irving's carefully contrived romantic public image of himself as caring little for industry and the management of his own career. The new generation of "poachers," with which Melville confesses complicity, appears as "the blossoms" reaping the beauty of Rip's legacy. The blossoms, however, not Rip, "take the fame" (a statement true of the *Typee* and *Omoo* Melville, but not of the fading celebrity of the mid- to late 1850s). Melville was likely pondering his own legacy and anonymity as he honored Irving's influence. From the vantage point of 1890 when he wrote the poem, Melville could recognize the generations that continued to bear Irving's influence stretching back to 1820, when *The Sketch Book* first appeared.

Reverence for the legacy of Irving combined with uncompromising ambition and high literary standards to form the common ground between Duyckinck and Melville. Duyckinck's circle received Melville so well not only because of the values he ostensibly shared with the group, but also because his contribution to the group was singular and unique, for he represented a new type of Knickerbocker. New Orleans critic Oaky Hall of the *Commercial Bulletin* astutely judged Melville "a sturdy Knickerbocker," maintaining the satirical connection to Irving, but also carefully associating him with Cooper and adventure: "There is a humor, and sparkle of rhetoric in his writings, which if he lives to be the man equal in years to Irving, Cooper and Paulding, will rank him as high on the chalk-notch of fame as they."[18] Melville thus represented the rough-and-tumble end of the spectrum of the Duyckinck circle, a real adventurer with a physical athletic bearing and tales of equally kinetic import.

A New York journalist describing the literary scene in an 1850 letter to a New Orleans newspaper said Melville was "taciturn, but genial, and, when warmed-up, capitally racy and pungent."[19] Indeed, Melville's connection with the Duyckinck circle was a means of spreading his originality and thus his fame, as Duyckinck helped link him in the popular consciousness to the adventure canon by calling him the "Defoe of the Ocean."[20] This encouraged other associations with world-class literature such as the comparison one reviewer made between *Mardi* and Jonathan Swift's *Gulliver's Travels*, capturing Melville's keen sense for weaving satire and allegory into outlandish travel narratives.[21]

Adventure was quite consonant with Melville's Knickerbocker identity. *Typee* and *Omoo* played on the sense of adventure as the "man about town," an image Melville himself was rapidly cultivating in his ninety-minute evening sojourns from six or six-thirty to seven-thirty or eight through the literary salons of New York City. Melville described *Omoo* to John Murray as featuring "'the man about town' sort of life, led, at the present day, by roving sailors in the Pacific—a kind of thing which I have never seen described anywhere."[22] "Roving sailors in the Pacific" tapped into the drifting bachelor image that Irving's fictional counterpart, Geoffrey Crayon, brought into vogue. Duyckinck loved the imaginative tropical relocation of the sort of nightly festivities he hosted and lived for, especially the Saturday night supper parties he held in his basement at 20 Clinton Place. Indeed, Duyckinck smiled knowingly at the bachelor's meanderings, rhythms, and social routines, as they appeared in *Omoo:* Tommo moved from his hut to the shed of the chiefs for relaxing conversation on his Polynesian island in the South Pacific "as if he were walking from the Astor House to the Saloons of the Racket Club."[23] Duyckinck's, a short four-block walk from his house on Fourth Avenue, was Melville's clear favorite of four gathering spots (which included Dr. John W. Francis's home on Bond Street; the home of N. P. Willis, editor of the influential *Home Journal*; and Frank's, an Italian hostelry at No. 5 Barclay Street, where Poe was a fixture) for the New York literati in 1847–48. Significantly, Duyckinck mentioned that Melville had been "a frequent visitor at no. 20" in a letter to his younger brother, George.[24]

Home to one of the largest and most impressive private libraries in the mid-nineteenth-century United States, 20 Clinton Place functioned as a resource of knowledge for Melville, whose ambitions pushed him beyond the romanticized autobiographical adventure novel into the metaphysical world of ideas. For whatever he lacked in formal education compared to the other Knickerbockers, he made up for through liberal borrowings from the Duyckinck library. Indeed, without that resource, Melville's corpus would look drastically slimmer in sophistication and scholarly import. The library combined with Duyckinck's connections to the biggest names in art, culture, and politics to furnish Melville with resources necessary for ambitious works like *Mardi* and *Moby-Dick*.

Perhaps the most dramatic introduction Melville had to Duyckinck's world of New York culture occurred on a pivotal night in their relationship on Broadway amid some of the most luminous figures in art and literature of the day. Duyckinck's connections and social graces were on proud display this evening of October 6, 1847, to celebrate the opening of several new rooms at the Art Union. The night's magic was pure Duyckinck, complete with the serendipity of bearing a "ticket of invitation" to the event and having the wherewithal to seize the moment: "Herman Melville dropping in, I carried him along, introducing him to Mr. Bryant and others. One of [Thomas] Sulley's bathing nymphs suggested Fayaway [the native beauty of *Typee*]. [Charles] Lanman introduced me to [William S.] Mount, the humorous painter . . . Mount and Melville were delighted with the living tableaus."[25] Melville, true to his nature, was drawn to the physicality ("living tableaus") of the art and enjoyed Mount's witty conversation, which potentially matched his own irreverent, "racy and pungent" humor.

Duyckinck's diary entry describing the event is among his longest, as it lovingly passes through the evening's events. Careful not to paint the outing as complete debauchery, he noted that "this occasion was purely canonical," defensively adding that the "punch [was] a liquor nowhere spoken against in Scripture."[26] Though signs of his doctrinaire side that would eventually alienate him from Melville surface, the entry nonetheless glories in plenty of sumptuous art, food, and big names to feast upon. He tells an amusing anecdote about an over-exuberant and unmistakably intoxicated speech made by George Colton of the *American Whig Review*, complete with Irvingesque caricature as the man "rivaled an infuriated Dutch windmill in the flourishes of his arms" with an equally circular story.[27]

Whereas Duyckinck personally escorted Melville to events like this, showing him his world in all its luster and excitement, Melville would do the same for him in the bucolic setting of the Berkshires. Duyckinck had introduced Melville to the art world through the dinners and the gallery showing. The editor's Young America circle brought the sailor in touch with the power brokers of antebellum American culture. Melville would return the favor and bring the dandy out of his familiar urban setting into nature. The bridge between the two was wit and laughter. Humor peppered their correspondence and released them from their conventional roles as author and gentleman patron. Duyckinck functioned as a kind of muse, inspiring Melville to conjure the wry exuberance from beneath his friend's staid editorial exterior. If he could make Duyckinck laugh, bring him to the Berkshires, and make him appreciate vigorous outdoor life, he had accomplished something.

On their famous three-mile hike on August 5, 1850, to the summit of Monument Mountain in western Massachusetts, with a group that included Hawthorne, his publisher James T. Fields, and Dr. Oliver Wendell Holmes, Melville struck a pose. After a brief rainstorm from which the group found shelter, Melville "bestrode a peaked rock, which ran out like a bowsprit, and pulled and hauled imaginary ropes" to the delight of the others.[28] The self-caricature was a great iconic moment both rollicking and boisterous—the soaking rain, the popping champagne, the exaltation of exertion and alcohol—within the context of the intellectual culture associated with Duyckinck's Knickerbockers. The two energies were equally fused at another moment when Holmes baited the group by paraphrasing the anti-American Anglophilia of Robert Knox's *Races of Man*, a provocation Melville all too willingly took on. Vigorously defending the American literature that very group represented, Melville's righteous rant anticipated that of the rural persona of the Virginian he would don for the same rhetorical purpose in "Hawthorne and His Mosses."

The effect on Duyckinck was unforgettable; he beamed on the way up to the peak despite reservations about traversing the rugged terrain. The rural charms of the trip touched him, perhaps making him feel the full influence of Melville, which he sensed throughout the fall season after his visit. He sent Melville a nineteen-dollar gift (approximately four hundred dollars in today's currency) of a dozen bottles of champagne in a basket with cigars ("Twelve . . . beautiful babies") as a token of his thanks, and perhaps a metaphor for the birth of a side of himself he had just discovered.[29] The strong effect Melville was having on Duyckinck appears in a letter he wrote to younger brother George: "I am getting less fastidious about many things," he confessed, "realizing that we have only a life interest and not a fee simple in the things of the world, finding more good in common enjoyments, thinking a good digestion infinitely better than an elegantly bound library. I have never enjoyed such extraordinary fine weather more than this season."[30] He expressed his appreciation for such "fine weather" by sending a thermometer to Melville the following summer of 1851, fishing for another invitation, which he received on August 29.[31] The second visit proved to be one of the most cherished events of his entire life, again equal parts inane drollery (seeking shelter from a storm in a barn without consulting the owner, the group began reading poetry aloud to the squawks of birds trapped inside, as they shouted "Turn 'em out!") and stimulating discourse on big ideas (Joseph Smith's company, he particularly enjoyed, as he found him a "thoughtful, sensitive man") as only a Melville experience could be.[32]

The two gifts indicate that Duyckinck's sense of humor was drier than we might have imagined. For as doctrinaire and idealistic as he was in his nationalistic promotion of American literature (his bizarre devotion to the self-righteous Mathews did not do him much good and, as alluded to earlier, in fact cost him a job), the freedom of the Berkshires under Melville's spell unleashed another side of him. Melville's outdoor sensibility, his robust pleasure in the basics offered Duyckinck an alternative to his role as "switch carrying dandy."[33] Duyckinck enjoyed the freedom from his urbane identity, a role taxing in its restraint and fastidious details, from clothing and a dizzying assortment of names and faces, to the finer points of prose in his authors' manuscripts and in the works he reviewed. The gifts were more than gratuitous. They speak to Duyckinck's deeper connection with Melville, which was achieved during a span of eighteen months as Melville's familiar "Dear Duyckinck" salutation replaced the formal "My Dear Sir" of his February 1849 letters to his editor. Duyckinck's younger brother George was Allan Melville's age, naturally drawing together the two sets of brothers in a fraternal circle during this period. Gansevoort had indeed been replaced in this new extended family.

The tone of Melville's August 1850 letter to Duyckinck after the editor's first visit to the Berkshires reflects the relaxed, jocose intimacy upon which their relationship now operated. In the letter, Melville roundly mocks him (in fun) for being trapped in the city with a kind of abandon and craziness usually reserved for brothers. "Do you drink Lime-water in the morning by way of stomachic? Do you use brick-bats for paper weights in the office?" he asked in a string of raucous questions leading him to an image of eccentric, bizarre behavior symptomatic of repressed city office life of the sort he would fully explore in "Bartleby, the Scrivener": "Do you & Mathews pitch paving-stones, & play ball that way in the cool of the evening opposite Astor-House?"[34] His reference to his own work of writing literally embedded in the stuff of the farm takes on the kind of domestic comic spin of "The Apple Tree Table," complete with the prospect of animal life inhabiting his writing desk: "Upon dragging [the desk] out to day light, I found that it was covered with the marks of fowls—quite white with them—eggs had been laid in it—think of that!—Is it not typical of those other eggs that authors may be said to lay in their desks,—especially those with pigeon-holes?"[35] The fun is also at his expense here, as he self-effacingly references his own authorial practice, with the eggs perhaps referencing the uneven sales and reviews that plagued his first five novels.

The letter gravitates back to what bonded Melville and Duyckinck so closely together at that moment: their shared experience in the Berkshires and the publication of Melville's first installment of "Hawthorne and His Mosses" in the *Literary World.* He playfully honors the Berkshire visit embodied by the champagne-as-babies gift right before discussing their literary offspring, the fruition of his essay in Duyckinck's journal. In keeping with the mood of Duyckinck's spirited (pun intended) visit, Melville riffs vibrantly on their "twelve . . . beautiful babies" in "that wicker cradle," as their progeny become a reflection of their relationship and even Melville's own best sense of himself as an author with "uncommon intelligence . . . in their aspect, and they seem full of animation & hilarity." Happy also with the printing of his essay ("far more correct, than I expected"), Melville finishes the letter promising to "drive to Hawthorne's to morrow, & deliver his parcels" which, unknown to him at the time, contained the most substantial progeny of his partnership with Duyckinck, copies of *Redburn, White Jacket,* and *Mardi,* as tokens of Duyckinck's appreciation for Hawthorne's hospitality upon that same summer visit.[36]

This relatively obscure letter to Duyckinck, I would argue, exudes the same kind of warmth and witty banter as those of Melville's celebrated correspondence with Hawthorne. Indeed, Melville's first known letter to Hawthorne similarly extends an invitation to relive the magic of the last gathering, metaphorically blending the alcohol with the literary: "we will have mulled wine with wisdom, & buttered toast with story-telling & crack jokes & bottles from morning till night."[37] He uses the same teasing and mockery, "Come—no nonsense. If you don't—I will send Constables after you," as with Duyckinck, showing just as much affection for his editor as for his new friend.[38] Indeed, Melville used the same mock-serious tone threatening to contact the police force in a similarly funny invitation to Duyckinck, reminding him to "by no means let George stay behind. If he does, I shall write to Chief of Police Matsell, to *send* him on."[39]

Melville's friendship with Hawthorne was exuberant, yet short-lived compared to his relationship with Duyckinck. The business between Melville and Duyckinck was real and ongoing, and profoundly influential to his writing and his life—with no shortage of affection, at least at this stage. Hawthorne may have been a new iconic, monumental literary celebrity to Melville, a kind of larger-than-life messianic savior of American literature, especially as seen in Melville's most bombastic moments of "Hawthorne and His Mosses." By 1850, however, just prior to the composition of *Moby-Dick*, Duyckinck's past with Melville was far richer, as it was imbued with the struggle and survival of navigating through the Scylla and Charybdis of the literary marketplace for the publication of five novels, every one of them embattled and difficult in their own way. Duyckinck had sheltered Melville from the wrath of the Methodists and John Wiley (of Wiley and Putnam), who lashed out at the anti-missionary sentiments of *Typee;* Duyckinck loyally supported and defended Melville in the press through the Toby controversy regarding *Omoo* and the critical outcry against the mixed form of *Mardi;* Duyckinck and Melville bonded in their mutual suffering through the concerted attack of literary charlatan and confidence man Thomas Powell. Indeed, Duyckinck, not Hawthorne, christened Melville "the Defoe of the Ocean," and publicized and nurtured his early career into renown. Perhaps the most telling difference from Hawthorne was that Duyckinck, hardly a literary snob, was his longest friend.

To say that Hawthorne and not Duyckinck was Melville's muse for *Moby-Dick* also misses Melville's willingness to share not only fraternal barbs with his editor, but his deepest melancholy. He wrote "Dear Duyckinck" on March 28, 1849, promising the proof sheets of the first volume of *Mardi*, but the letter exceeded such business. Melville's prose becomes lyrically nimble in describing "the Fourth day of the Great

Boston Rain, & how much longer it is to last the ghost of the last man drowned by the Deluge only knows."[40] His next line anticipates Ishmael's "damp drizzly November in my soul"[41] on the first page of "Loomings" in *Moby-Dick*: "I have a continual dripping sensation; and feel like an ill-wrung towel—my soul is damp, & by spreading itself out upon paper seeks to get dry."[42] Thus, Melville was close enough to Duyckinck to find a lyrical vein and follow it to the darkness in his heart, an unusual show of vulnerability between men, even for the relatively expressive epistolary conventions of antebellum America. That notorious melancholia would hit its nadir after the publication of *Moby-Dick*, and rise the next year to a fountain of fury in the pages of *Pierre*.

KRAKENS IN THE WAKE OF LEVIATHAN

It may have been Duyckinck who took the majority of the blows in *Pierre*, but bigger krakens lurked deeper. Melville's anger toward the Harpers, which had grown from their initial rejection of *Typee*, along with Melville's own ungodly capacity for self-loathing, formed the real root of his tirade. Like a brother, Melville went back to Duyckinck. The despicable exploitative Harpers, and even the beloved Hawthorne, by contrast, never played that role for him. The only "clean break" of the early 1850s was from Melville's British publisher. This was a time distinguished by Melville's anger at himself and the Harpers. These years were also notable for the speed with which Melville and Duyckinck recovered from the most visible dispute of their careers.

Parker blames Duyckinck's crony and right-hand man, Mathews, a curious suspect to be sure, for Melville's alienation from his editor in the early 1850s.[43] Parker argues that Melville saw himself becoming Mathews, a loathsome fate he carefully avoided. Melville, like so many others, tolerated more than he enjoyed the prickly, obtuse company of Mathews. The thought of taking on the role of subservient disciple horrified him. Mathews and Duyckinck were not at fault, however. Melville's target was more a sensibility to which they were prone. They could drift into self-righteous, inflexible indignation, energies especially potent in the Harper Brothers. Melville satirized this sensibility in much of his fiction, from the missionaries in *Typee* to Peleg and Bildad, the capitalist Quaker owners of the *Pequod*. Their pretentious pieties failed to hide their ruthless self-interest, much like the Methodism of the tight-fisted

Harpers. Variations of this attitude appear in Glen Stanly of *Pierre,* a figure fit for the gathering of dandies in "The Paradise of Bachelors and the Tartarus of Maids."

Melville's parody of Duyckinck in *Pierre* (particularly in Book XVII, "Young America in Literature," and Book XXI, "Pierre Immaturely Attempts a Mature Work") similarly burlesques such self-important high-mindedness. What distinguishes his attack in *Pierre,* however, is the exposure of his own similar flaws. His target was not the popular market that aggressively catered to the masses with no aspirations for high art like the one Henry David Thoreau aims at in "Reading" in *Walden,* which takes on weeklies like the *New York Ledger,* and sentimental fiction like that of E. D. E. N. Southworth. Melville was instead attacking Duyckinck's aspirations to high art and neglect of the mass market, a sin to which he himself confesses. Melville suggests his own inadvertent complicity in Duyckinck's arrogant trivialization of the realities of the literary market. In this vein, he vented on his and Duyckinck's own outsized ambitions in *Pierre.* This is crucial, as it makes sense of the function of Melville's fictional reviews in the novel—exaggerated opposite diagnoses of Pierre's actual condition—as barbs against Duyckinck's gaudy reviews of Melville early in his career. Indeed, Duyckinck struggled with the pressures of popularity just as Melville had. His Wiley and Putnam American Library series, according to G. P. Putnam biographer Ezra Greenspan, "was not a major success" since Duyckinck, not unlike Melville with *Moby-Dick,* "was aiming over the head of the mid-century reading public" and "occupied a publishing niche too narrow to guarantee significant commercial success."[44] The double-bind of popularity and quality plagued him as well as Melville. Like Melville, Duyckinck refused to sacrifice his ideals, which meant he was not always a commercial success, as George Haven Putnam's statement about the American Library series shows: "the publication as a whole produced a deficiency instead of a profit."[45]

In *Pierre,* an exaggerated version of the same problem that plagued Duyckinck emerges from the perspective of "the Romantic author imagining himself as high priest charged by god to bring forth Truth," as Andrew Delbanco says, whose embrace of the hermit artist role (echoed in Melville's permanent move to his country home in Pittsfield) only rendered "a blocked and stupendously pretentious writer . . . indifferent to a world that generously returned the indifference."[46] Before such ambition takes hold, Pierre initially has no sense of the professional demands of authorship in the marketplace. Pierre begins as an amateur, arrogantly assuming writing to be easy work, "and that it is not altogether impossible to receive a few pence in exchange for his ditties."[47] Pierre naïvely regards writing for money as a way of retaining his privileged past and avoiding a working-class occupation like that of "The mechanic, the day-laborer, [who] had but one way to live; his body must provide for his body." He instead gleefully embraces the idea of "letting his body stay lazily at home, send off his soul to labor, and his soul would come faithfully back and pay his body her wages."[48] Pierre's hubris is class bound. He naïvely believes his genteel background will exempt him from the work of "many a poor be-inked galley-slave, toiling with the heavy oar of the quill, to gain something wherewithal to stave off the cravings of nature; and in his hours of morbid self-reproach, regarding his paltry wages, at all events, as an unavoidable disgrace to him; while this galley-slave of letters would have leaped at delight—reckless of the feeble seams of his pantaloons—at the prospect of inheriting the broad farms of Saddle Meadows."[49] Pierre's arrogance is closely associated with Melville's own self-awareness that in writing *Pierre* he finds himself in the middle of a project (writing for the masses) he has terribly underestimated, perhaps due to the privilege and consequent complacency following his relatively easy success with *Typee*. Melville's new disrespect for popular fiction grew from his recent alliance with Hawthorne and the ruin of *Moby-Dick*, his high-art magnum opus (dedicated to Hawthorne himself, who famously denounced domestic novelists as a "damn'd mob of scribbling women").[50]

Melville's realization that *Pierre* was bound to fail springs from his own idealization of his craft as romantically insulated from the reality of material necessity within the economic networks of production in the marketplace. Melville gives full voice to this naïve, immature, and impractical sense of literary business through his protagonist author. Far from sending off his soul to toil while resting his body at home, writing becomes nothing short of self-induced slave labor to Pierre. His writing chamber is a dismal, cramped, prison-like place. Hardly a parlor for lounging and soul searching, it is instead a "most miserable room" with "a plank, paper, pens, and infernally black ink, four leprously dingy white walls, no carpet, a cup of water, and a dry biscuit or two." The dismal scene makes Pierre regard the work of writing in disgust and reproach as "the most miserable of all the pursuits of a man, and say if here be the place, and his be the trade that God intended him for."[51] Significantly, his anger springs from the economic pallor of "the trade that God intended him for," which casts the writer as a prisoner within "four . . . white walls" with his customary ration of bread and water ("a cup of water, and a dry biscuit or two").[52] In this sense, Melville was the architect of his own authorial prison.[53]

Whereas Melville mocks himself for aiming too high and alienating common readers in *Moby-Dick*,[54] the villains in *Pierre* bear the distinct marks of superficial fashion-conscious publishers and promoters. Ever fascinated with the stuff of material production that becomes literature (as in the paper mill of "The Paradise of Bachelors and the Tartarus of Maids"), Melville lampoons the process of literary production in a firm that "recently abandoning the ignoble pursuit of tailoring for the more honorable trade of the publisher (probably with an economical view of working up in books, the linen and cotton shreds of the cutter's counter, after having been subjected to the action of the paper-mill), had on the daintiest scalloped edged paper . . . addressd him a letter," which suggests to "dress your amazing productions in the library form."[55] "Library form" is an unmistakable reference to Duyckinck's American Library series. Duyckinck's dapper attire betokens his concern for literary appearances—the production and packaging of his authors (a concern, in all fairness, not without its literary as well as commercial significance)—as the very fabric of his publications.[56]

Melville's villains in *Pierre* arise out of his sense of being prevented by an unjust system from producing his very best work. Pierre's "burning desire to deliver what he thought to be new, or at least miserably neglected Truth to the world; and the prospective menace of being absolutely penniless, unless by the sale of his book he could realize the money" are also Melville's.[57] Emory Elliot has recently rejected a critical tradition of collapsing Melville and Pierre into one, by claiming that Melville's humor at Pierre's expense distances author from character, and that Pierre never resorts to spiritual or philosophical thought to rescue himself from despair.[58] Despite differences, the chief anxiety plaguing both was the prospect of writing "the Gospels of this century" only to "die in the gutter."[59] This is the dark, skeptical underside of Pierre's sunny resolve "to give the world a book, which the world should hail with surprise and delight."[60] Melville eerily foreshadows the rejection he received from London publisher Richard Bentley. Pierre's letter, like Bentley's, voices skepticism in the author's capacity to produce a book for mass consumption "Upon the pretense of writing a popular novel."[61]

Pierre's premature attempt "to write a mature book" is precisely the mistake Bentley suspected when Melville offered him the proofs of the new novel. Bentley doubted that *Pierre* would perform any better than *Mardi, Redburn, White-Jacket,* and *Moby-Dick* for good reason: these novels had brought the publisher a loss of 453 pounds. Bentley could therefore not afford to pay a lump sum for the copyright, and offered Melville the less than desirable deal of publishing his "new work [*Pierre*]" on a joint account with payments of half profits as they arose. Even under such a deal Bentley could not hope to reduce his losses by more than 100 pounds. Bentley's offer, sent on March 4, 1852, insulted and offended Melville not only because of its stinginess, but because his publisher had clearly lost faith in him as an author: "I fear," Melville's publisher told him, "your books . . . are produced in too rapid succession."[62]

In April, Melville wrote Bentley back to renegotiate the terms. In so doing, he argued that *Pierre* was an entirely new work, like nothing he had done before, "treating . . . utterly new scenes & characters; . . . and very much more calculated for popularity than anything you have yet published of mine."[63] Like Pierre, who begins his book with the idea of reinventing himself both personally and professionally, Melville promises that the author of poor-selling books can be forgotten: "let bygones be bygones; let those previous books, for the present, take care of themselves. For here now we have a *new* book, and what shall we say about *this?*"[64] With all the hopefulness and naïveté of Pierre, he attempts to deny and flee his past of public humiliation and rejection by asking, "If nothing has been made on the old book, may not something be made on the new?" Melville even goes so far in this appeal to suggest that *Pierre* appear under a pseudonym, "'*By a Vermonter*' say, or '*By Guy Winthrop.*'"[65] Such a new work warranted a new authorial persona, Melville reasoned, to disaffiliate *Pierre* from his now tarnished reputation. Pierre's own escape into the anonymity of New York City is the fictional expression of this professional urge.

Bentley's reply terminated negotiations with Melville, citing that not only would publication under his imprint require the original half-profits deal he offered, but that the novel would be subject to substantial revisions without Melville's consent—a policy of "silent-editing" which is humbling to any writer, to say the least. *Mardi* and *Moby-Dick* would have been more suitable for mass consumption, Bentley told his author, "If you had . . . restrained your imagination somewhat and had written in a style to be understood by the great mass of readers—nay if you had not sometimes offended the feelings of many sensitive readers you would have succeeded in England."[66] In *Pierre*, Melville lampoons such motives in the publishing firm of "Steel, Flint and Asbestos," referencing the stuff of cold manufacturing and construction materials for mass production. The fire imagery in the firm's name—steel and flint make sparks for fire and asbestos does not burn—implies that their business is logically and intuitively oxymoronic, wholly antithetical to the heat and flame of serious literature. *Pierre* nonetheless was Melville's attempt to capitalize on the very market he attacked; Melville knew domestic romances were selling in huge numbers at the time, and wanted to boost his declining income.[67]

Melville does not attack the "literary marketplace" as some monolithic entity in *Pierre*. His assault, while pitched at himself, Bentley, and the Duyckinck circle, was intensified by his dealings with the Harper Brothers. The seeds for his anger were planted early in his career, when in 1845 the Harpers refused to publish *Typee* because they were certain that not a word of it was true. In 1944, Melville's niece Charlotte Hoadley recalled that "One thing I do know, the Harpers refusing it calling it [disparagingly] a second 'Robinson Crusoe' embittered his whole life."[68] The Harpers' acceptance of *Omoo* in 1846 was in many ways Melville's vindication for their earlier rejection. Forging such a contract under such ill will was a bad omen. They would refuse his request for an advance for *Moby-Dick* in 1851, claiming that he owed them nearly $700. Stung, he promptly secured a massive loan of $2,050 for 5 years at 9 percent on May 1, 1851, driving him into deeper debt. After the disastrous reception of *Moby-Dick*, the Harpers responded to Melville's bid to publish *Pierre* by maliciously offering him an unheard of 20 cents on the dollar for all profits after costs were covered. Rather than refuse him outright, they presented him an offer he couldn't accept, a low-ball bid that aggressively undercut their usual half-profits arrangements, which was the going rate in the antebellum American book market. The problem was that Melville accepted their pathetic offer.

Despite being married to the well-to-do daughter of a judge (Lemuel Shaw), Melville had driven himself into nearly irretrievable debt to fund his literary career by the time *Pierre* was due to come out. His anger at his financial situation, stemming from his own reckless financial decisions, the Harpers' abuse, and the disastrous reception of *Moby-Dick* were all heaped onto Duyckinck, not unlike Ahab's heaping of all the world's sin onto the White Whale. This debacle typifies the transformation of the publisher's role from a confidant and friend like Murray into an increasingly alien and faceless business dealer. As proto-corporate publishers like the Harpers moved away from personal relationships with their authors, editors filled the gap by working closely, and even intimately, with their authors. Melville did not know the Harpers personally as he did Duyckinck; they were never capital companions. Much of Melville's venom, therefore, was directed at Duyckinck, a humanized target and the nearest representative of the literary market. The Hawthorne "dollars damn me" letter indicates, as demonstrated above, the emergence of an authorial self-image renouncing the popular market and his existing friendship with Duyckinck. His refusal in February 1851 to add a short riff (a "dash of salt spray," as Duyckinck called it) or pose for a daguerreotype for Duyckinck's *Dollar Magazine* ("to see one's 'mug' in a magazine, is presumptive evidence that he's a nobody") bears a much harsher tone, for example, than his playful pleading ("on bended knee, & with tears in my eyes, deliver me from writing ought upon this crucifying Romance of Yachting") two years earlier to be released from reviewing Joseph C. Hart's tedious and infinitely digressive *The Romance of Yachting*[69] for Duyckinck's *Literary World*.[70] Melville's anger toward Duyckinck could have been precipitated by a face-to-face argument, as Parker and Brian Higgins suggest.[71] However, the confrontation, if it occurred, did not in the long run "damage him more than his negotiations with the Harpers," as they claim.[72] Certainly writing Duyckinck into the manuscript as the joint editor of *Captain Kidd Monthly* was done on impulse, since Melville had written him cordially the same month he made the notorious additions to the manuscript. Though out of town during a proposed visit, "I will be glad to call," he promised, "at some other time—not very remote in the future either," kindly acknowledging Duyckinck's recent gift: "The nut-crackers are very curious and duly valued."[73] This from a man who penned the following sentiments that very month: "drop my arm now—or I'll drop you," Pierre threatens Duyckinck's fictional counterpart: "To the devil with you and your Daguerrotype!"[74]

Pierre thus threatens to obscure their enduring friendship that would continue years after the assault. The last blows in the debacle were Duyckinck's understandably harsh review, which was met by Melville's cancellation of his subscription to the *Literary World.* Melville would eventually settle into writing poetry, which, as Parker argues, was not an afterthought, but a serious and long vocation for Melville.[75] It is fitting, therefore, that he trusted Duyckinck in 1860 with his manuscript of collected poems "as a veteran and expert in these matters, and an old acquaintance, to lend something of an overseeing eye to the launching of this craft—the committing of it to the elements."[76] Duyckinck followed through in earnest, submitting the manuscript to two New York publishers who unfortunately rejected it.[77] This request for Duyckinck's assistance is neither sudden nor surprising since Melville had resumed visits to (and thus his friendship with) Duyckinck as early as 1854.

The 1852 fracas seemed an ancient memory by then, as the old magic of their friendship permeates Duyckinck's October 1856 diary entry of a Melville visit. Melville was in top form, racy and pungent as ever, peppering the evening with a scandalous tale of one Judge Edmonds and his entanglement with "female convicts," resulting in an "orgie of indecency and blasphemy"; the "atheisical" strains of Robert Burton's "passages on some sacred matters"; and of course, "sailor metaphysics" rounded out "a good stirring evening—ploughing deep and bringing to the surface some rich fruits of thought and experience." Melville said of Emerson, "I love all men who *dive*" into metaphysical oceans, and likewise, there can be no question that Duyckinck also held the profoundest respect for a man capable of "ploughing deep."[78]

By 1860, when Melville had covertly turned in earnest to writing poetry, Duyckinck was the one to whom Elizabeth revealed her husband's "profound secret," knowing that he represented her husband's best chance at finding a publisher for his manuscript simply entitled, *Poems.* Melville had left her and brother Allan in charge of placing the manuscript, as he had gone on a voyage around Cape Horn with his other brother Thomas. He had sincerely hoped that he would find a copy of his *Poems* waiting for him at his destination in San Francisco, but was sorely disappointed to find a letter from Elizabeth explaining that their attempts to place the assignment had miscarried. Significantly, Duyckinck provided all the help he could to meet that end, offering the manuscript first to the well-reputed Scribner publishing company, and then, undaunted by their rejection, to Rudd and Carlton. The latter's refusal inspired Elizabeth to prod Duyckinck to send it to Derby and Jackson, a publisher with family connections, "The first named being a brother-in-law of 'Toby' of Typee memory."[79]

There is no record that Duyckinck declined to pursue this lead; in all likelihood he did, but the tie to Toby (Richard Tobias Greene) was tenuous at best, for his memory had likely faded in the thirteen years since the publication of *Typee*. Further, Duyckinck's pitch, had he made one, may have missed the mark because Toby's brother-in-law was not James Derby, the firm's partner, but Chauncey, one of the four Derby brothers. Lizzie's slip may have been more consequential than trivial. Such networking, termed "social linking" in Robert Putnam's theory of social capital building, pays greater financial dividends than internal bonding with an exclusive coterie, but only if the connection is manifestly precise and valid.[80] An approach that misidentifies the familial connection upon which to establish a business proposition appears disingenuous and often derails trust. Thus the prospect of Duyckinck rushing into James Derby's office to persuade him to accept a manuscript because the publisher was the brother-in-law, when in fact he was not, of Melville's shipmate from thirteen years prior was doubly doomed to fail. This is all clear in hindsight, as it must not be forgotten that it would have been unconscionable for Duyckinck not to pitch the manuscript to Derby, armed as he assumed he was with Lizzy's apparently powerful familial and literary connections.

Duyckinck was not likely to have withdrawn support for Melville out of spite for past differences. Indeed, just prior to this failed attempt at placing *Poems* in 1860, there is ample evidence of the editor's good will and support toward his former author. Duyckinck wrote to his brother George in July 1859, reporting that "Allan Melville had been here with an entertaining account of his Virginia travels," a visit made of course due to the good standing of Herman with his editor, who jocosely added in the letter that "Herman is doing nothing in particular."[81] This was certainly intended to sound silly to Evert's brother George. But it also reveals Evert's willingness to play the editor role to Melville's author at this late date, checking on, and complaining about, his writer's productivity. Interestingly, this was the time when Melville was hard at work on the *Poems* manuscript, which was effectively kept secret from Duyckinck, who would not find out about his project until the 1860 letter from Lizzie. Perhaps he sensed a covert operation underfoot, one that would intimately involve him as the intermediary playing an instrumental role in placing the manuscript. In September 1859, Duyckinck reminded brother George, "You will of course see Melville and as certainly give him my regards."[82] In January 1860, Melville borrowed several books from Duyckinck, an otherwise perfunctory exchange Duyckinck recorded with relish. Conjuring up old times, the staid editor vicariously gloried in the colorful audacity of Melville's quip that "the mealy mouthed habit of writing of human nature of the present day would not tolerate the plain speaking of Johnson, for instance, in the Rambler—who does not hesitate to use the word *malignity!*"[83]

The duo again were spending the sweet spot of summer together in 1861, on July 1 visiting the navy yard for the reception of James H. Ward, captain of the ship *North Carolina.* The occasion prompted Duyckinck to write a somber and reflective entry in his diary about the onset of war ("who shall fathom the iniquity of this rebellion?" he asks). Two days later the mood lightened, as younger brothers Allan and George arrived for an excursion to New Rochelle, a whimsical escape as lyrical as the Monument Mountain hike. They enjoyed "hospitable open handed entertainment—the beauty of nature, the tranquility of the landscape stretching to the blue waters of the sound reflecting the azure of the skies a happy relief to the war agitation of the times." Celestial rather than martial fireworks lit up the sky, as a comet flashed forth "a brilliant apparition in the north," in George's words. Following the dazzling spectacle they indulged in "A stroll through the woods a rest on the rocks, a glass of blackberry wine . . . a long talk on the piazza looking out on the Sound—a fine dinner."[84] It was all he could do to tear himself away from the temptation to spend the evening at the home of their friend and host Richard Lathers.

By 1862, Melville was still freely borrowing from the Duyckinck library, and warmly inviting his editor for social visits, brewing "some whiskey punch" so that they might "settle the affairs of the universe over it."[85] Evidence surfaces as late as 1863 that Duyckinck not only knew of the ambition that went into *Moby-Dick,* but had a nuanced enough appreciation of it to recognize Melville's ideal reader in Hugh Willoughby during one social occasion on Fire Island. Duyckinck saw in Willoughby one who "when he is not telling stories or chuckling or talking with his boy Hugh [Jr.] . . . he is reading Moby Dick and is just such a reader as Melville would be delighted with and make a chapter of."[86] This could hardly have come from a man permanently offended by *Moby-Dick* as an assault on his moral righteousness, as Parker has suggested, nor one always put off by a sense of the novel as violating his ideal of genial literature for the masses he envisioned for Putnam's Library of American Books series, nor forever jealous of Melville publishing his masterpiece with Harper's, as Edward Widmer imagines.[87] Widmer's notion of Duyckinck as "a pioneering but flawed broker of American culture, incapable of going the distance with Melville, but important for inspiring him," misses the final two decades of their lives together. Those decades were not marked by spectacular fireworks in publication history, but with the quiet failure of *Poems* and the bolder achievements of *Battle Pieces* (1866) and *Clarel* (1876). The depth of their bond at this time is well illustrated by the candor with which Melville rejects Duyckinck's request to write a book review for him. "Though I would like to please you, I have not spirit enough," he says, graciously declining. In the next breath he invites him to visit with his brother Allan and his family: "if convenient, pray join us."[88] In 1869, the two attended the trustees of Sailor's Snug Harbor annual dinner to close the last big social event they shared of the 1860s. It would also be the last public engagement they would attend together, fittingly on the occasion of erecting a monument, a massive sculpture, in honor of the nautical life.

The sincerity of such admiration that began with their Knickerbocker bond was deeper and more heartfelt than can ever be found on the pages of *Pierre* or Duyckinck's scalding reviews. Indeed, the two gravitated back to one another sooner than those documents might have suggested. Later, when Duyckinck's health faltered, Melville was by his side. His name consistently appears on the register of visitors to the editor's home starting in April 1876. The series of fortnightly visits would continue until August 16, 1878, when Melville attended the funeral of his longest literary friend, bidding farewell to the most capital companion of his personal and professional life.[89]

Part 2 ~ Married Interests

3

DAVIS, INC.

Rebecca Harding and L. Clarke Davis's Reform Magnum Opus

As Washington Irving's and Herman Melville's careers have shown, intense negotiation and conflicting interests characterized most author-publisher relationships from the period; authors were grateful to befriend their editor-publisher, and deep, long-term bonds like the Melville-Duyckinck relationship were even more rare. What happens when the author's prime literary partner is a spouse? Can spousal partners (or surrogate spouses) offer their counterparts who are professional authors, especially women, better types of support, inspiration, and guidance than traditional author-publisher relationships? Whereas Irving and John Murray embodied the tension between America and England, requiring the careful negotiation of gentility and capitalism, of manners and money, the couples of this and the following chapter never had to strategize to overcome such differences. The two authors of Part 2 were focused not so much on reconciling differences with or wrestling power from their literary partner as they were wedded to the same goals of reaching the broadest audience for the largest social impact and the most lucrative financial return. Whereas Melville's literary radicalism and Evert Duyckinck's commercial conservatism were constantly a source of tension that their friendship had to endure, the Davises and E. D. E. N. Southworth–Robert Bonner were teams with no inherent polarities, but instead with mutually shared interests that resonated with harmony.

Economic aspects of publishing and artistry were essential to the successful literary partnership of the Davises, which was forged at the intersection of high and low cultures. Together they would reach two seemingly unbridgeable literary markets through popular and elite presses. At the beginning of her career, Rebecca Harding Davis was poised on the brink of elite status of the sort Melville enjoyed in the first decade of his career. Her future in the world of serious literature beckoned; the intermediaries and support networks were in place, and her pen was flowing. At the age of thirty-one, the Wheeling, West Virginian's first publication, "Life in the Iron-Mills," appeared in the April 1861 *Atlantic Monthly*, which immediately placed her in the inner circle of the literary elite, prompting her meeting with Ralph Waldo Emerson and the Alcotts, and sparking a correspondence with Nathaniel Hawthorne. A close friendship also bloomed with Annie Fields, wife of *Atlantic* editor James T. Fields of Ticknor and Fields, Boston's most prominent publishing house. Davis's first connections in the publishing world thus consisted of intellectuals and sophisticates far removed from the sort of popular fiction that appeared in weeklies like the *New York Ledger* or *Peterson's Magazine*. Then, in 1862, she received a fan letter from L. Clarke Davis.

Clarke entered Davis's life as both her most loyal and enthusiastic fan and as an associate of *Peterson's Magazine*. He appeared to represent and even promote popular fiction to her in an irresistible cocktail of love and money. With ties to the publishing world, Clarke added an intriguing new dimension to Davis's author-publisher struggles that otherwise had been like those that prevailed over the majority of the industry at the time, following a pattern of intense negotiation like Irving and Melville. Indeed, such authorial chess matches with Fields, her first publisher, between money and motivation, aesthetic experimentation and the conservative *Atlantic* readership, colored Davis's main literary partnership early in her career. She had angled for better compensation as Irving had, and rebelled against editorial control like Melville, though not in tones nearly as strident. In these ways, literary partnership in her early career was author-publisher driven. Then love walked in.

Clarke would not only supplant Fields as Davis's primary literary partner, he would nurture her career from the position of her domestic partner and spouse. As her husband and literary advocate, he was thus capable of inspiring one of the most socially significant feats of her career. As her publisher and friend only, Fields would never have had the compassion and understanding of her personal priorities and struggles to support her reform writing that would change asylum laws forever. Yet most biographies lament the correspondence that eventually led to the hasty marriage in an ominous Wheeling March blizzard in 1863 and forever altered the trajectory of Davis's career toward popular fiction. As a reader for Charles J. Peterson, Clarke naturally encouraged Davis to contribute to *Peterson's Magazine*, a weekly known for sensational stories and serialized novels. A long relationship with that magazine ensued, marking a turn in her career generally lamented by modern readers.[1] Were it not for Clarke, Davis would have enjoyed a career associated with the educated elite of the *Atlantic*, according to the standard view, cementing her status among canonical authors like Margaret Fuller and Henry James rather than popular *Peterson's* sensationalists like Anne S. Stephens.[2] Most histories claim her innovations in the genre of social realism and her approach to literature as art rather than money all vanished upon the entrance of Clarke, the man guilty of dragging her career into hack "potboiler" writing because she fell in love with him at the most financially needy point of his adult life.

Despite the distance from social and political activism she established early in her career that earned her the label of "parlor radical," the second decade of Davis's career tells a different story. Her artistic vision was profoundly conjoined with social activism, to which Clarke was fully committed. Her writings from the late 1860s through the 1870s prove she was hardly a detached and ambiguous critic of general social ills, complacent in her role as money-making popular author. Her reformist agenda takes on a decidedly radical literary activism during this time that, significantly, coincided with her work with Clarke. In this chapter, I examine how Davis's writing benefited from Clarke's legal mind, and how Clarke's own career bore the mark of Davis's literary sensibility. In particular, Davis's own temporary yet debilitating bout with mental illness alerted her to the rampant corruption of asylums, inspiring her to launch a legal and literary collaboration with her husband for one of the most effective cultural and institutional reforms in American history. Her serialized *Peterson's* novel *Put Out of the Way* (1870) grew out of a nationwide controversy two years prior in Clarke's *Atlantic* article, "A Modern Lettre de Cachet," which exposed the common practice of committing sane individuals to mental institutions (usually for economic reasons) with no legal recourse.[3] *Put Out of the Way*, significantly, is deeply embedded in Davis's own ongoing interest in capitalist reform, as it directly links what she would later call "The Disease of Money-Getting" (1902) to such false imprisonment. Davis's literary subjects—primarily the economically disenfranchised who are stigmatized on the margins of society—not only directed Clarke's legal interests. Her favorite rhetorical proto-realist tropes and techniques also persistently appear in his own writings, from the *Atlantic* article to his own novel, *A Stranded Ship* (1869). Clarke's eventual gravitation away from the legal profession toward positions as editor and critic in the literary world testifies to Davis's influence on the development of his own professional career.

The depiction of Clarke's negative influence on Davis's "literary" fiction for the *Atlantic* has been handed down from 1960s literary history to more recent scholarship reaffirming that "though he was proud of her talents, he did not understand her artistic vision," as only "several of Davis's contributions to *Peterson's* are of as high quality as her *Atlantic* submissions."[4] One critic condemns Clarke for "hampering her artistic development" by coercing Davis into writing "reformist didacticism" with "journalistic speed" to supplement his low income, which he was forced to augment with two editorships and a postal job.[5] The argument that Clarke pressured Davis into more lucrative and less literary writing to supplement his salary overlooks their socially responsive collaboration. Indeed, Davis's best reform writing, in terms of its direct role in transforming statutory legal code, was inspired by her work with Clarke.[6] Such writing, furthermore, craftily utilized the highbrow venue of the *Atlantic* for access to the power brokers of elite culture in tandem with the popular *Peterson's*, which provided an indispensable link to the masses for their reform efforts to truly take hold.

THE ECONOMICS OF REFORM WRITING

To dispel the myth of Clarke's negative influence on Davis, one need look no further than the evidence that she had already turned toward more lucrative writing long before receiving her first fan mail from Clarke.[7] Indeed, Davis had already established herself at *Peterson's* well before Clarke solicited her work there. She chose to place her work with *Peterson's* early in her career because the rate of pay dwarfed what Fields offered her at the *Atlantic*. She never looked at this as a compromise to her artistry, but as a natural consequence of a successful career. For an author whose primary subject was the tragedy of exploited labor under unfair wages, Davis was hardly naïve to the variance in the prices her work could command in the market, especially between those of the *Atlantic* and *Peterson's*. Davis's self-deprecating comments about her

Peterson's writing are often cited to prove she sacrificed her art for commercial fiction.

However, sentiments like Hetty's in "The Wife's Story" ("she felt herself inspired with poetry, and had written miserable rhymes—vapid and pretentious") reflect instead her humble attitude toward authorship. Averse to the romanticized transcendental notion of individually inspired "genius," Davis despised such arrogance in other writers and disabused her son from it as he embarked upon his own literary career.[8] Davis did not consider her *Peterson's* fiction inferior because it was driven by economic necessity. Instead, she felt as if she were finally realizing her true market potential precisely because of her maintenance of high literary standards. She articulates this position in a letter to her son Richard warning him of the financial risks inherent in playing to the crowd. She counsels him not on how to realize his full literary talent, but on the necessity of exploiting it to maximize the full potential of his earnings from his reputation in the literary market. Her advice breaks down the dichotomy between literary and hack writing: "Begin to write because it is 'a lot of money' and you stop doing your best work. You make your work common and your prices will soon go down. George Lewes managed George Eliot wisely. He stopped her hackwork. Kept her writing novels and soon one each year brought her $40,000 . . . Mind your mother's advice to you—now and all the time is 'do your best work—even if you starve doing it.'"[9] Financial interest is never in question. While she assumes that writers should always write to make money, she is careful to distinguish between good and bad literary capital. She insists that compromised writing for quick cash, however tempting, does not provide the long-term financial stability of writing to one's highest standard of quality. Writing to one's full potential will eventually pay off, whereas compromise degrades an author's reputation. Davis maintained such high standards in her own fiction, approaching it with the same deliberate pragmatism that characterized her business dealings. Critics, however, have seen her as an inept businessperson.[10] Cast as "confused" and "naïve" in her negotiations with editors such as Fields, she allegedly was financially victimized and "underpaid" throughout her career despite evidence to the contrary.[11] "It is not inspiration—it never was that—without practice, with any writer from Shakespeare down . . . real success takes time and patient, steady work," she advised her son, signing off unsentimentally to resume her own work: "I had to stop my work to say all this, so goodbye dear old chum."[12]

Teaming with Clarke on reform issues was born as much out of commercial enterprise as moral reform. From a distance the two objectives might appear laughably at odds, rendering the kind of absurd image of Walt Whitman fueling the composition of his grisly temperance novel *Franklin Evans* with several flasks of whisky.[13] Unlike Whitman, Davis actually believed in the reform measures she was advocating. Many like her found reform writing compatible with the commercial world of professional letters, and thus "openly tied their literary professionalism to reform."[14] Lydia Maria Child, for example, courted a mass readership in her appealing "Letters from New York" to promote abolition, while Fuller used her position as book reviewer for Horace Greeley's *Tribune* to forward her reformist agendas. Fuller celebrated authorship's new connection to reform writing, envisioning a movement inspired by "love . . . which calls the poet from his throne of Mind to lie with the beggar in the kennel, or raise him from it; [and] which says to the Poet, 'You must reform rather than create a world.'"[15] Fuller's validation of literary labor's compassionate moral function to diagnose social ills and prescribe their cures resonates with Davis's socially responsible sense of authorship. Such service to the greater good was not without its material rewards. For Davis, this meant securing her rights to the fruits of her labor was not so much exploitative capitalism or rampant materialism as it was smart business of the sort she counseled to her son. Furthermore, doing business with Clarke, the most trusted and beloved person in her life, made it especially meaningful and effective. Clarke shared his wife's view that fiction was not only an ideal vehicle for legal imperatives, but that the reform impulse for social justice brought out the more engaging aspects of fiction itself. Davis's defense of victims of economic and social injustice and exposure of corruption in both written and unwritten codes of behavior were rhetorically consistent with the finer and more dramatic flourishes of her fiction. Indeed, many of the *Atlantic* publications known for their social philosophy could have been comfortably placed in the more narrative-driven *Peterson's*.

Not only was there considerable compatibility between Davis's writings for the *Atlantic* and *Peterson's*, but also between her domestic role of wife/mother and professional author. As her long and successful career showed, the domestic role of wife and mother and the artistic role were not in debilitating conflict.[16] For example, Clarke's polemic introduction of the appalling lack of legal constraints against the false commitment of sane individuals to mental asylums sparked a frenzy of public interest in the topic that effectively fueled the sale of Davis's *Put Out of the Way.* The success of both documents reflects the power of the couple's domestic intimacy, which, for Davis fostered a more nuanced understanding of the arguments at stake and for Clarke a deeper sensitivity to the human injustice inherent in the issue. Each wrote better, with more balance of passion and reason, because of the presence of the other. Davis could effectively assume the role of literary professional not only as Clarke's wife, but also as Richard's mother. Her maternal advice and sage literary wisdom blend harmoniously in Davis's correspondence with Richard. Under Davis's tutelage, Richard would establish himself as a famous public figure; he had his mother to thank for his literary work ethic. The recipe for success is quintessential Davis in its foregrounding of the importance of human sympathy, humor, and the sharpening of skills through real practice, all packaged with a pragmatic punch aimed at disabusing the young man of any pretensions to romantic notions of authorship.

The "patience" and "steady work" Davis encouraged in her son's writing were also indispensable to her success in business. Davis's shrewd refusal of a $100 advance from Fields early in her career illustrates her savvy given the vagaries of trade courtesy (publishers' first rights to authors) then very much in flux. Refusing the advance enabled her to entertain competitive offers in the open market. An acceptance would have been like a professional marriage vow of loyalty to Fields only, closing off future opportunities and thus severely limiting the development of her career. Indeed, she wanted him to value her voice and vision beyond capital to establish the *Atlantic* as a continuing outlet for her work, yet remain free to accept higher bids should they arise.[17] Thus she could avoid breaking a promise to him she did not want to keep. Davis consistently wrote for *Peterson's* throughout her career, especially when she needed the money most. Her "dedication" to the *Atlantic* was anything but loyal as she continued to market her writing to the highest bidder in a free market of self-interested professional authors. In fact, Davis received a tantalizing offer of $300 from *Peterson's* for a story she had written in two weeks in 1862, just one short year after her $50 debut publication of "Iron-Mills" in the *Atlantic.* She wrote her *Atlantic* editor to inform him that he had been outbid by the popular ladies' magazine.

In a bold business maneuver, she denigrated the more frivolous pieces commonly published in *Peterson's*, an assertion that does not contradict her own aggressive reform fiction's critical realist innovations in such popular works as *Put Out of the Way*. She urged Fields to increase his payments because "If I wrote stories suitable for other magazines I could make more."[18] He responded by offering her $8 per page, to which she replied, "I accept your offer to write solely for the A. M."—a promise she happily broke on more than one occasion shortly thereafter (within the following year) and throughout her career. Davis knew she was an exception to the rule that as the *Atlantic*'s "literary tastes tended more toward realism," as Anne Boyd observes, "the kind of stories that many women were contributing were deemed less important."[19]

Davis's business expertise was on display later in her career as she again successfully capitalized upon the erosion of the gentleman publisher's code, the mutual recognition of editors and publishers of their "first rights" to an author's work. Using her pseudonym to her advantage, Davis published the same story in two different journals, generating double returns. Of course, this raises ethical questions of professional integrity today, but the rules of the writer's trade were not yet firmly established in the 1860s during the early commercialization of letters. Business ethics were in flux, as the patron system gave way to a literary market in which writers worked as entrepreneurs with no loyal ties. This is especially true in Davis's willingness to submit the same weird-but-true story in two journals. "Ellen" first appeared in *Peterson's* by the author of "The Second Life" in 1863. Davis sent the *Atlantic* the same story two years later in 1865, when they solicited a true story about the war. The *Atlantic* published "Ellen" by the author of "Life in the Iron-Mills." *Peterson's* defended Davis by claiming that their story was fiction based on real-life events, while the *Atlantic* piece was "the bald facts" of "Ellen's" history.[20] The cover-up worked and Davis profited. Ironically, Davis would publish an essay at the end of her career in 1902 for the *Independent* called "The Disease of Money-Getting." Apparently her own entrepreneurial guile was not part of this hampering illness.[21]

The double publication of "Ellen" blurs the boundaries between popular fiction and "serious" literature in the Davis canon. Tillie Olsen's suggestion that Davis abandoned artistry for money and acquiesced to financial pressures by writing popular trash as a "professional workhorse" becomes dubious when an identical story was suitable to both the highbrow conservative tastes of the *Atlantic* editors and the pulpy sensationalism of *Peterson's* editors.[22] Davis's "serious" writing, such as "Iron-Mills," employed the sensationalized "realism" of popular literary modes. With its penchant for sensationalism and spectacle, "Life in the Iron-Mills" functions like a *Peterson's* tale, particularly in the pulpy depiction of Hugh's tragic suicide and the repulsive Deborah, whose deformity and filth overwhelm her introduction. *Peterson's* relied heavily on gothic and mystery stories, the conventions of which appear throughout Davis's fiction. Without the philosophizing of Mitchell and the men touring the iron mills, "Iron-Mills" bears the look of a typical popular ladies' magazine story. Davis, however, never underestimated the popular audience and refused to reserve her "intellectual" and socially relevant material only for educated, mostly male, elite *Atlantic* readers. *Put Out of the Way* would signal the appropriateness, and indeed the necessity, of *Peterson's* to carry a narrative like "Iron-Mills," both racy and of major social and legal consequence.

THE GENESIS OF *PUT OUT OF THE WAY*

Writing for money was always part of Davis's conception of authorship and her realistic ethos that spread to other dimensions of her life. The promise of long-term financial stability and independence from writing, I suggest, enabled her to recover from the most significant emotional and professional breakdown of her life. She drew on that experience in her collaboration with Clarke to prevent the placement of sane individuals in asylums in what would become the most effective reform writing of her entire career. After marrying in 1863, the Davises immediately moved into Clarke's sister's home in Philadelphia. Clarke's income was insufficient for them to live on their own, so the new couple was forced to share living space with relatives. Lack of funds, in fact, precluded any honeymoon. The living situation with Clarke's sister Carrie Cooper, her husband, and small children was not amenable to Rebecca's plans for writing and managing a home of her own. Although there is no evidence of outwardly expressed animosity between the Davises and the Coopers, Davis made a point of escaping housework and helping Carrie with what amounted to tasks for the betterment of the Cooper household. Domestic labor was especially alienating to Davis, since the children and the home itself were not her own. She sought refuge in the Philadelphia

Public Library, where she could write in order to supplement Clarke's meager income.

The struggle to produce profitable literature and have a baby in a home not truly her own contributed to a nervous breakdown in June 1863. Throughout the winter of her pregnancy, Davis's physical and mental health fluctuated, sometimes incapacitating her. She spent much of her time bedridden, which she said was "like the valley of the shadow of death," feeling "afraid of the end."[23] Significantly, Davis's physician advised her not to engage in "the least reading or writing for fear of bringing back the trouble in her head."[24] This anticipated the treatment prescribed for "hysteria" by writer/physician S. Weir Mitchell, whose prohibition of Charlotte Perkins Gilman's reading and writing inspired the horrifying story, "The Yellow Wall-Paper." Although it is unclear whether he treated her directly, Mitchell was a close family friend of the Davises in Philadelphia and commonly treated the mysterious female "hysteria" by severely isolating the patient and abruptly cutting off all literary activities.

Of course, Davis was not rehabilitated by such therapy. What most likely returned her to health was the fact that she *did* write during this period. Her dark pregnancy yielded an extremely reflexive piece, "The Wife's Story," which was published shortly after the birth of Richard Harding Davis in April 1864. Literary production, plus Clarke's promise (which she reported to her close friend Annie Fields, wife of publisher James, "If I get well we are going directly to live by ourselves—it is all clear now. *You* know what that means to me"), were tokens of future economic autonomy that buoyed her.[25] Her sense of success both as a mother with the healthy birth of her child and as a writer with the completion of a publishable manuscript coincided with the end of her illness. By the fall of 1864, the family of three moved out of the Coopers' residence into a home of their own, bringing Davis full reign over her domestic sphere as well as a less crowded writing environment for the first time since her marriage.

After the move, Davis was still actively interested in gaining as much capital from her writing as possible to alleviate the financial burden. So she more vigorously cultivated her relationship with the editors at *Peterson's Magazine* for whom she had written a sensational murder mystery called "Murder of the Glen Ross." *Peterson's* boasted "the largest circulation of any ladies' periodical in the United States, or even in the world," with 140,000 subscribers.[26] Davis's interest in publishing for the magazine was driven by its economic base, which was larger than that of the *Atlantic*. *Peterson's* trumpeted its power to pay writers "more for all its original stories than all other ladies' magazines put together."[27]

Such unprecedented financial rewards now available to women set up the ethical dilemma Davis placed at the center of "The Wife's Story." Davis knew this was a philosophical and cultural problem of immense importance to readers interested in the market's impact on the domestic sphere. The subject was not only timely; it was worthy of producing passionate prose, since the issue had recently touched her own life. The protagonist of the story dreams of becoming an artist. In the dream, the character Hetty writes an opera, only to watch its first production fail miserably, much to her public humiliation. At the low point of the dream, after having lost it all in the cultural market (including her husband to a heart attack during the performance!), she wakes up to embrace the security of motherhood with new zest. What looks like a rejection of public professional writing for the safety and security of motherhood is more emphatically a rejection of the Emersonian myth of the divinely inspired artist, as Hetty's worst sin is artistic egotism: "No poet or artist," she says, "was ever more sincere in the belief that the divine spoke through him than I."[28] Hetty's attempt to isolate herself from her immediate social network of her husband and child represents exactly the kind of disaffiliation and self-reliance in the name of artistry that Davis disapproves of. Like "Life in the Iron-Mills," "The Wife's Story" critiques this sort of blind, radical individualism that possesses the character with artistic propensities. The delusions of absolute transcendence above the imperatives of economic and social relations are projected as deadly. This is not a conservative, antifeminist promotion of fawning female dependence so much as it is a warning against transcendental notions of artistic production.[29] Davis herself showed that one could both meet the domestic responsibilities of antebellum motherhood and produce appealing literary merchandise as a professional because "The Wife's Story" appeared in the June issue of the *Atlantic* following the birth of her son in April 1864. Davis showed by her own example that the production of art does not necessarily sever the writer's social and familial ties.

Family ties indeed would help Davis recuperate both professionally and psychologically. While her illness was enmeshed in her professional urges and her confining domestic situation at the Coopers, the remedy appeared to be a reassertion of her authorial power by fearlessly reflecting on her very own psychological derailment for her subject matter, and by capitalizing on her husband as an invaluable resource. By 1868, Davis's mental breakdown and sense of vulnerability was fresh in the couple's memory. Now safe from the tandem forces that attended her breakdown five years earlier of potentially hostile in-laws and the risk of losing her professional literary—and thus profit-earning—role, she and Clarke could assess the experience at a distance and take stock of how fortunate they were that Davis's health and career recovered and relations with the Coopers remained amicable. Davis and her husband were well aware that their privileged retreat to the Jersey Shore during Davis's darkest hours was essential to her recovery, and that most women in her position would not have had access to such a second home. As a lawyer, Clarke knew of innumerable cases at the time in which family discord led to the perfectly legal practice of summarily confining sane individuals to mental hospitals, a process then requiring only a doctor's certificate without examination. If they had shared a home with a family less sympathetic than the Coopers and conflict had arisen, Davis herself, and even her mentally stable husband, would have been vulnerable to being "put out of the way." Davis fortunately escaped such a fate, as she essentially wrote herself back to health under the care of Clarke, who was responsive to her demands and honored her liberty. Clarke catered to her needs during her illness with sympathy and aid that would extend into their next literary project.

LEGAL AND CREATIVE COLLABORATION

As so much of writing is self-reflexive, and mined from personal trauma as well as triumph, so too were the publications of the Davises in the late 1860s. Clarke's 1868 "A Modern Lettre de Cachet," now a great document in the history of investigative journalism, laid out the legal argument in the *Atlantic* exposing the absence of laws preventing the confinement of sane people in mental institutions. The article also accomplished the psychological objective of exorcising the lingering demons of Davis's breakdown by marshalling their forces to advocate for the mentally ill. The Cooper residence was a chaotic, confining environment not conducive to the sort of peace and tranquility Davis cherished for her writing.

Clarke arranged for her writing desk at the Philadelphia Public Library precisely for her to escape this environment, which may very well have contributed to her breakdown. Indeed, her confinement to the Coopers' home offers a parallel experience providing Davis imaginative access to the ways in which captivity within the world of the asylum, as *Put Out of the Way* illustrates, can induce madness in a sane individual. As Davis's frightening struggle with mental illness touched her life deeply, she could easily imagine the horror of being confined in an asylum, and at once appreciate her liberty and sanity, while arguing more fervently on behalf of others who had been robbed of them. Further, her past illness imbued her approach to the subject of life in a mental hospital with a sense of urgency and immediacy that prompted her to join forces with Clarke with new zeal to crusade for social and legal justice.

Clarke's aim was to educate the elite about the issue, focusing on the medical and legal communities. This was primarily a professional male audience, a fact registered in the angry retort from the *Medical and Surgical Reporter* in May 1868, which attempted to discredit his argument by claiming it "contains some evidences of having come from the pen of a lady."[30] While Clarke stirred controversy through his *Atlantic* article among a narrow male elite audience, Davis would spread it to the widest audience possible, including significantly more women readers, in her *Peterson's* serial novel. The gender issue that the *Reporter*'s rejoinder points toward was significant. Fanny Fern's *Ruth Hall* (1855) includes a character, Mary Leon, whose husband discards her by falsely imprisoning her in a Lunatic Asylum, where she dies a torturous death. Ruth tours the asylum, discovering a disproportionate number of female patients there. She inquires about one, whose husband took her children, only to learn that in such matters, "the law you see, as it generally is, was on the man's side."[31] The tour guide regards the woman chained in her cell with restrained optimism, noting, "we don't have to whip her *very* often."[32] Fern witnessed such atrocities firsthand when she toured an asylum in New England in 1862, commenting in the *New York Ledger* on how female patients vastly outnumbered men.[33] Men were clearly exploiting gaps in the law to falsely commit women to asylums at a far greater rate than women were of men, or within the same gender, a fact oddly obscured by the selection of male victims as the central figures of both Clarke's article (Morgan Hinchman) and Davis's narrative (Richard Wortley, loosely based on Hinchman).[34] Yet the Davises were perhaps more crafty than antifeminist, since male victims would have appealed more directly to the male legislators who eventually did change the law. Although they did not call attention to it, the Davises were more than aware of how women directly benefited from the laws their writings ostensibly changed.

Interestingly, Wortley is feminized in Davis's novel, while Clarke's article does not foreground, or even hint at, the relevance of gender. All his pronouns are male, and, significantly, all but one of his innumerable anecdotes describes a male victim of false incarceration. On the surface, he can hardly be said to be writing on behalf of women.[35] However, his collaboration with Davis to write *Put Out of the Way* for the predominantly female audience of *Peterson's* clearly speaks to a subtler appeal to both audiences and thus addresses both male legal/medical and female moral and domestic concerns. One can speculate that such an omission was intentional. Clarke's mid-nineteenth-century male audience might have balked at explicit charges of gender bias to account for the disproportionate amount of women in asylums. It is also probable that Davis's women readers would have sympathized with Wortley's feminized character, as he is hopelessly stuck in a state of powerless captivity, a condition anticipating Gilman's "The Yellow Wall-Paper."[36] Shattering the rigid divide of conventional separate spheres ideology that denounced professional collaboration between men and women, Clarke borrowed Davis's favorite rhetorical techniques that animate her novel to heighten the pathos of his legal essay. In turn, her humanized fictional portrait armed women with the facts of this issue—its arguments, its legality—gleaned from Clarke.

Such covert feminism in the Davises' reform agenda was subtly detected in other misogynistic strains in the *Reporter*'s attack on Clarke's "A Modern Lettre de Cachet" beyond their accusation that it came "from the pen of a lady."[37] In particular, the *Reporter* claims that asylums are really quiet and orderly, and that Clarke's rendition was guilty of the sort of sensationalism ("unutterable things . . . wails of anguish, disheveled hair and clanking chains") associated with the type of lurid gothic fiction that Davis herself wrote on occasion for ladies' magazines.[38] But the rejoinder commits its own sin of delving into the lurid details common to dark reform.[39] The *Reporter* casts asylums in the institutional role of protector of the community from the criminally insane, an interesting trope that inadvertently aligns sanitariums with prisons and penal corrections rather than health care. "Within a month of the time," the unnamed author argues, "of the appearance of that article, full half a dozen cases came under our observation of homicides, suicides, and casualties committed by, or happening to insane persons for lack of a 'Lettre de Cachet' [a document authorizing immediate imprisonment or execution without trial during the French Revolution]." He then goes into grisly details of the "brutal assault of a little girl eight years old" and vicious murders, describing the sexual perversion of "an insane woman, in an almost entirely nude state, who had for some time been wandering about in a demented condition [and] was run over by a train of cars."[40] This from a medical doctor, who describes individuals of the sort who could be his very own patients in the most demonizing and dehumanizing manner imaginable as "half-witted," crazed, "demented lunatics." This representation of the mentally ill bluntly distances the medical community from even remotely approaching them with humanity and respect. If anything, this rebuttal actually proves the Davises' point that the medical community's attitude toward the issue was inherently unjust and unsympathetic.

Clarke's method of conjuring sympathy from readers not likely to grant it in his article was to draw from his wife's arsenal of rhetorical techniques for critical realism. The impact of Davis on Clarke's article is immediate and obvious. His appreciation of the realism in "Iron-Mills" that exposed social injustices is evident in the opening stages of his exposé. The slow approach to the asylum, lingering on details of the physical surroundings designed to highlight social injustice and capitalist inequality intrinsic to this evil institution, is unmistakably borrowed from "Iron-Mills." For this was the story that struck him as so astonishing, so moving, that he vowed to marry its author. Indeed, Davis's stunning gothic lurid details of the dark satanic mills echo those of Clarke's description of the asylum. Like Davis, Clarke aims to rivet the reader to shocking images of inhumanity: "There in the fierce glare of the noonday sun, we saw the figure of a young man chained to a stake, in the yard." The animalistic qualities of his subject are pronounced, much in the way of Davis's wolfish Hugh Wolf and his groveling, slovenly companion Debra. Clarke's figure is "strangely clad and moaning . . . [walking] to and fro to the extent that his chain would permit."[41]

The *Reporter*'s claim that Clarke's piece was written by a woman was designed not only to discredit its author as a non-specialist, but also to target the piece's sentiment and sympathy, features that dominate Davis's fiction. Clarke makes the point, for example, of showing how inhumane it was that this chained figure was made a spectacle of, much in the way Davis indicts the gentlemen touring the iron mill for gawking with philosophical wonder and not a little morbid fascination at the laborers. Clarke objects to exposing the "not violent or vicious, but simply insane" to "the jeers and jibes and curious stares of the thousands," whose unsympathetic gaze is metaphorically figured in "the burning rays of the sun." Inhumane institutionalization, as in so much of Davis's work, bears the mark of social class, as the man is "not wealthy" who strains against his chain like a leashed dog in the yard of a "not altogether unpretentious mansion."[42]

Clarke then moves into a sharp comparison between due process and the lack thereof in committing sane persons to such horrific institutions. If the artist Hugh is miscast in life as a laborer in an iron mill, then the prospect of anyone "among us, however pure, wise, or influential . . . upon the certificate of a single physician, committed to the cell of a lunatic asylum" is an image equally jarring. The whims of fate in both capitalism and the medical/legal system, the Davises both argue, can tyrannically ruin lives. The "enemies, the cupidity of relatives, the treachery or ignorance of a physician" can leave a perfectly sane citizen institutionalized according to the superannuated fifty-year-old statutory code. The attack on the medical community dominates the first half of the article with sallies against the corrupt physician, who "ignorant, besotted, armed with that mighty weapon, a diploma from a medical school, holds us at his mercy."[43]

The year after his article appeared, and perhaps inspired by its success, Clarke would publish his only novel, *A Stranded Ship.* It addresses many of the issues that arise in the article, and also reflects more of the influence of Davis's fiction. Luke Conner, the protagonist, is a murderer who confesses to his crime, yet is found not guilty by an incompetent jury. Here, Clarke exposes flaws in the legal system, as he had in his article on asylum abuse, while also depicting his victim in an economically disenfranchised condition. Like his wife's best fiction, Clarke's book highlights the dangers of idealistically flinging oneself into the free market. For example, Luke "resolved to go out into the world and to make his hands earn the bread he ate . . . to go where his crime was unknown and where, under a new name he could remain unquestioned and trusted by 'honest men.'" He flees to dig for gold in San Francisco, and, like Davis's Hugh Wolfe in "Life in the Iron-Mills," he is an outcast among the men with whom he works. Financial futility and social ostracism go hand in hand for Luke as they do for Hugh. Rumors abound about his identity, and he spends his days "digging and washing, but scarcely getting out sufficient gold to support existence from day to day"; he is a recluse, suffering from "solitude [that] oppressed him beyond endurance."[44]

Luke's obsessive "thirst to find gold" supplants "human love and fellowship," becoming "that one passion that filled his life up, took all his thought, and occupied his sleep."[45] Shortly after Luke leaves the crew to work on his own, they strike gold and do not share it with him. He eventually boards an Australian trader, and increasingly shows signs of alcoholism, another social ill commonly targeted for reform. Clarke portrays alcoholism—true to the central reform objectives of Davis, Inc.—as a symptom of a weak judicial system and brutal economic forces. Luke is "out of work, desperate, reckless . . . seeking employment and finding none . . . down to his last dollar, after two years labor in the mines." He then resolves to join the English in the fight over "foul deeds done in India" in order to "die like a soldier" with honor, a suicidal tendency echoed in Lot Tyndal and Hugh, two of his wife's characters who take their own lives.[46]

In *A Stranded Ship* Clarke also employed the pulpy narrative intrigue common to his wife's stories as his protagonist saves a comrade's life and returns to America in hopes of starting anew. On the voyage home, his ship sinks and he is picked up by Professor Daunton, the man who had originally served as prosecuting witness against Luke. Luke falls in love with his daughter Margaret, but thinks himself unworthy, as he is still wracked by his sin.[47] The professor then tells Margaret about Luke's crime, and she grows ambivalent toward her new husband. The moment finally comes for Luke to prove himself when a stranded ship offshore bobs in the current, the professor too weak to save the people aboard, and others too cowardly. Clarke brings the narrative tension to a fever pitch, as Margaret calls Luke a "murderer" and thus gives him his chance to finally die with honor and atone for his sin: "'My friends,' he said, 'I am sorry I was wrong, and this good wife is right. I will carry a line to the ship.'"[48] In an act of physical strength and daring, he dives directly under the raging surf and successfully brings the passengers to shore, saving the life of George Lawrence, the man whom he believed he had murdered years before. While Clarke's novel is undeniably flawed as a work of fiction (strained, tedious, improbable), it serves as a useful glimpse into the rhetorical techniques he shared with his wife, and thus further insight into their style of literary activism. Like Hetty of "A Wife's Tale," Luke undergoes an inner transformation, drifting into a life of excessive self-destructive individualism, for which he is punished (much of it self-inflicted), ultimately to return to a socially functional domestic role. As in "A Wife's Tale," the conclusion to *A Stranded Ship* never follows through didactically on the judicial and capitalist corruption the vast majority of the narrative indicts. As in so many of Davis's tales, social reform is just as important as inner reform in Clarke's novel.

Clarke's use of his wife's techniques for nonfictional legal argumentation is much more effective than that of his prose fiction. His deployment of juxtaposition, for example, is reminiscent of how Davis sets pure visionary artistic dreams against the dirty air of stupefying incarceration in "Iron-Mills." Specifically, "the refined intercourse of society, dreams of art," and "the wholesome air of the outer world" clash against the soul-killing stuffy world of "the lonely cell . . . densely populated with the insane."[49] Both pieces bring the reader into the presence of an inconvenient truth that advanced civilization and technological progress tend to mask. Employing an almost Brechtian aesthetic, they expose injustice in all its glare and dissonance to shake middle-class readers from their complacency, tearing open the cocoon-like gauze of their comfortable existence.[50] Like a good lawyer, Clarke uses rhetorically well-placed documentary evidence in achieving his aim in the article, as seen in his dramatic unveiling of the physician's brief, shockingly terse form letter and bond. His diction draws directly from the stuff of dark reform, as the documents themselves are of "monstrous proportions," however silent and covert, like the *lettre de cachet*, "that old letter of France that consigned its victim to the Bastille."[51]

Wielding a rhetorical flourish worthy of his wife's best assaults on capitalism and its horrific, even gothic effects, perhaps the most nefarious of the documents Clarke presents in the article is the bond. An economic seal of fate, the bond reflects how "even these charitable asylums may have an interest in your living death." Yet another stunningly simple certificate with profound influence, the bond encourages the "involuntary servitude [of] granting to physicians such immense powers" of corrosive graft that give way to horrifying "natural consequences." In his most overt revelation of his wife's influence, Clarke maintains that "the lawbooks are full of such cases, and so well known have they become that *writers of fiction* have found in them material for their work, such as their wildest imaginations would fail to suggest."[52] "I'll have you committed!" was such a common refrain in the popular fiction at the time that it had become almost a cliché in the cultural lexicon. Davis's most obvious nod to Clarke appears in her description of the power of the doctor's certificate, a puff acknowledging his notorious article and confirming her alliance with it: "That printed slip . . . has all the power of a *lettre-de-cachet* in the worst days of the old regime."[53]

The second half of Clarke's article offers a series of anecdotes, but centers on the story of Morgan Hinchman, a true story stranger than fiction and thus the model for *Put Out of the Way.* Hinchman's wife's family had him committed soon after his marriage, upon which he had merged his wife's stock worth between $10,000 and $12,000 with his own farmland worth roughly the same amount. The wife's family protested when Hinchman put his wife's stocks into his farm, "what he conceived to be a judicious use of his wife's estate" and a perfectly legal action. Shortly thereafter, he was arrested and confined to the Frankfort Lunatic Asylum, wherein family, friends, and even "an old servant" were barred from visitation and correspondence: "they had consigned him to a living death." The family had "concocted this scheme for the purpose of obtaining his property"; Hinchman eventually "escaped through his uncle's [financial] aid."[54] The signing doctor never saw Hinchman prior to his committal. The court eventually ruled in Hinchman's favor, awarding him $10,000 in damages.

Davis's signature direct address, so famously deployed in "Iron-Mills," is also on display in "A Modern Lettre de Cachet." It alerts the reader to this social injustice of economic domination, married property in the case of Hinchman, and treacherous heirs scheming for their elderly father's estate in the second anecdote. Davis's Hugh and these victims all find themselves incarcerated in various forms of demonic institutions portrayed as living hells. Clarke's appeal to the reader draws on the rhetoric of fear, as he claims this could happen to you: "Consider this evidence, you who are today enjoying freedom from your sanity—consider it well, and then pause before you order new furniture, or an Arctic dream of Church's (painting), or a painted poem by Hamilton . . . should tomorrow find you an inmate of a mad-house, and you vainly beat against the iron bars of your cage." Such purchases, he warns, could lead to the same fate of the elderly gentleman whose greedy heirs commit him to prevent him from spending their inheritance. All your behavior (as "you vainly beat against the iron bars of your cage") will be used as evidence to prove you are insane, a trap that renders futile at the least, and self-incriminating at the worst, any attempt at self-expression, whether verbal, written, or physical. Language and law thus become useless tools for self-defense. Further, Clarke argues, it is hard to shake the association with the mad-house once the victim is presented to the jury: "vagaries of confirmed madmen, and their howls by night [haunt him]; if he can so put the past away from him, with all its attendant horrors" and achieve poise before the jury, "he may have some chance."[55]

It is precisely this hope that drives Richard Wortley's story in *Put Out of the Way*. In the novel, Davis brings the legally defenseless predicament of neutralized and disempowered communication raised by Clarke to nightmarish, Kafkaesque levels. Wortley's plans to support his true love Lotty in married life with his burgeoning art career are mercilessly dashed by the treacherous rival Fred Leeds, whose scandalous secret first marriage abroad (a clear echo of Rochester and Bertha Mason in *Jane Eyre*) is known only by Wortley. Leeds and his corrupt father, whose aim is to seize Lotty's lucrative inheritance, thus seek to put Wortley out of the way. They commit him to an asylum with their too easily obtained signed doctor's certificate. A perfectly sound future in painting, an occupation defined by its capacity to communicate subtlety through a deeper and wider range than language itself, in this case is wrecked, due to no fault of Wortley's own, by marauding capitalists willing to exploit lax laws regarding the commitment of "friends" to asylums. The capitalist condition can potentially devastate any honest entrepreneurial pursuit, but artists in particular are especially vulnerable. Wortley's powers of expression, both verbal and artistic, are stolen from him; try as he may, at one point in the story he cannot even convince a benevolent and kindly Quaker that he is sane.

The key elements of Clarke's argument—the lack of medical professionalism, the financial motives behind the abuse of the asylum system, the graft of payoffs to doctors and asylums, the threat to individual rights and liberty couched in nationalistic terms—are all present in *Put Out of the Way*. Davis makes positive innovations on each point, indeed adding altogether new, more radical angles completely absent from her husband's article. Her capitalist critique, as one might expect, is broader and deeper than her husband's. She is more sophisticated, for example, in ascribing the cause of the asylum manager's cold indifference not simply to incompetence but to a deeply human reaction against the horrifying displays of suffering to which he is constantly exposed. Being hardened to the pain of others is a process of dehumanization itself that renders the manager incapable of feeling. His position systematically strips him of the capacity to sympathize. The ironically named Dr. Harte, bloodless to be sure, could be a flat stock villain. Davis, however, rounds out the psychosocial edges of his identity in terms of his occupational demands, thus indicting the larger capitalist ethos. The narrator observes in him a "wooden manner too often common to men whose daily routine brings them into contact with suffering. One wonders whether the indifference, assumed at first for prudence, has not penetrated deeper and deeper, till the whole man is actually hardened into a wooden puppet, only to be set in motion by duty, or what he thinks is duty . . . The last place to look for genial temper, or quick sympathies, is in the actual manager of any charitable institution."[56] We learn in the following chapter that Wortley is not out to vilify medical personnel. "I do not blame you for admitting me here," he says to Dr. Harte, "this is the fault of the law." But Wortley does castigate Harte for failing to examine him upon admittance, as Davis sidles in a point on behalf of women: "even delicate women, whose mental derangement arises from physical causes, receive no medical attention, but are left to the sole care and companionship of such women as they would employ in their kitchen."[57] The major sin such a charitable institution commits is a lack of sympathetic companionship as embodied by Harte, with whom Wortley and the narrator ironically sympathize.

Capitalist corruption, according to the narrative's logic, conditions asylum managers to be inhumane. Indeed, the asylum has become a means of seizing family fortunes through a web of bribery and graft between physicians and asylum owners. Both Davises relay anecdotes about patients being released upon the stoppage of payment to the asylums. The asylum itself in *Put Out of the Way* is not above capitalizing on its patients for profit: "'My clothing are in rags,' said Dick, stretching out his shirt-sleeve. 'What provision do you make for clothing your prisoners?' The little man was all alive with politeness. 'You can purchase any article you wish from us, Mr. Wortley.'" Financial incentive is even the key to Wortley's liberation. Dr. Harte fears the "great embarrassment" of a public trial once the writ of habeas corpus (a request to bring a person before a court for investigation of illegal imprisonment) finally arrives, and thus hastens to discharge Wortley, whose ostensible symptoms of abuse would likely spark a scandal. "The publicity of a trial is more distasteful to us than to you," Harte says to the Leedses, who attempt to remove Wortley to another private hospital prior to the arrival of the writ.[58] Harte saves his reputation and money, as Wortley's case would have incurred considerable fines against the institution.

Davis is concerned with capitalist corruption from the very beginning of the novel, as she characterizes Ned Leeds as a man of false fronts deceptively using fashion as a mask for destructive purposes. Mrs. McIntosh, the maid of Charlotte Hubbard's father, remembers Ned when he visited Mr. Hubbard to go hunting and fishing. She describes him with "his diamond rings and flesh-colored gloves, his shirts were only fronts, Charlotte! Shams, worn over flannel; and half the time there were no socks under his French boots. You see, I superintended the wash. Oh! I know what Ned Leeds' sort is well!" The readers of *Peterson's* also knew his sort well. Stephens's editorial influence on the magazine brought fashion into sharp focus for female readers, from its playful approach to heightened femininity in its fashion plates—dress patterns of the latest styles were often included in issues—to its moral cautionary tales warning against fashion as a mask for destructive purposes.[59] Designed to deceive Lotty into thinking them wealthier than they are, the home fashions of the Leeds residence aid Ned's attempts to marry her as part of his elaborate scam to seize her estate. Thus the "silver glittered miraculously," yet Ned's father Fred "wears even his own hair gray when dye's so cheap," a detail lost on the bedazzled Lotty, fully taken by this false show of money through the home's pretentious fashion—"beauty, music, culture, and quiet ease"—so that the real capital, "the lead mine . . . seemed such a wretched heap of poor and common metal!"[60]

The very first page of Davis's novel falls right in line with Stephens's editorial policy cautioning readers of nefarious intent fashionably cloaked. (A similar warning appears in Melville's Claggart of *Billy Budd*, who cloaks his black heart in a mantle of genteel respectability.) Davis employs this anti-capitalist theme not merely as a false lead to her real topic of asylum abuse. Instead, she frames asylum corruption economically, just as she had found capitalist corruption the cause of the many social ills she diagnosed in her critical realistic fiction. The explicit didactic purpose of the story then takes over roughly halfway through; up until this point, the signs of a reform agenda are masked behind a domestic tale, replete with a conventional plot involving an heiress (Charlotte Hubbard) to a fortune (in lead mines), a false lover (Ned Leeds) with a sinful past, and a true lover (Richard Wortley) as pure as his art and his care for his invalid mother. Davis only explicitly engages the reform issue when the evil father-son duo of Fred and Ned Leeds pay $50 to the corrupt Dr. Molker (portrayed regrettably in a sickening anti-Semitic stereotype of greed complete with garish phonetic rendering of his Yiddish accent) to sign a certificate to have their "friend" Dick Wortley committed.

Perhaps Davis's most significant contribution well beyond the scope of Clarke's article is her capacity to humanize the mentally ill. The looks of pity and horror aimed at Wortley as he rides the train to the hospital represent a myriad of interpretations, making Wortley himself a radically plural symbol to which innumerable meanings are applied, not unlike the parade of reactions to the doubloon ranging from the sacred to the profane in Melville's *Moby-Dick*. His silence is interpreted as "melancholia so far, though he may become violent at any moment"; another detects that "he is growing violent, sir . . . his face is very much flushed, and the eye is excited. You can always detect insanity by the eye, sir! I have a great deal of experience"; and still another more kindly, yet equally wrong, view is voiced: "The elder [the escorting police officer] is a man of great refinement and feeling . . . I have no doubt that the poor young man is his son." In a nightmare of miscommunication in which his best intentions are used against him, Wortley's protest only calls attention to the profoundly unsympathetic, flippant, and thus inaccurate judgments of the general public toward the mentally ill. Even the most sympathetically inclined in the populace read him wrong, as Wortley's attempt to conscript the aid of a kindly Quaker astonishingly fails: "The young man deceived me with his calm manner" into thinking he was sane, he confesses, but quickly recants: "he thinks he was put in by an enemy? Poor fellow."[61]

The true spirit of reform, according to Davis, must come from this very populace, a point she poignantly dramatizes in an elliptical, lyrical, and touching chapter (22) that provides the key to Wortley's liberation. Upon his first failed attempt to escape, he had dropped a note to his friend Judge Cathcart, explaining his entire predicament. One of the major concerns in Clarke's article that Davis would reinforce in her fiction was the severe restriction of correspondence (in many cases, completely prohibited) between patients and potential advocates, such as their friends, relatives, and legal counsel. Again, derailed or misperceived communication is precisely what makes the asylum patient's situation so inescapable. With the conduit of one small person, in this case a schoolgirl, we see the significance of but one sympathetic intermediary in bringing about justice. Jessy is a vision of the determined, imaginative Davis herself: "There was a certain softness and stealth in all that Jessy did . . . with her long-lashed, grey eyes, ready tears, and low voice. But she would generally have her own way," which Davis shows in her resolve to take the discarded letter, thrown into a mud puddle by her apathetic schoolmate Hester. Jessy then opened this vital line of communication connecting Wortley to his liberty, and "smoothed the crumpled paper and sealed it in a clean envelope, directed in her own clear hand, and then strolling out at noon, she dropped it in the post-office box."[62]

Once Wortley is discharged and in the hands of the Leedses, the son, inexperienced in such matters, considers killing the man who knows too much. "'No Fred!' the older man said, 'I've lived longer than you; and I know that a man who breaks the law is worsted at last. So far we've had the law on our side. Put the knife up.'" With the law in their support, Davis highlights the dire social consequences of the legally defenseless predicament of victims like Wortley. The father-and-son criminals are not even ashamed or fearful enough of the law to do what any self-respecting sensational serial villain would at this point: attempt to kill the witness to their crimes. Ned Leeds's counsel is wise considering that the case was closed the next morning since Wortley was not put "before the Honorable Court, the said Richard Wortley having been discharged from medical custody." The narrator's following three-word paragraph, "What a farce," is the first emphatic editorial break from the third-person narrative established from the beginning of the novel. With this explicit bias shown by the narrator, the veil of objectivity is broken with the bitter acknowledgment that such violence is above the law. Here the narrator decries how the law has allowed such bitter endings for people like Wortley. Criminals manipulate every angle of the system in a series of evasive moves, rendering efforts to apprehend them farcical, much like Wortley's own attempts to explain and defend himself after being labeled insane. The law thus fails to protect the liberty of the innocent from the treacherous. Davis protests that "the law faces us like a dead wall" in an image of unresponsiveness that calls to mind the dead wall reveries of Melville's Bartleby in the law office on Wall Street. Melville's story also savagely exposes the hypocritical inadequacies and farcical concatenations of the law all at the cost of humanity, the ultimate "dead letter," like Wortley's crumpled note lying in the mud puddle.[63] Indeed, Wortley's quiet ending—his marriage to Lotty and reclusive rural life away from politics and contemporary life—reinforces the call for reform through the implication that the institutionalized urban world is uninhabitable in its current state. His simple agrarian life anticipates what Davis extolled decades later in an article entitled "The Disease of Money-Getting." In it she supports satisfaction rather than surplus ("Why should I slave fer money I don't need?" asks one farmer in the piece), much as Henry David Thoreau does in *Walden*'s "Economy," another agrarian jeremiad lamenting capitalist corruption.[64] Davis's conclusion complements and vastly enriches the rather dry bureaucratic call to arms: "The whole subject is worthy of official notice and reform," Clarke's denouement intones.[65]

Davis herself had access to sensitive and responsive legal representation through her husband, a resource protecting her from being committed to an asylum against her will or from being forced to undergo any treatment she did not want. In some ways being institutionalized and thus cut off from Clarke's counsel would have been her worst nightmare, for he offered both legal protection and the warmest sympathy of anyone in her life. Davis, Inc., as it were, was thus a literary and legal team that arose out of their belief in the power of compassion for recovery and recuperation, a pattern they skillfully applied to the reform of rampant abuse of asylums through their respective professions. The pragmatic style with which Davis managed the financial business of her career shines through in her aggressive, savvy advocacy of capitalist victims "put out of the way" in asylums. The capitalist frame of reference for the Davises was not just another social evil attached to their reform agenda. It indeed was the larger problem that lay behind asylum abuse, the common thread tying together all the players in the system, from estate vultures, to corrupt doctors, to cold asylum directors. The laws their work helped to change testify to the depth of their own financial partnership and professional relationship, and its effectiveness in both argumentation and rhetorical style. Davis benefited from Clarke's detailed knowledge of the legal arguments and common defenses surrounding the issue, while his inspiration—and his best rhetorical tactics—for advancing this reform came from his long admiration for his wife's advocacy of the economically disenfranchised and socially marginalized. His own stylistics in "A Modern Lettre de Cachet" bear the mark of his wife, just as the shape of his career would veer away from the law toward editorial work and dramatic criticism. His article, interestingly, is precisely the intersection of these two careers, and thus reflects more than any of his works the strength of his wife's influences combined with his own. *Put Out of the Way* should be viewed with equal admiration for its socially responsive, supple style that straddles the literary and the legal worlds so adeptly. The Davises helped stop the commitment of sane individuals to mental institutions, and thus were pioneers in uncovering such centuries-old corruption, leading to greater scrutiny of the system and a higher degree of accountability. That alone, to most socially conscientious readers, should suffice as evidence of great literature produced in collaboration between the husband-and-wife team of Rebecca Harding and L. Clarke Davis.

4

CAPITAL BONDS

The Compassionate Partnership of E. D. E. N. Southworth and Robert Bonner

Whereas the stable marriage of the Davises was so instrumental to their literary success, E. D. E. N. Southworth masterfully reassembled the shards of her shattered marriage into world-famous fiction critical of married life's worst flaws and a business partnership composed of its very best features. Although not married, Southworth and Robert Bonner shared a capital bond forged in the business world that proved stronger than marriage, enhancing both their personal and professional lives. The chapter entitled "The Awful Peril of Capitola" in Southworth's *The Hidden Hand* speaks to how the two were conjoined. It depicts the notorious criminal Black Donald breaking into Capitola's room with the intention of raping and perhaps murdering her. Her quick wit saves her life as she swings into a stagy domestic performance for him in which she insists that she serve him dinner and provide religious counsel. This is all an elaborate trick to maneuver him over a trap door, which she deploys by chapter's end, sending him into the dark oblivion below. The scene is profoundly reflexive of Southworth's predicament as a woman writer: "And I have been reading you," Capitola's arch villain Black Donald says, indicating that he is aware of her charade, to which she quips, "Well, I hope the page was entertaining."[1] Capitola's lines are carefully planned to please, yet reflect her true feelings, much as Southworth was skilled at entertaining while also voicing her cultural preferences. Capitola actually does admire Black Donald, as indicated both by her resistance to plans for his execution and by the horse and money she provides him in the end.[2] She tells him she likes a man who strikes fear in people, and he replies by saying women are attracted to men with "the spice of the devil" in them (*Hidden* 390). Though she enjoys his power, analogous to Southworth's own fiction, to "make people's hair stand on end," she refuses his association with the devil and instead spins out a religious justification worthy of Southworth's own yarns (*Hidden* 386).

Such characteristics are not devilish, she argues, but rather exude Christian boldness and courage. She does well to clean up his moral conscience according to the Cult of True Womanhood, justifying his crime as bold economic marauding typifying religious virtues, not criminal vices. This is a wonderful parody of true womanhood, as Southworth tips her hand to the reader to indicate that her true heart lies with Black Donald and not with conventional piety. Indeed, Capitola herself does not really believe the Christian dogma behind any of this, as it is only part of her ploy to subdue him. But she does admire him and justifies his economic savagery in tones worthy of Southworth's admiring letters to her publisher Bonner, also a fearless and notorious figure of the market.

Southworth's close relationship to Bonner and her handsome salary have been well documented,[3] and testify to the fact that the publisher's "best authors were also his best friends," as Mary Noel notes.[4] Bonner not only lent his writers money, especially Harriet and Leon Lewis, and gave lavish Christmas bonuses, he offered to hire a substitute to fight in place of Southworth's son in the Civil War, attempted to pass a bill to allow Southworth to divorce her estranged husband, and vacationed regularly with her family. Bonner was loyal in sickness and in health, as he promised to "pay [Southworth's] salary and with more pleasure than now" if she "should be incapacitated from writing for years."[5]

The politics of such care and devotion appear to reflect a benevolent paternalism, yet their economics defy a neat replication of separate spheres relations. My purpose is to demonstrate that, far from a separate spheres arrangement, the author-publisher relationship between Southworth and Bonner was more equitable than a traditional marriage at the time, as their shared commercial goal of winning, and maintaining, a mass readership fostered compassion through the mutual recognition of the freedoms and challenges necessary for success in this business venture. The satisfaction Southworth derived from her dealings with Bonner was directly correlated to her own power to produce a profit for herself and the *New York Ledger*. This pattern is echoed in her fiction, especially in tropes of artistic production in which supportive, liberating love functions as a necessary condition conducive to economic vitality. I locate such patterns in the chapter "Art and Money" in *The Lost Heiress* (1854), and throughout the virtually unknown novel *The Artist's Love* (1872), which elaborate on the condition of popular antebellum female authorship encoded in Capitola's confrontation with Black Donald in *The Hidden Hand* (1859). Southworth's image of autonomy and resourcefulness has been well established—mainly through the autobiographical content of *The Deserted Wife*—by Joyce Warren, Noel, and Joanne Dobson. I add that such autonomy was leavened with the equally important ingredients of supportive, liberating love visible in her model of ideal patronage for artistic production.

DOING BUSINESS WITH BONNER

For building the *Ledger* into the most lucrative weekly newspaper in the United States during the entire nineteenth century, Bonner's standards for selecting authors were laughably bad.[6] In an early 1880s conversation with veteran publisher J. C. Derby of Derby and Miller (publisher of bestselling author Fanny Fern), Bonner only half-jokingly said he considered two things when judging manuscripts: handwriting and sentence structure. When asked about the abominable penmanship of Horace Greeley, Bonner said in that case, sentence structure was the deciding factor.[7] Bonner's phenomenal wealth earned from the *Ledger*'s record-breaking circulation of 400,000 in January 1860 did not arise from his capacity to know when he was in the presence of a quality manuscript.[8] Instead, his ability to poach rising stars on the brink of greatness in the increasingly profitable weekly serial fiction trade undoubtedly contributed to his success. Bonner was in fact better at playing the authorial stock market than at assessing the subtler tones of prose fiction.[9] But was this the whole story? His real talent lay in his method of retaining his authors, especially women. His business ethic was masterfully tailored to the professional and personal demands of his most powerful female authors, particularly Southworth. His methods were consonant with the new authorial identity women writers like Southworth were forging during the market revolution of the 1850s, when transforming economic conditions upset traditional gender roles, especially among the more profitable occupations open to women.[10]

Bonner was a sentimental favorite among his authors of sentimental fiction because, unlike his competitors, he loved them. Southworth and

Bonner's partnership was as warm as it was profitable: she made him famous with the astonishing success of *The Hidden Hand,* first serialized in 1859 and twice more by Bonner to maximize profits for the *Ledger* before it was finally published as a novel in 1888. Though designed to appear like economically disinterested humanitarian philanthropy, Bonner's human touch was of course made possible by Southworth's ungodly work ethic.[11] Their bond was far more complex than her simply enjoying playing the "lady author" to his "gentleman publisher," for in such arrangements, women were sheltered from money matters and executive decisions. Southworth instead worked directly with Bonner on equal footing as a business partner out to make the *Ledger* as profitable as possible. Both understood the delicate interdependence of their author-publisher relationship, demanding the sort of risk and trust Herman Melville symbolized in the monkey-rope in *Moby-Dick* (1851): "individuality is now merged in a joint stock company of two," Ishmael muses: "If your banker breaks, you snap."[12] While Southworth knew her work for Bonner was a capital venture in which she played perhaps the most crucial role—for what is a publisher without a writer?—she was nonetheless driven by a curious combination of love and money, since her astute writing, like Ishmael's dexterity with the monkey-rope, was what Bonner relied upon for his livelihood. As a professional author, she was driven to write as much and as profitably as she did not only to feed her family, but also to return through her labor the financial love Bonner had publicly proclaimed to her in her lucrative exclusive contract. Rather than a genteel system of artistic patronage, theirs was a progressive business partnership, a capital bond that would amass the largest readership in the history of American weeklies. From such an equitable business relationship grew a congenial friendship that extended into their leisure lives.

Ironically, Southworth produced profitable sentimentality in her fiction, just as she sought it out in her life as a balm for the coldness of the capitalist condition that forced her to the brink of starvation in the 1840s. It was then, in the wake of being abandoned by her unemployed husband Frederick Hamilton Southworth, that she struggled to feed her family with meager schoolteacher's wages while pregnant with her second child in Washington, D.C. *The Deserted Wife* (1856) has drawn an abundance of commentary correlating the novel with this experience.[13] *The Lost Heiress* (serialized in 1853 and published as a novel the following year) has received little attention and *The Artist's Love* (1872) is virtually unknown, yet they dramatize the business ethic in her letters by staging dilemmas of artistic production mitigated by broken interpersonal relationships and fraught material necessity.[14] Such figures correlate with the distinct pressure of writing under economic peril, even to the brink of death by starvation, a personal experience Southworth repeatedly drew upon and which characterizes so much of her work.

Southworth turned from school teaching to writing for survival; she wrote hungry and she wrote for money. Before signing with Bonner, Southworth and Fern, who would become the most famous of his contracted authors, initially wrote for patriarchal, authoritarian publisher-editors whom they openly despised. Their early jobs were incarcerating, as their publishers curtailed their sense of professional and artistic freedom: William Moulton of the *Olive Branch* clung to Fern despite Bonner's gaudy offer that dwarfed her current salary.[15] In the same spirit as Moulton, Henry Peterson, editor of the *Saturday Evening Post*, censured Southworth for writing "immoral" fiction. He refused to publish one of her numbers of *The Deserted Wife*, for example, citing the impropriety of attempting "to interest us in a character who could force a young girl into a marriage against her tears and protestations."[16] Viewing her work on the level of representation alone, Peterson continued to badger her in 1854. "The Missing Bride," he complained, should have "a sensible and noble instead of a weak and foolish woman" as "your *best* character, in the artistic sense of the word."[17] Using fiction as a means of social control here, Peterson's patriarchal objective to indoctrinate female readers with an ideal sense of womanhood in the stories betrays his facile appeal to art here. As a bad business partner, Peterson, like Moulton, came to represent nothing less than an unwanted suitor, or worse, a possessive husband in a once-promising marriage turned rancid. Add this to Southworth's burden as a single mother and the stage was set for the entrance of Bonner, an entrepreneur in the guise of a romantic suitor, a fierce advocate, yet warm and loyal with an ethically spotless private life.

Bonner's morals were impeccable; he neither drank nor smoked, owned the most coveted prize racehorses in the nation and never raced them for money,[18] remained a loyal husband to his wife and children, was a dedicated elder of his Presbyterian church, and projected an image of a clean-cut Scotsman well assimilated to the capitalist condition of antebellum print culture. He offered a unique style of advocacy for his authors, combining traditional gentility with new age capitalism. He cared for his authors while savagely marauding the market on their behalf, implementing competitive techniques and advertising strategies unheard of at the time—one of which was to spend as much money as possible on advertising while allowing none in the *Ledger.*[19] This typified his business ethic of unrestrained competition and promotional pyrotechnics off site, while locally maintaining an impeccable appearance that expunged all signs of the grubby marketplace[20] both in his private life and in the pages of the *Ledger.* With absolutely no advertising, the *Ledger* was uniquely distinguished from all other weeklies published in the nineteenth century. Further, no ads meant Bonner's authors did not have to compete for the reader's attention in a cluttered and distracting format, lending their pieces an intimate, even book-like presence fostering a relatively unmitigated medium between author and reader. Bonner thus showcased his stars in the most reader-responsive format possible.

Bonner possessed a "perfect understanding of the great new reading public that was growing up in America."[21] He neither censured Southworth nor chastised her; the two continually worked together with those readers in mind, in what would prove to be a much more successful marketing strategy than Peterson's. Southworth was aware of this, and therefore asked him to silently edit (i.e., to make alterations without her consultation) her story "Eudora, or the False Princess," because she felt its narrative pace dragged: "I think it so necessary to conclude the first number at some startling point in the story that I should advise you in the event of the first number being too long to *cut it down* so as to end the number just where the dreadful accusation of poisoning the whole family is brought out against the heroine." Keeping reader satisfaction in clear view as the common interest, and thus bond, between her and Bonner, she trusts that, "Providence permitting, the interest of the work shall continually rise."[22] In cases like this, she reciprocated her artistic freedom by granting his editorial freedom. She even suggested having a ghost writer "enlarge on that part [of 'Astrea'] and write the story out to its proper length" to finish a number to meet deadline when she was stricken with smallpox; she lauded his capacity to satisfy her request, pleased "with the episode written by your confidential assistant. That girl-hunt in the Cyprus swamp was very good."[23]

Southworth's disputes were rarely with Bonner, but mostly with recalcitrant readers, who represented a small minority of her audience. She reacted to complaining letters Bonner provided, for example, arguing that "we should not judge the half-million of readers, who *being satisfied, say* nothing, by the half dozen who complain of [unimportant] details"; the same criticism, she notes, has been made of "Walter Scott, Charles Dickens, Victor Hugo, and George Eliot."[24] This is not the voice of a woman who passively "accepted conventional views of noncompetitive, feminine behavior," as at least one critic has assumed.[25] She was aggressive about reaching her readers, and took pride in the "half-million" she "satisfied."

Without tyrannical artistic constraints, Southworth felt at liberty to speak her mind; she would have never made such comments to Peterson, whose business manner cast her in a distinctly inferior role. Bonner had economic incentive to offer more artistic and editorial freedoms to her and to serve eagerly her requests since she in fact was the source of the *Ledger*'s popularity. In this sense, Southworth was the agent of change, and not the fawning, overly grateful dependent that her gushing letters ("You came to me and saved my life," one says)[26] would make it appear. Such joy in writing for Bonner is not indicative of her role as his minion. If anything, the discourse governing much of their correspondence that borrows from the language of matrimony in fact revises and extends its traditional definition to something more modern and progressive. In the same letter she defines specifically the benefits she drew from his entrance into her life, dawning "a bright glad morning" in which she "found independence, sympathy, friendship and honor and an occupation in which I could delight."[27] In this sense, Southworth's incentive to stay with Bonner and write her best for him was built on her desire to maintain the business equivalent of an ideal male domestic partner, one that could accommodate for and honor the fact that she was a professional woman—note her emphasis on "independence" and "occupation"—in an era in which women rarely commanded significant capital in the market.

Southworth was overjoyed to write for Bonner. He was not only a welcome relief from the strictures of Peterson, but he also offered Southworth a source of friendship as a true confidant that had been missing in her life since her husband left her. As in her novels, she too was a "deserted wife," but hardly a passive one helplessly tied to the railroad tracks. Instead, she was, like the heroine of *The Deserted Wife*, a successful professional artist and popular entertainer, first establishing her value economically in the market *on her own* before the hero's entrance.

Indeed, the husband's return in that novel, like Southworth's own life, was predicated on her having amassed financial independence and thus a measure of female power uncommon in the era. Power and money are not without their allure, and indeed, Bonner only emerges when her financial worth is established. This does not imply that love, therefore, was out of the question; the binary was never so mutually exclusive between love and money for Bonner. Indeed, the business opportunity to mutually enrich one another made the love possible; the mutual appreciation thus grew from it, as Bonner looked upon Southworth with the same wide-eyed wonder as she looked upon him: she was his hero (masculine ending intended) as much as he was hers.

This sort of capitalist marriage in many ways was the model for how good author-publisher relations could be in the nineteenth century. Southworth, for example, turned down a rival's offer to write for $10,000 per story for a weekly called *Saturday Night*. Her language is rooted in the discourse of matrimonial devotion, vowing that "even without the [five-year] contract, honor, gratitude, old habit, and my own best interests and my sacred friendships, bind me fast to the Ledger."[28] With careful emphasis upon her "own best interests," Southworth presents herself as an independent businessperson driven by her own personal development rather than self-sacrifice. Stating her decision in terms of "sacred friendship" humanizes their relationship in what the culture conventionally sees as a morally unclean market, thereby elevating their commercial enterprise. Money does not disappear in the equation, however, as both understood that the sacredness of that friendship, the filial love that is so potent in so many of her letters to him, was forged from capital. Southworth was loyal to Bonner out of much more than reflexive conformity to conventional gender codes; blind obedience to an abstract notion of masculinity according to separate spheres ideology was not her source of attachment either. If she were so conventional, she never would have left Peterson, her first employer, and thus, according to a strict reading of gender codes, her "true" hero. Rather, she knew the dynamics of her relationship with Bonner offered her unique levels of artistic freedom and editorial latitude that an upstart like *Saturday Night* would likely be unable to match. Bonner was financially savvy enough to embrace a nonjudgmental, equitable, supportive relationship for his best female authors with minimal moral censorship.

It is not surprising, therefore, that Fern, his most opinionated feminist pundit who openly questioned the stodginess and rigidity of gender codes (particularly the stultifying effect of marriage on female ambition), developed her voice to its most subversive amplitude in the *Ledger*. Bonner's relationships with Southworth and Fern should not be misconstrued as lived versions of the gentleman rushing to the aid of a lady in need, however much they liked to frame their relationships that way in letters and fictional figures. Indeed, their radical reformulation of gender roles is often obscured by genteel language. Their warmth with one another, I would submit, was as genuine as any in the history of author-publisher relations in the United States, and it was generated by a mutual interest in literature as a commercial enterprise.

Publishers like Ticknor and Fields or *Harper's Monthly*, whose interests were not so explicitly commercial as they were literary, personified the older late eighteenth- and early nineteenth-century image of the gentleman publisher. They thus tended to alienate women writers. The commercial interest of a publisher was directly proportional to how congenial he was to women authors. For as clean as his personal life was, Bonner was never an insider among the most respected gentlemen publishers in the nineteenth century. His displays of economic power through advertising clashed with the staid, sedate houses of Boston, typified by Ticknor and Fields which catered to admired yet unsalable sophisticates like Nathaniel Hawthorne. Another fascinating contrast to Bonner's business style is reflected in the correspondence of Melville with his publishers. Author-publisher relations were fraught with insecurity, insincerity, and strategizing, plaguing Melville to the extent that he made them the satirical target in the second half of *Pierre; or, The Ambiguities* (1856). The very opposite characterizes the Southworth-Bonner correspondence, which was open, spontaneous, transparent, and emotionally engaged. Its priorities were clear: please the readers to sell more papers, and support one and other in the process. "American women writers . . . have often written within a gendered tradition of entrepreneurship . . . associated more with moneymaking than with art-for-art's sake," which for Southworth was a condition not restrictive but liberating.[29] Southworth and Bonner thus unleashed their imaginations on the market, as they shared a passion for stretching the boundaries of the commercial.

Indeed, feats like filling the entire May 6, 1858, edition of the *New York Herald* with advertisements for the *Ledger* spoke to Bonner's willingness to bring his market dominance to the level of public performance. This was a landmark in the history of self-promotion and publicity, anticipating Goodyear's twentieth-century display of power and technology in flying blimps over stadiums filled with 100,000 people and televised to millions more. Such extensions of the definition of the commercial world through such overt celebrations of capital and territorial dominance of his competition seemed a glaring mismatch with eighteenth-century notions of the gentleman publisher. For Bonner was advancing a Gilded Age version of the gentleman publisher prototypical of twentieth-century corporate marketing strategies.

Bonner's relation to capital was geared toward the grand spectacle, as much as Southworth's fiction writing was. In this sense, they shared the same objective and played their politics accordingly, which is to say, to the middle.[30] Bonner's editorial statements, therefore, were mainly methods of controlling the *Ledger*'s public profile and maintaining its image for as broad an audience as possible. Such a statement appeared in the *Ledger* in 1859, prompting the claim that "even so liberal a man as Robert Bonner" was "really" sexist.[31] In the editorial, Bonner denounced women who pursue professional careers. He aligned their radical independence with lascivious indulgence in the passions, intimating that such women are also sexually promiscuous, and thus anti-marriage: "The so-called 'strong-minded women' of the day, with their 'independent' platform, self-condemned as infidels, as contemners [sic] of marriage and its obligations, as the advocates of the 'largest liberty' in the indulgence of the passions."[32] But we know he is selling papers here—note the drama in the voice, the excessive piety, and the mention of sexuality in the dark reform trope that so dominated the centrist politics of the *Ledger*. We know, indeed, what he actually did to advance and nurture some of the most subversive public voices in the history of female authorship in the nineteenth century. We know that any pious defense of the institution of marriage he expressed was severely undercut by his willingness to change the law to allow for divorce in Washington, D.C., and further liberate not only Southworth from her superannuated matrimonial ties, but all women from unwanted marriages.

Bonner's actions speak louder than his words, just as Hagar's successful professional singing career is far more striking in *The Deserted Wife* than her eventual marriage. Indeed, Warren's point about Southworth can equally apply to Bonner: "it is true that the fairy-tale reconciliation is not what interests Southworth. She is much more interested in the economics of Hagar's story."[33] Likewise, Bonner was much more interested in the economics of women's lives, and did what he could to make marriage conform to their (and of course his own) economic interests rather than the reverse. Southworth's response to the suggestions that she might marry after her return from England reflects her financial priorities. In a letter to Bonner, she ironically appropriates the language of matrimony to describe her resolve to remain a Southworth and thus maintain her brand name so closely associated with the *Ledger* in the public eye. Though the potential suitor was "as near Christian perfection as any human could approach . . . I will remain as I am, E. D. E. N. Southworth, and you will never lose your contributor," she promised Bonner.[34] The implication is also that married life would bring her a source of income through her new husband, thus threatening to end her writing career. This vow signals a resolute sense of her identity as a professional author wedded to her commercial interest first. It moralizes and justifies her economic interest and personal livelihood that provided not only friendship through Bonner, but also the canvas upon which she expressed her creative passion.

PRODUCTIVE SENTIMENTS AND SENTIMENTAL PRODUCTIONS

Indeed, Southworth's loyalty to her professional identity is also loyalty to Bonner. The larger pattern in Southworth's letters in which she "couched the financial dealings with Bonner in terms of friendship rather than business" was not ascribable to a domestic anti-professional temperament in which "she was far more comfortable with a personal rather than a strictly commercial relationship," as one critic argues.[35] Southworth was not uncomfortable around money, business, or financial dealings. Instead, she found professional life could provide a source of comfort and warmth that conventional married life often falsely promised. She did not simply transform Bonner into a spouse, but more complexly, imagined him as brother, banker, confidant, emotional counselor, employer, and colleague as well: a business partner with a heart. She "learned to intertwine private and professional matters" in her relationship with Bonner, as Susan Albertine notes.[36] In its most ideal form, her association with Bonner as embodied by her position with the *Ledger* was better than a traditional marriage, especially in the context of the American mid-nineteenth century.

Southworth's unusual circumstances as a writer wielding unheard of power in her relationship with her publisher appear at odds, however, with her seemingly straightforward traditional values. Take, for example, her expression of thanks to Bonner for arriving at an opportune time to facilitate her escape from the unsavory Peterson: "If all men were as prompt and spirited in defending the women dependent upon them, as you are then we should all be very glad to leave our rights in the hands of our *brave, big brothers*."[37] The compliment is designed to flatter Bonner's gentlemanly pride, but troublingly does so at the expense of women's rights. Her statement, upon closer inspection, is conditional: "if" advocacy were to function universally like Bonner's, women's rights should be gladly handed over to such allies, given that virtually all of the capital in the market was wielded by men at the time. Thus men could either work in support of women, like Bonner, or not, like Peterson. While I find Southworth's sentiment is more progressive here than it appears, placing her politics in the historical context of rising market culture is essential to fully understanding such statements otherwise easily cast off as "traditional" or conservative.

It makes little sense to argue over whether Southworth was "progressive" or conservative without a clear view of the cultural preoccupations and the currents of intellectual history that shaped her time and situation. According to June Howard, "Sentimentality remains a powerful element of popular literature, and one can scarcely find a canonical author—including [Henry] James—who is not drawing on or in dialogue with the tradition."[38] For example, Melville's *Pierre*, like *The Lost Heiress*, offers a critique as well as a deployment of sentimentality's form. The terrain is too broad to cast the question in narrow progressive versus conservative political terms when we consider Herbert Ross Brown on the influence of the Scottish Common Sense philosophers,[39] the formalist sophistication of "human connectedness" Dobson illustrates in the fiction itself,[40] and how sentimental sympathy rises during the market revolution to make "fellow-feeling" compensate for "the distance and hostility separating individuals in a world of commodity transactions."[41]

A shift in cognitive styles under capitalism to construct a humanitarian discourse was a key to the rise of sentimentality.[42] Southworth's enterprising spirit emerged just as "Sentimental sympathy began to flow out along the veins of European commerce in search of its victims."[43] Sentiment reacted against the rise of empirical science.[44] Such currents in intellectual history help explain why an author like Southworth and Fern, her more radical feminist colleague at the *Ledger*, would opt for marriage endings in their fiction. At stake for them was not a binary of progressive versus conservative values, but the more complex challenge of how to celebrate the market's liberating powers and defend the human spirit from the reification of the almighty dollar. Hence, much of Southworth's fiction is dedicated to humanizing the female need, often figured in male artist figures in her fiction, for economic independence.

The Deserted Wife has been hailed by critics as one of Southworth's masterpieces of fiction on the theme of female power and economic independence because of the heroine's staunch individualism and potent professional career. It first appeared in weekly installments for Peterson's *Saturday Evening Post* in 1849. In 1853, Southworth wrote *The Lost Heiress*, also for the *Post*. It received as much praise and notoriety as *The Deserted Wife* at the time, yet contemporary critics are drawn to the more pronounced feminism of the earlier novel. *The Lost Heiress* actually garnered her as much praise, and ultimately the attention of Bonner. When Bonner signed Southworth, he promised her new work would surpass the appeal of "even 'The Deserted Wife' and 'The Lost Heiress,' which [had] been considered her most popular works."[45]

On the surface, *The Lost Heiress* appears to be the least interested in women's economic independence. At a closer look, it shows a deep concern for the emergent patron-artist relationship in the context of the mid-century market revolution and thus sheds much light on Southworth's relationship with Bonner. *The Lost Heiress* is in many ways a cautionary tale for future artists, as it warns against the romantic myth of the individual, autonomous genius. Excessive self-reliance and dependence on intuition are punished in the story. Management rationally carried out with the aid of an astute consultant and wealthy investor in the project, the tale instructs, is as essential as creativity for the successful production of art. The rise of market culture by the 1850s signaled such a change in the condition of authorship. "The old tradition that writing was not a trade, but an avocation for ladies and gentlemen," notes

Frank Luther Mott, gave way to a new generation of "young writers" who "wanted money." One perennially exploited writer from the time, Fitz-James O'Brien, testified to the rampant abuse of authors in the market, and the necessity of astute financial management of one's career when he picketed for higher wages, marching up and down Franklin Square with a large sign that said, "ONE OF HARPER'S AUTHORS. I AM STARVING."[46]

Indeed, the most didactic elements of *The Lost Heiress* describe such damaging effects of idealizing and thus neglecting the hard realities of the market. The novel reads like a parable of Southworth's own professional career, as she extols the virtues of her own successful business ethic. The story does not promote eighteenth-century forms of patronage in which the artist's occupation is insulated from the rigors of a consuming public, with monetary aid permanently supplied by a wealthy donor. It does not make the opposite mistake, however, of idealizing self-reliance and autonomy of artistic production. Instead, it wholly acknowledges the benefits of a figure, like Bonner, who might serve as artistic consultant, financial supporter, and loyal psychological advocate. Southworth's "professional behavior," like that of many women writers at the time, "frequently depends on a willingness to receive advice from mentors," as Albertine has argued. But too much emphasis on their conformity to a "traditionally female position in relation to their male publishers" can obscure how women applied market-specific skills in business management, particularly compromise and negotiation, in executive decisions within those author-publisher relationships.[47] Southworth envisioned the ideal publisher in this novel, interestingly enough, before she even met Bonner.

In *The Lost Heiress*, Falconer O'Leary is an estranged lover and sculptor working in Rome after leaving his true love Maud, presumably for good. He seems to have good reason to do so, as Maud's father Daniel Hunter, the governor and highly esteemed gentleman, had years earlier refused to sign a reprieve to save Falconer's father from capital punishment. Hunter is "a man for a woman's worship," idealized and glorified into a larger-than-life, god-like figure.[48] He appears poised to grant the man freedom, and then refuses to do so with a long speech advocating the hard truths of capital punishment, arguing for its function to prevent future crime rather than reform, which, he says, is the work of the Bible and thus the provenance of women's domestic roles as pious civilizing influences (*Heiress* 54). Any appearance of conventional separate spheres didacticism evaporates when the commercial management of the artist's role takes over as the novel's paramount concern.

The vacillating female power in the early part of the novel indicates that Southworth was sublimating her concern for her public role as professional author into her fiction. Market culture's influence on women's public roles is highlighted through Augusta's attempt to sway her husband into granting a reprieve for O'Leary. In a moving passage, the narrator intones "that a lady's word has decided the destiny of empires and of individuals." Her "power is greater with his excellency than that of any other human being alive. She is the woman that can lead the lion, if any created being can" (*Heiress* 48). This is a red herring, however, as she capitulates to Hunter and concedes, "I have not the power" (*Heiress* 64). Southworth takes the focus off Augusta's power to effect change through her husband by explaining the circumstances of the shopkeeper's murder that William O'Leary has been charged with. Upon William's execution, his mother Norah becomes psychotic; she pleads at length to no avail for her son's life directly to Daniel Hunter in a gesture of female futility and rage that comes directly on the heels of Augusta's political impotence. This is Southworth at her best, as she veils social protest in episodic popular fiction. Indeed, here is a situation in which "husband worship" is seriously questioned through the torture these women endure, yet masked by the superficial (if not satirically facile) appeal to female obedience to male authority. Amy E. Hudock's insight about Southworth's fiction in general applies here specifically: "Southworth could question 'husband worship,' and still appear, on the surface at least, to be writing a traditional, conventional 'moral' lesson for young girls."[49]

Perhaps one of the most difficult moments in *The Lost Heiress* for a modern reader to bear is the scene shortly following that overtly instructs that a wife's duty is to obey her husband. But the details bear out Hudock's theory, and come to represent, I would argue, more than just rebellion against oppressive gender roles, but a model for self-assertion and negotiation akin to the sort demanded of Southworth in her dealings with publishers. Daniel Hunter sends Augusta to her room when she insults his mother. She obeys, deciding to triumph over herself with almost religious pride in her willingness to act knowing that the others would misinterpret it as obedience. He then demands that she apologize to his mother: that, she says, is a cross she can't bear (*Heiress* 114–15). Biblical, higher motives (not servile ones) make Augusta agree with Daniel's demand for her public apology, but she will be humiliated because his mother's daughters will misinterpret it as servility and not the act of self-possession and higher calling to control that she knows it really is (*Heiress* 117). The reconciliation with the mother-in-law creates a bond—they embrace in sympathetic tears—that is confirmed monetarily when Augusta inherits a fortune and puts her in-laws into a comfortable life (*Heiress* 118). Southworth's deft control of the scene highlights the galling injustice of Daniel's commands, and promotes the notion of reconciliation, not blind obedience, to forge bonds that eventually open economic channels for financial expressions of amity. "Godliness is profitable in all things," proclaims Ellen, Norah's virtuous daughter, later in the novel (*Heiress* 352). The scene is less interested in Daniel's power than in Augusta's triumph despite his tyranny and her ability to connect sympathetically with her mother-in-law, whom she previously assumed to be a permanent enemy.

Maternity and money also come into play when Norah O'Leary, the maniacal mother of executed criminal William O'Leary, abducts Augusta and Daniel's daughter, who is the heiress to Augusta's fortune. Maud is thus as precious economically as she is angelic (*Heiress* 123). Norah gives Maud to Ellen to raise, along with her son Falconer O'Leary, who becomes a political activist avenging his father's death by opposing the views of Daniel Hunter. Norah eventually puts Maud up for adoption; Augusta and Daniel later adopt her without knowing she is Maud (years had passed and the child had grown) in a coincidence common to the serial fiction of the time that featured family separation and reunion intersected with mistaken identity.

As Ellen raises Maud and Falconer, a bond is forged between the two reminiscent of that of Heathcliff and Catherine in Emily Brontë's *Wuthering Heights*. In a crucial foreshadowing of the precarious predicament Falconer will find himself in as an adult during his artistic career, he drops his sketchbook at the age of ten down a precipice (*Heiress* 218). In his career, he will lose his inspiration and have to find it again, but not without help. Maud risks all to retrieve the sketchbook, anticipating how his artistic career will be fueled by her love in the form of letters he receives while toiling at his art in Rome (*Heiress* 221).

Falconer's career speaks directly to the sins, according to Southworth, of a mismanaged artistic career. He strays from those who support his art to follow his political and creative whims with no deliberate plan except to indulge his "genius" whenever he pleases. He is neither farmer, nor charismatic demagogue, nor sculptor, as he dabbles too superficially and inconsistently at all three. He does more sculpting than farming, moving from his art to his speeches, leaving the farm in the hands of the "old ignorant negroes" (*Heiress* 331). Only after great struggle does he learn to rely less on his "genius" and more on his management of "time and money" (*Heiress* 331).

In an extended meditation on authorial subjectivity that covers the last third of the novel, Falconer learns how to succeed in his artistic career and in love, both romantic and filial. Exiled in Rome on a government appointment after Hunter interceded upon his marriage to Maud (Hunter was unaware of her true identity as his daughter up until the moment she approached the altar), Falconer discovers he has an unknown patron whose identity is revealed to be Daniel Hunter in the chapter titled "Art and Money." But success is not won through a patron alone. Hunter's financial and emotional support, like Bonner's, facilitates but does not determine success that is ultimately left up to his ability to win a favorable market reception. Significantly, Bonner's artistic counsel is figured in the character of the Major, Falconer's supervisor, who readily disabuses the young artist of the notion that the soul and work are mutually exclusive entities: "Throw a little more *soul* into your Virginius, and that group will make you famous," he says to Falconer, who initially finds the soul incompatible with "*work*" because he is love sick: "Yet not upon the artist's *work!* Alas! In this bitter hour, what cared the boy for his fame? In this bitter hour when he felt that she who gave all the value to it, was gone for ever [as he falsely assumed Maud was dead]" (*Heiress* 449). Falconer's best work is eventually fueled by a healthy and true love. He is inspired by the knowledge of Hunter's support once his identity is revealed to him, and Maude's love, which blooms precisely when his masterpiece sculpture for the Capitol—and for *capital,* a favorite pun of Southworth's also found in Capitola's name—is complete.

The Capitol statue tops Falconer's other great work, Virginius, which is originally flawed because it is distorted by his lovesick mood. Originally odd and imbalanced, the Virginius statue in the early stages reflects Falconer's obsessive longing for Maud despite wrongly assuming her dead in the early stages of the project. Upon the disclosure of Hunter's identity as his supportive patron, however, and once fortified by Maud's letters expressing her love, he makes Virginius look "glorious and

God-like" in keeping with the original Roman myth. Southworth clearly advocates the power of love to inspire great art, but is careful not to mystify the process of artistic production. She shows the damage reckless egotistical and naïve trust in talent alone can do to the finished product, a pitfall she carefully avoided in her own career. Restraint is also essential: it is symbolized by the waves of the ocean Falconer wants to cross from Rome. He resists returning to Maud, however, until his work is completed, whereupon he ships out on the vessel carrying his sculpture. His diligence in sculpting and letter writing to Maud are clearly reflexive of Southworth's own practice of keeping up her correspondence that gave her the strength to make her weekly deadlines for the *Ledger*.

Hunter's Bonneresque loyalty weathers Falconer's bouts of individualistic perversity that distract him from his art and lead to his prejudiced political opposition to the governor. Falconer demands the Major heap the full scale of his sins upon him in all their agonizing detail. Marianne Noble has traced such patterns in *The Masochistic Pleasures of Sentimental Literature*, in which she notes that pain, in this case Falconer's guilt, can function as religious transcendence and an atonement of sins. Further, Falconer's extravagant and dramatic self-flagellation in the scene reaches breathless, pitched cadences reminiscent of the sex act itself; he wants more, the Major says enough: "*Beast!* that I was! I could thump my own head against the wall!" The Major replies, "Nay, nay, now don't assault yourself at that rate" (*Heiress* 453). Falconer cries, "Oh! My God! This is too much! Too much," but apparently not enough, for he commands the Major to continue delineating his cruel miscalculation of his father-in-law's character, joyfully proclaiming, "This is really heaping coals of fire on my head" (*Heiress* 456). As Noble remarks, "when twentieth-century male masochists engage in theatrical rituals of violence against the self as a form of transcending the self, they are imitating in parodic ways patterns established in sentimental works" like this one. "Masochism as a sexual practice," she continues, "and as a form of erotic fantasy would not have taken the forms it has today were it not for the sentimental literature that provided many of its most characteristic images."[50] Falconer glories in his confession because it exultingly rids him of his guilt and thus brings him closer to Maud, the erotic object of desire toward which his masochism is projected. The Major's harsh medicine thus provides him with an anguish to savor in an experience as orgasmic as it is cleansing: "Oh, sir, why do you cease? . . . Proceed—do not spare me!" (*Heiress* 455).

The Lost Heiress ends with Falconer, his sins appeased, wedding Maud upon his return to America with his masterpiece sculpture commissioned for the Capitol in Washington, D.C. Falconer's engagement gift to Maud is a pearl necklace purchased from his earnings; the diction describing the jewels is decidedly economic: "He condensed, crystallized the labor of years in that one costly offering, and laid it on their feet. They represented—not so many thousand vulgar dollars—but painful days and nights of toil and study—glorious days and nights of inspiration!" (*Heiress* 498). Falconer proclaims, "every gem here stands for days of toil—of an artist's priceless toil! Yes! And priceless love, too" (*Heiress* 498).

The capstone of the novel is economic unity: Maude gives him the deed to the estate, not to glory in her dependence upon him as modern readers might assume, but to marry symbolically their fortunes together, his artist's labor in the form of pearls to her inherited land. They join forces financially, consummating their mutual capital power. Matching his generosity in giving the whole of this artistic labor to her, she gives her entire property to him, to which he registers shock. "What of that?" she responds in language that is at once financial and affectionate: "Are not our interests *one?*" (*Heiress* 499).[51] The word "interest" here puns on both the return on an investment, drawing on the notion of economic self-interest, now combined and mutual, and their romantic interest, or desire, for each other. In Southworth's letters, much of the seemingly self-denying tones that appear worshipful of Bonner in fact enact this same ritual of triumph in shared success, wealth, and privilege, all generated by a complex web of intermediary aid and disciplined yet visionary production of an in-demand product. *The Lost Heiress* encodes how Southworth enjoyed loyalty, warmth, and "kinship" with Bonner, yet maintained her professionally independent identity through her narrative power to escape the shackles of the institution of marriage, a pattern figured in Capitola's confrontation of Black Donald in *The Hidden Hand.*

Whereas *The Lost Heiress* promotes the galvanizing power of love for the creation of art, "The Awful Peril of Capitola" in *The Hidden Hand* presents the power of narrative as a force capable of preserving the lives and dignity of both author and reader. Returning to the scene so reflexive of female authorship that I discuss at the opening of this chapter, Capitola's response to Black Donald's aggression ("Take care girl! No bad names! You are in my power! at my mercy!") speaks volumes: "I know my position; but I must continue" (*Hidden* 390). The first clause of her reply indicates her poised confrontation of the hard truth of her position as Black Donald's "caged starling." Her circumstance is emblematic of women's captivity under possessive male tyranny endemic to the nineteenth century, particularly within the confines of the institution of marriage. The second clause, "but I must continue," refuses silence, and thus passive submission to such conditions, instead choosing to continue speaking/writing for empowerment within them. Capitola's control over the scene through her narrative power echoes Southworth's own capacity to use narrative the same way. "I must continue" to tell this tale, Capitola says, much in the spirit of Southworth, who knows her position as a woman within the culture's prevailing gender politics, but must continue to use her access to domestic discourse for her survival. For however admiring Capitola is of Black Donald, he is potentially dangerous, much like the mass market itself. Southworth's power to entertain the masses with Black Donald's wild spirit harnesses forces, especially racy subjects and their attendant disapproving readers, with the power to devour her unless she deftly deploys the rhetorical piety of domesticity.

The Artist's Love similarly voices Southworth's appreciation for bold economic enterprise, but justifies it through her more genuine belief in the power of filial love. It is the tale of the rural Marie Serafinne who finds herself deserted by Roland Talbot, artist and father of her child, who returns to his agency after completing a collection of landscapes and portraits of his new love Marie. She insists on staying with her grandmother out of loyalty to the dying woman, refusing his offer to come with him to the city. When her grandmother discovers Marie is pregnant, the old woman offers to find Talbot and extract as much money from him as possible; her motives are purely economic.[52] The grandmother dies and Marie is left in a freezing house with little food; she loses consciousness and awakes with her frozen premature newborn pressed to her bosom. In a near false confession, she says she was likely the murderer, though she can't recall the act. To Marie, being hanged for murder would be a "trifle" given the abject freezing and starvation she regularly suffers. This condition embodies the economic terrors of a loss of resources to stay fed and sheltered, especially with a baby (*Love* 61).

Public defender Ishmael Worth takes the case and refuses to let her die, especially "with an undeserved stigma upon her name" (*Love* 65).

Worth is the Bonner figure of the story, facilitating Marie's freedom in such a way that he does not outright save her, so much as enable her to make a living independently for herself. Indeed, when Marie finds work on her own for a rural family of German anti-intellectual capitalists called the Burgers, she channels the spirit of her baby in a great moment in Southworth's fiction that merges spiritualism and economics, mysticism and business. The child/angel completes her domestic chores for her, thereby enriching the family and Marie with her extraordinary labor. The love of her child enables such labor to be miraculously completed (*Love* 88), thus raising her status on the Burgers' farm: the "power of work in her was money in the pocket of the laboring farmer" (*Love* 91).

Talbot returns after searching the world over (and after a stint studying schools of art in Rome like Falconer) and they settle in London, where she is a "modern spiritualist" communicating with her "spirit child." Southworth considered such "modern spiritualism" not at all at odds with Christianity, but rather a natural extension of it. She found such mystical forces with the power to regenerate characters from illness and madness "divinely prefigured in the laying on of hands."[53] If miraculous results issue from the same pattern ("I prayed for it, believed in it"), she reasoned, then why does one have to be blasphemous and the other sacred? Her faith, Helen Papashvily argues, "seemed not so much faith in God or faith in herself as just faith in Faith—a kind of militant optimism, peculiarly American, in which to want and to believe and to expect and to deserve equaled to receive."[54] She poured such optimistic faith into Bonner both personally and financially, and he returned the sentimental investment, as it became the key in some crucial ways to their entire relationship. The support and love that characterized so much of their partnership is also reflected in her supportive readership, whose outpouring of sympathy that coincided with the recovery of her child's health is directly linked to such faith: "Next my child contrary to my own opinion and that of the Doctor's got well [as] friends crowded around me, offers for contributions poured in upon me."[55] However much Southworth liked to mystify such power in faith, the warmth from Bonner and her readers nonetheless is very much rooted in the material reality of her own popularity as an author, which I have noted is the direct result of her ardent work ethic and realistic management of her career.

The Artist's Love portrays Southworth's economic power in her domestic efficiency, as tasks are mysteriously accomplished with the aid of her "modern spiritualism," justifying Southworth's mysticism that is so much at the heart of her sense of authorship. For without access to her dead child, her voice would not sing like a harp, and her economic power would not be realized. The power to write also had the power to make domestic work disappear. Southworth indeed wanted to continue channeling spirits in her writing, as depicted in the novel's happy ending, which features a marriage that embraces and fosters Marie's special skill.

Southworth was as acutely aware of the economic benefits of such good marriages as she was of "the parallels between bad business and bad marriages," as Ann Ingram notes.[56] In "Marriage and Divorce," the preface to *The Deserted Wife*, Southworth touts the virtues of "PRUDENCE" to avoid "ending in bankruptcy of heart, home, and happiness," and of "FIDELITY" to thwart "business [corruption], embezzlement of funds, &c., and hence broken marriage, faith, and deserted families."[57] Southworth's dedication to Bonner embodied these principles; it was built on mutual risk and trust in business competence. Melville's meditation on the monkey-rope describes how these principles animate the dynamics of relationships throughout society's myriad transactions, from medical and pharmaceutical to legal and financial. The author-publisher partnership between Southworth and Bonner models the humanitarian and financial potential of such transactions during a phase in American history when literature was becoming big business and the old patron model was vanishing. Between the sheltered patronage of old and the new mythic promise of complete autonomy was where their arrangement lay. The myth of the autonomous producer never really existed, as intermediaries can be found in even the most self-reliant of authorial careers. Even Walt Whitman, a notoriously individualistic self-promoter, hired out most of his printing or had it done for free by friends. Weathering the market with an intimate companion, as Southworth had, was still preferable to going it alone in the increasingly brutal and competitive book trade of the 1850s.

Not all author-publisher relations at the time were so amiable, intimate, and thus profitable as Southworth and Bonner's. By comparison, open hostility and exploitation characterized Harper and Brothers' treatment of Melville; Henry David Thoreau's relationship with Ticknor and Fields was distanced and fraught with frustration. The Southworth-Bonner partnership proves how powerful shared economic interests can be when humanized; how affection can motivate labor, and thus drive and sustain success. If, as Thomas Merton has said, "Compassion is the keen awareness of the interdependence of all things," then Southworth and Bonner's mutual compassion arose from their keen awareness of the economic interdependence intrinsic to their positions as author and publisher serving each other as well as a mass readership.[58] Within this market setting, they were true collaborators in a business relationship on more equal footing than traditional marriages. Their relationship therefore radically departed from the conventional gender roles of gentleman author and lady publisher that appeared to replicate separate spheres codes of behavior. Compassion for each other and their readers served their profit motive and made the *Ledger* and Southworth's literary career smashing successes in what combined into perhaps the most lucrative engine for popular fiction of the entire nineteenth century. Such success demanded bravery, risk, and imagination in both Southworth's fiction and Bonner's promotional strategies to extend the market to astonishing new dimensions. Southworth and Bonner's market-driven powers of imagination forged a capital bond anticipating the modern democratizing effects of mutual financial interest on imbalanced gender codes of behavior. For Southworth and Bonner, commercial enterprise brought both money and meaning, capital and compassion, to their lives.

Part 3 ~ Literary Partner as Parent and Kin

5

OUR WAYWARD SON

Emerson and Fuller's Tutelage of Henry David Thoreau

The literary partnerships illustrated in Part 2 were remarkable for their innovative and progressive refigurings of the stultifying marital arrangements common to the antebellum United States by placing women on equal footing as business partners and collaborators with their male counterparts. Part 3 of this book examines literary partners as metaphorical parent figures in Henry David Thoreau's career, and then as siblings—both rivals and advocates—in Fanny Fern's career. Whereas Part 2 detailed how power was effectively balanced by the actual and figurative married interests of literary business, this chapter and the one following explore the more problematic power struggles of Thoreau's and Fern's respective literary partnerships. Thoreau's quarrels with Ralph Waldo Emerson and Margaret Fuller, and Fern's altercations with her brother N. P. Willis, testify to this pattern. Fuller's maternal tutelage, along with the father-son dynamic of the Emerson-Thoreau relationship, was initially forged upon a deep communion of spirit and craft, but economic concerns, especially the challenge of securing gainful employment for Thoreau in the literary market, thwarted the high hopes of transcendental Concord's best son.

Thoreau must have known such fate was looming, for upon hearing his mother's reply to the question of what he should do after graduation from Harvard, he burst into tears. Even in his youth, Thoreau sensed he was going to face trouble as an adult in the market seeking employment. He always resisted leaving home, so her telling him, in no sentimental terms, to "buckle on his knapsack and set out to seek his fortune" was more than he could bear.[1] E. D. E. N. Southworth also approached professional life reluctantly, even painfully, albeit in a far worse state of financial desperation than Thoreau. And unlike Southworth, Thoreau has not been heralded for his efforts as a professional author. His youthful tears foretold his many commercial shortcomings, from the hapless fate of *A Week on the Concord and Merrimack Rivers* (1849) that left his own shelves stocked with unsold copies produced at his expense, to the narrow yield of two publications (a review, "Paradise to be Regained," and a single article, "The Landlord") following his assault on the New York market, to the glacial composition process that kept *Walden* under construction for more than six years, to his decision to leave much of his best work hidden in his private journal. His corpus consists of a mere two published volumes, perhaps the fewest publications of any major American writer besides Emily Dickinson. Like Dickinson, he has been understood as an author who willfully, and scornfully, fled the market after briefly testing the waters. Aside from a string of unusually bad luck—Evert Duyckinck leaving his post as editor of Wiley and Putnam's Library of America series shortly after giving his blessing to Thoreau; *The Boston Miscellany of Literature and Fashion* going out of business shortly after publishing Thoreau's "A Walk to Wachusett"—his efforts to succeed as a professional author nonetheless persisted throughout the 1840s in particular, during which more than these two promising leads abruptly vanished, and his own decisions, along with faulty guidance, derailed him.

This chapter focuses on the missteps in Emerson's, and to a lesser extent Fuller's, literary parentage of Thoreau. The faults in Emerson and Thoreau's professional relationship, which frequently left Emerson mystified, were not so much the result of Thoreau's excessive autonomy or lack of vocational ambition. Rather, they were the combination of unfortunate timing and two major limitations of Emerson's guidance: a provincial sense of a literary marketplace based on the one in which he had made his start decades earlier, and a conflation of the business practice attending his own privileged status as established professional author with that of a neophyte like Thoreau. Emerson's promotion of Thoreau was further hampered by his sense of him as his perpetual wayward son, a professional project perhaps impossible to fit comfortably in any conventional vocation available at the time. During one full year from 1844 to 1845 when Thoreau neither published nor lectured, Emerson registered his disappointment in the tones of an exasperated parent, frustrated by Thoreau's unfulfilled potential: "Henry is a good substantial child . . . the only man of leisure in town."[2]

This image of Thoreau as perpetual child casts him as naturally unfit for the professional world. The common tableau of Thoreau as the isolated transcendental naturalist miscast in New York City in the iconic moment of his professional collapse, senseless to the business of writing and ethically hostile to the commercialization of his own mind, obscures how closely he worked with those who could best help him succeed from the very beginnings of his career.[3] Thoreau's career triumphs and disappointments were always deeply connected to Emerson, who adopted him as his heir apparent and savior of *The Dial*, whose slim circulation of 220 he hoped would swell under his hand.

Thoreau's autonomous transcendental persona might lead us to see his faulty career decisions as bold ideological stands of self-reliant rebellion. Instead of philosophically principled individual renunciations of the market, such decisions were often poorly executed attempts at earning payment for his writing and openly courting as wide an audience as possible. Steven Fink's biography of Thoreau frames his life according to the literary business of his pursuit of fame, usefully unveiling what is commonly missing from studies focused on the internal, ideational development of his aesthetic and psychological sense of self as author.[4] This market perspective supports my focus on the most crucial decisions Thoreau made under the influence of Emerson and the forces that converged to form a perfect storm of missed opportunities and false leads, resulting in a demoralizing series of unfulfilled expectations that fractured their personal relationship.

"THE DELICATEST OF ALL EXPERIMENTS"

Not the least of Thoreau's troubles was that, among established authors, Emerson was arguably the least successful promoter of aspiring writers of the entire American nineteenth century.[5] Despite his lack of success in this area, Emerson's keen interest "in modifications to the various callings of men, and the customs of business," along with his own successful career shift from Unitarian minister to full-time writer and lecturer, made him particularly susceptible to the temptation of discovering and growing young authorial talent.[6] Ushering young talent into the literary marketplace was a role with which Washington Irving, by contrast, was not only comfortable, but also wildly successful, turning the patronage of literary novices into something of an art form.[7] From 1841 to 1848, the time of Thoreau and Emerson's closest intimacy, Thoreau epitomized

Emerson's "special parish" of "young men seeking their way" but finding instead a volatile and cold literary marketplace.[8]

The 1840s were the most significant years of Emerson and Thoreau's relationship, and thus the most pivotal for Thoreau's career. During this time Emerson undertook in earnest the development of Thoreau's career, a venture he acknowledged in an 1843 letter to Henry James Sr. was the "delicatest of all experiments, experiments of men and intercourse . . . which one can never be sure will prosper."[9] Thoreau's career indeed resembled that of an experimental subject, as Emerson would place the young author in three radically disparate writing environments—his own home, New York, and Walden Pond—and measure, mostly with profound disappointment, the results. The results of the experiments were volatile, as Thoreau's greatest accomplishments and bitterest defeats, his most and least productive years as a writer, took place during that decade. Thoreau stayed in Emerson's home on two occasions, each under extremely different conditions, particularly with respect to his position of power and authority, totaling four "experiments," two domestic, one rural, and one urban, to see which would be most conducive to the nurturance of the apprentice's nascent genius. The first domestic situation cast him in the role of adopted literary son from 1841 to 1843, as he lodged quietly in the alcove at the top of the stairs, working as a general handyman and assisting with *The Dial*, in Emerson's stately Concord abode purchased with money from his deceased first wife's estate. The other stay in the Emerson home from 1847 to 1848 put Thoreau in the role of surrogate pater familias while Emerson toured Europe at the height of his international celebrity. Prior to this, he moved in with Emerson's brother William on Staten Island, New York, in 1843, tutoring William's son and searching for publishers interested in his writing. He then returned home to work at his family's pencil factory, and later, from 1845 to 1847, took up residence at Walden Pond, where he composed *A Week*. Upon Emerson's return from Europe in 1849, the two had grown apart, due mainly to the fate of *A Week* and Thoreau's perceived lack of support from Emerson.

Thoreau's unstable occupational identity during the 1840s prompted Fuller—the only person besides Emerson to respond as honestly, deeply, and thoroughly to Thoreau's writing for the sake of improving it—to note how he was "very fond of the classics and an earnest thinker, yet intends being a farmer."[10] Her comment is telling in that it alludes to the various vocations Thoreau fully immersed himself in, never superficially dabbling since he considered his time (that he called "life") allocated for work of all sorts—from surveying, to working Emerson's garden, to splitting wood—to be nothing less than sacred. Such immersion and intensity no doubt had financial potential, as he was at his most commercially effective when he worked to enhance the efficiency and productivity of the family pencil-making business. It was a challenge, not unlike that of the economic puzzle of subsistence living at Walden Pond, wedding his love for conceptualizing ever-more efficient engineering designs with the handiwork of its practical application. His joy in making a good abstract idea come true physically, which crucially distinguished him from Emerson, is seen in his confession that engineering improvements in pencil production had penetrated his dreams.[11] He immersed himself in the project of professional authorship with the same vigor and total commitment, but it was neither consistent nor sustainable given the guidance that conditioned it. So when Emerson implied in Thoreau's eulogy that he was never cut out to be a poet, if obviously not a captain of industry, like Fuller's farmer reference, he did not mean Thoreau lacked talent and appetite for authorship. Both Emerson and Fuller indeed saw these attributes in him, and thus invested considerably in nurturing them.

Fuller's style of mentorship mainly was meted out through her high editorial standards and brutally honest feedback on what she found to be the disjointed, generically amorphous prose and tepid (at best) poetry he submitted to her for publication at *The Dial*. Fuller's feedback, had he more readily applied it without Emerson's interference, may have led Thoreau to better understand the demands and conventions of the literary market. Had she taken to him personally, she indeed may have proven the more effective literary parent (particularly as a prose stylist) of the wayward Thoreau. The genuine mutual intellectual stimulation and care between them is often overshadowed by Thoreau's weak first impression upon her, which failed to distinguish him from other withdrawn, intelligent young men she had encountered.[12] Never intending to drive him away, her editorial rejections actually invited revision, which he did not pursue because of Emerson.

Fuller indeed showed signs of deep sensitivity to Thoreau's development on her own accord, despite Emerson forcing Thoreau past her onto the pages of *The Dial*. Immediately after the founding of *The Dial* in 1835, and before Fuller could establish some sense of editorial authority, Emerson's obsession with seeing Thoreau in print began to overshadow her own efforts on his behalf. Emerson arranged for the poem "Sympathy" to be Thoreau's debut appearance in the journal's first issue. Only after safely confirming these plans did he inform Fuller of them. Further, Emerson himself also revised Thoreau's first prose publication, a literary critical piece entitled "Persius," for that first number. "Can you put it in Number One?" he asked Fuller not once, but twice in consecutive letters.[13] When she consented, Thoreau "recorrected" the changes Emerson had made and submitted it to Fuller. This was an early sign of Emerson's tendency to be more interested than Thoreau in seeing his protégé's work in print. Emerson's pressure to publish *A Week* in 1849 had particularly dire results, which I discuss later. The event prompted Thoreau's April 15, 1852, journal entry that registered his astonishment at "how many there are who advise you to print! How few who advise you to lead a more interior life!"[14] Indeed, Emerson was guilty of forcing Thoreau into print not only against Fuller's will, but frequently also against Thoreau's.

Although such circumstances chilled Thoreau's relationship with Fuller considerably—he was not *her* discovery after all—he did value her and was deeply influenced by her vision. The distance he acknowledges in their relationship in a passage appearing in "Friendship" within *A Week* masks an undercurrent of shared interest: "I am glad to help her, as I am helped by her . . . If this person could conceive that, without willfulness, I associate with her as far as our destinies are coincident, as far as our Good Geniuses permit, and still value such intercourse, it would be a grateful assurance to me."[15] Frequently overlooked is Thoreau's emphasis on the "value such intercourse" maintains for him in his dealings with Fuller, who at seven years his senior was a model of self-reliance worth emulating. The circumstance of her lawyer father's death when she was eighteen made pressing demands on the professional dimension of her sense of the transcendental authorial vocation, thus making her career successes shine all the more brightly in Thoreau's eyes. He would have been intimate with such details, as he was close to Fuller's younger brother Richard, sharing with him a fifty-mile-round-trip hike to the summit of Wachusett Mountain, an early formative experience in his development as a writer that eventuated in the essay, "A Walk to Wachusett." That essay was the first step toward the discovery of his own independent voice as a participant-observer naturalist/cultural critic philosopher that would reach its fullest expression in *A Week* and *Walden.*

Thoreau meant more to Fuller than other Emersonian protégés. Convincing evidence of the influence of Fuller's *Summer on the Lakes* (1843) on Thoreau's *A Week* has been demonstrated. Not only is there significant overlap between their approaches toward nature, Indians, and Christianity, in many ways, *Summer* inspired him, functioning as a muse that breathed life into his prose.[16] At this crucial phase in his development, Thoreau considered *Summer* the best transcendental work he had read. Fuller's sensibility for nature writing was a closer match to his, particularly her penchant for grounding her sociocultural criticisms into the details of nature, a movement closer to Thoreau's penchant for burrowing into the soil than Emerson's expansion outward toward the formation of abstract laws. This aesthetic kinship may have brought them together for a closer, more profitable professional partnership. Fuller's ever widening sphere of influence, which extended to Europe, would have undoubtedly aided Thoreau. She brooded over "The Service" for five months before rejecting it, far longer than other submissions she summarily dispatched with little or no explanation during her editorship of *The Dial.* Indeed, she provided not only valuable detailed feedback for making the piece more palatable and thus commercially viable, but also forthrightly invited him to revise and resubmit. "Yet I hope you give it to me again, and if you see no force in my objections, disregard them," she wrote, in a spirit both encouraging and flexible.[17] She would later show such sensitivity in a letter to Emerson in which she suggested giving a rare complimentary copy of the journal to Thoreau "for his frequent aid" as one seeking the publication of his work.[18]

Were it not for Emerson's advice to begin another project, Thoreau might have actually pursued revisions on "The Service," thus providing a chance to establish himself on firmer ground with Fuller. Instead, he wrote "A Natural History of Massachusetts," a piece that initiated a break from Emerson in subject and method, particularly in the physical immersion in nature as the impetus for his larger generalizations. Emerson found fault in it, complaining to Fuller that he did not "like [his] piece very well."[19] The discrepancy lay in Thoreau's use of direct observation as the basis for his discussion of nature, a significant departure from the

Emersonian method of treating nature as a large, abstract concept. In a letter to Thomas Carlyle, Emerson confessed to his love of the abstract, "the remoteness of my writing from real life," yet wondering what good contemporary issues, if not direct experience in nature, might do for his work, as such "an intrusion it is into another sphere & so much loss of virtue in my own." "If I can at any time express the law & the ideal right," he reasoned, "that should satisfy me without measuring the divergence from it of the last act of Congress."[20]

Squeamish about too much trafficking in "Temperance or the Abolition of slavery," Emerson certainly had no intention of dirtying his breeches with Thoreau on any of his epic four-hour walks, much less even wrapping his mind around trekking fifty miles to Mount Wachusett, which formed the basis of his latest essay. By experiencing it directly, Thoreau was converting nature into "real life," a gesture too earthy for Emerson, whose love of the abstract he openly admitted and defended. Indeed, this distance would be expressed in Emerson's difficulty in burying the dead and dealing with their physical remains. Not surprisingly, Emerson delegated such chores to Thoreau because of his capacity to carry out such tasks meaningfully and with the utmost respect. Thus it was Thoreau, upon Emerson's request, who would arrange for the burial of Emerson's retarded brother and search the cruel shores of Fire Island, New York, on July 19, 1850, for the bodies of Fuller, her husband, and their infant son, who along with her latest manuscript, vanished in a shipwreck.

Emerson's vision of Thoreau was thus an odd mixture of literary savior and manure-hauling gardener and handyman, as evidenced in the patron's letter to his wife Lidian sent from London in 1848. At one point he calls on Thoreau as the leader of a cadre of young minds he hopes might save Bronson Alcott's fledgling journal, the *Massachusetts Quarterly*, which "will fail unless Henry Thoreau & Alcott & Channing and Charles Newcomb—the fourfold visaged four—fly to the rescue." One page later he puts a shovel in his hands. "Henry," again at the top of his list of names he considers for such jobs, "& Mr Hosmer must advise & act [as] The main object is the trees; and there is a good heap of manure, & more to be made by bringing peat to the sewer in the garden . . . I hope Henry will not decline."[21] How could he? After all, Emerson traveled to England on the condition of Thoreau lodging and dining in exchange for the management of the garden and execution of household chores and mechanical maintenance.

But Thoreau was first and foremost a thinker and a writer of tremendous potential in Emerson's eyes. As their relationship grew, and as it became more apparent that he was struggling at professional authorship, the roles played by this wayward literary son increasingly diversified. Like Emerson, Fuller also recognized Thoreau's unique transcendental sensibility, as she made more special concessions for him than any other rising star in the Concord circle. But her attitude never approached the scale and magnitude of Emerson's style of patronage, which fully embraced the young author as a family member. He first funded the opening of the twenty-one-year-old Thoreau's Concord Academy, then lodged him for two years, then placed him in the residence of his brother William on Staten Island for another, then situated him in his own vacated paternal role while he traveled Europe for yet another, finally purchasing the land by Walden Pond where Thoreau would live deliberately. For the better part of a decade of his forty-four years, Thoreau called Emerson land home.

Emerson and Thoreau's peaceful communion could not exist in the wider market for literature beyond Concord that would dictate the fate of the young author's career. Their transcendental companionship met its fiercest challenge when Emerson began promoting Thoreau in the New York literary market. This was a transition no doubt difficult for Thoreau, one freighted with the significance of a parent fitting his child for entrance into public life away from home. Emerson's decision to send Thoreau to Staten Island to tutor his nephew and pursue his literary career came after Thoreau had spent his first two years living with the Emersons. His stint in New York yielded a publication, "The Landlord," that may well have driven him to tears. Like the hard truth in his mother's words, facing the sight of his own writing in the well-respected, yet no less mass-market, venue of the *Democratic Review* was more than he could take. The popular press, and perhaps more to the point, his attempt to write according to its conventions a tale of a genial, warm-spirited landlord who betokens America's promise as an ever present and welcoming host to the oppressed, sickened him. He refused to send a copy home to his family, noting that it was not "worth fifty cents."[22] This incident, significantly, speaks to Thoreau's general response to advice first from his mother "to set out to seek his fortune" and later from Emerson, who sent him off with his paternal blessing.[23] "And now goes our brave youth into the new house," he announced to his brother who was to host him, "the new connexion, the new City." Rather ominously, he remarked that "I am sure no truer & purer person lives in wide New York," warning of his "village exaggeration of the value of facts."[24] His point forecasted Thoreau's collision with a market whose imaginative powers were focused on creating demand for unnecessary products rather than appreciating the value of facts.

"I was born to stay at home," Thoreau admitted in one of his more deeply personal letters to Fuller after his move to New York in May 1843, "not to ramble . . . These kindly but too determined persons, the air of Wall street, the . . . crowd in Broadway, the endless rustle of newspapers all make me feel not the value of their classes but of my own class—the supreme need of the few worshippers of the muse—wild & sacred—as counteraction to this world of material ephemeral interest."[25] The teeming market culture in America's biggest city only intensified Thoreau's transcendental faith. Emerson never sent Thoreau into the literary marketplace to domesticate and profane this otherwise "wild & sacred" spirit. Instead, he was hoping to appease his request on March 1 for "meditating some other method of paying debts than by lectures and writing which will only do to talk about—If any of that 'other' sort should come to your ears in New York will you remember it for me?"[26] Emerson acted upon his belief that Thoreau, with the right introductions, might instead find the sort of success he himself had enjoyed there years earlier. Such expectations were instead stymied by very unfortunate circumstances, exacerbated in several instances by suspect advice from Emerson himself.

Only after failure began to set in did Thoreau's aversion to commercial authorship mount. He did not go to New York with such misgivings, but instead gamely embraced the challenge of fulfilling his mother's and Emerson's great expectations. "As for money matters I have not set my traps yet," he wrote in an encouraging June 8 letter to her, "but I am getting the bait ready."[27] In 1843, Thoreau was also eager to please Emerson by appeasing his persistent desire to see his young apprentice in print. Thoreau would bitterly scorn this demand after 1850, and perhaps rightly so since Emerson rarely told Thoreau to withhold a manuscript for further revision before submission. Emerson resisted his pupil's penchant for plodding through the composition process and poring over his manuscripts for extended periods of time. Rather than work with this impulse, Emerson actively fought against it. Emerson registered his frustration with "the scale on which his studies proceeded," which he estimated "was so large as to require longevity," a formula that "wants a little ambition in the mixture."[28]

Emerson knew, perhaps too late, that Thoreau worked on a grander scale and slower pace than a magazinist, or even lecturer, the transcendental equivalent to writing for a popular weekly given the lyceum circuit's wider audience than that of *The Dial*. Attendant to this longer view of his literary projects was an attitude toward work and its material reward that became the cornerstone of his experiment in deliberate living at Walden Pond. Thoreau always enjoyed the fruit of his labor, not despite, but because of, his abstemious approach toward consumption visible throughout his writings. His ascetic predisposition led Emerson to regret that Thoreau did not eat and drink with the same hearty gusto as most men. In this vein, Thoreau would attack John Field in *Walden* for his mindless overwork and equally mindless overeating. Thoreau deeply savored his material rewards in so far as they were fair and proportionate to the quality of his product. His letter to Horace Greeley, for example, gushes heartfelt gratuity and a deep sense of relief at finally being paid by *Graham's Magazine*—they had held him off for nearly two years due to an unforeseeable budgetary crisis—for his essay "Carlyle."

There was no better metaphor for his ideal sense of writing than in going "a-berrying," an activity whose significance is easy to underestimate given Emerson's infamous summation of his protégé's professional prowess. Emerson likely felt entitled to make the "captain of a huckleberry party" joke in his eulogy since Thoreau had made the same one at his own expense so often. Those who knew him best were likely not offended, but instead understood that much of his wit, interestingly, deals in self-referential occupational subjects. They ranged from anointing himself with the professional title of "self-appointed inspector of snowstorms and rainstorms," to the laughably amateurish author whose writing, as prolific as it is unpublishable, is "of no very wide circulation, whose editor has never yet seen fit to print," to the unsalable Indian baskets story, to his quip about his own library holdings increasing by the hundreds with the unsold copies of *A Week*.[29]

In one unfinished book-length project that Thoreau labeled "Notes on Fruits," he pokes fun at his own vocational quirks: "I served my apprenticeship and have since done considerable journeywork," dryly delivering the punchline, "in the huckleberry field."[30] The jesting continues, but we know it betrays a deeper ethos about the education he would gain from his botanical studies, and his sense of a profit that never involves the exchange of money. "Though I never paid for my schooling and clothing in that way, it was some of the best schooling that I got and paid for itself," he writes.[31] His unassuming persona here matches the idle lounger of *Walden*, a slacker who freely spends (his days) while owing nothing compared to his farm-poor Concord neighbors shackled in the chains of their mortgages. Harvard is superfluous when all we need is a huckleberry field, for "*there* was the university itself where you could learn the everlasting Laws, and Medicine and theology, not under Story, and Warren, and Ware, but far wiser professors than they. Why such haste to go from the huckleberry field to the College yard?"[32] In *Walden*, he would similarly claim that trees are better than scholars. "Instead of calling on some scholar," Thoreau writes, "I paid many a visit to particular trees, of kinds which are rare in this neighborhood, standing far away in the middle of some pasture, or in the depths of a wood or swamp, or on a hilltop . . . to pine groves standing like temples."[33] Herman Melville would also make the same claim for whaling ships functioning as Ahab's university, also with tongue in cheek, yet very much interested in the project of ennobling this setting as one ripe with pedagogical potential.

Thoreau says berrying is not an education valuable only in the consumption it offers separate from the process itself, "for going a-berrying implies more things than eating the berries": the work of gathering them, slow and deliberate, yet fully immersed in nature leaves him richer than those "at home [who] got nothing but the pudding, a comparatively heavy affair—but I got the forenoon out of doors—to say nothing about the appetite for the pudding." The experience of the picking, like the process of keeping and amassing the thousands of pages in his notebooks after 1850 on the "Dispersion of Seeds," "Wild Fruits," and Native American Indians, rewards him far more than faster-paced, commercially driven writing, whose authors figuratively "got only the plumbs that were in the pudding, but I got the far sweeter plumbs that never go into it."[34] Those "far sweeter plumbs" could very well be the best insights of his journal that never went out for publication and never made it into the pudding of the finished product.

But in the early 1840s, nearly a decade prior to his dedication to his journal and long-term projects like *Walden* so closely connected to it, Thoreau was more intensely engaged in generating a commercial product. Producing the pudding was his primary concern rather than holistically finding a slow ritualistic significance in picking its fruit. Concocting such literary confections, albeit transcendental ones, particularly in his venture to New York in 1843, conformed perfectly to Emerson's constant advice to print. The first step was connections in the literary market, and Emerson, approaching the flower of his career, was flush with them.

NEW YORK PROSPECTS

Emerson's contacts for Thoreau ranged from the rich and famous to the over-rated and ultimately trivial. The former was embodied by James, whom Emerson boldly wrote on May 11, 1843, "I should like both for Mr. Thoreau's and your own sake that you would meet and see what you have for each other."[35] The latter consisted of Thoreau's other first contacts in New York, Giles Waldo, another Emersonian protégé who ran a credit-checking business with William Tappan and his father Lewis. In his spare time, Waldo wrote verses and sent them to Emerson, who was perhaps too receptive of them, agreeing to print them in *The Dial*. In a packet he had Thoreau deliver to Waldo, Emerson brought the happy news that "the letters and fragments of journal" were not only acceptable for publication, but also indicative of a promising literary career.[36]

Thoreau proved a better judge of talent than Emerson in this case, as he loathed Waldo and his associate William Tappan, whose contributions to literature amounted to virtually nothing. In their meetings in New York, Thoreau relentlessly barraged them with questions, lording his superior intellect over them rather rudely, as Waldo's report back to Emerson indicates: "My interview with Thoreau has shown me how desperately ignorant I have been content to remain of books. He found that on this subject, in regard to 'this scholar stuff' there could be but little sympathy between us—at least that he had nothing to learn of me while I must owe everything of him."[37] Likewise, Lewis Tappan tattled on Thoreau for his intellectual bullying, with his bruised ego as evidence of how the Concord saunterer "left many questions sticking in my shield."[38] Emerson was displeased with Thoreau's behavior, which nonetheless did little damage to his own career, as Tappan and Waldo were such inconsequential players in the New York literary market as Thoreau had sensed. Such badgering was not beyond Thoreau either. His venom calls to mind Hamlet's abuse of Rosencrantz and Guildenstern. He was not known to suffer fools gladly, especially those whose talent had been drastically overestimated by his own patron, an insult of sharing rank (as fellow Emerson disciples) with such dolts. Thoreau's irritation was likely directed at Emerson's growing collection of promising youths, as Waldo and Tappan only represented a procession of others eager for his tutelage. That very month of May 1843, Emerson had taken up Benjamin West Ball, for example, to make into a genius, according to Ellery Channing's letter to his sister-in-law Fuller. With the absence of "oakum-brained Thoreau" from Concord, Channing wrote, Ball was the most promising young graduate in town, a twenty-year-old fresh from Dartmouth whom Emerson found irresistible.[39]

A more successful and promising contact in New York was with James, whom Emerson had met on a lecture tour of New York. In this case, Emerson had written a wonderfully persuasive letter setting up the meeting. Assertive and direct, yet warm and personal, the introduction had more than the desired effect. Emerson's request dated May 6, "I should like both for Mr. Thoreau's and your own sake that you would meet and see what you have for each other," was met with a prompt reply from James only five days later in his enthusiastic May 11 response: "I shall right gladly welcome Mr. Thoreau for all our sakes to my fireside, or any preferable summer seat the house affords—and will so advise him at once."[40] Thoreau's respect for James shines in his reflection on the meeting, which was in many ways the antithesis of his interrogations of Waldo and Tappan. Instead of questioning, he was the one being questioned, but with a spirit to make "humanity seem more erect and respectable. I never was more kindly and faithfully catechized. It made me respect myself more to be thought worthy of such wise questions," his letter to Emerson read. Thoreau even voiced a preference for James's style of patronage, noting how it bore none of Emerson's impatience and pressure associated with his advice to print that had grown to irritate Thoreau: "I know of no one so patient and determined to have the good of you. It is almost friendship, such plain and human dealings."[41]

James was eager to provide the support and publicity Thoreau desired, yet in a stroke of dreadful misfortune, James was called away from New York for the summer and departed for Europe the following October. Although James appeared to be the most promising lead of all Thoreau's New York contacts, his promotional efforts were also severely limited by Thoreau's hostility toward the Fourierist communitarian social reform that so many New York transcendentalists, like Parke Godwin, espoused. Thus, James never put Thoreau in touch with Godwin, since Thoreau's transcendentalism was ill suited to the systematic reform and utopian communal thinking sweeping the intellectual circles of New York at the time.[42]

With Waldo and Tappan, and now James, as dead-ends, Thoreau, inspired by Fuller's "The Great Lawsuit"—the first contemporary writing he found worthy of praise, calling it "a noble piece"—was especially receptive to Emerson's solicitation of a piece for *The Dial.*[43] Writing once again for his coterie of like-minded intellects was welcome relief from the alienating encounters of his New York setting. Such inspiration to submit to *The Dial* may have been deceptive, as "A Winter Walk" was a perfectly salable piece for the New York market, with a ready taker in John O'Sullivan, editor of the *Democratic Review.* Thoreau had just published "A Walk to Wachusett" treating similar subject matter in *The Boston Miscellany,* a promising outlet for his future work with a mass-market audience and high salaries for its authors, and thus an excellent option for "A Winter Walk." The journal financially collapsed, however, in yet another uncanny stroke of misfortune for Thoreau, and ceased operation after the February 1843 issue. An excellent opportunity at a paid publication still remained with the *Democratic Review.* O'Sullivan invited Thoreau to submit precisely the sort of writing upon which he was thriving at the time, "extracts from your Journal, reporting some of your private interviews with nature, with which I have before been so much pleased."[44]

Significantly, the error was not Thoreau's alone, for Emerson had requested something from him for *The Dial* at once. Blind to what the piece could command in the paying New York market compared to *The Dial*'s provincial circulation and attendant nonpayment of its authors, Emerson pushed Thoreau to send "A Winter Walk" to the Concord periodical. Also diverting them from this opportunity with the *Democratic Review* was that O'Sullivan made his invitation for nature writing, Thoreau's strong suit, in the context of rejecting a book review, "Paradise (To Be) Regained," which Thoreau was determined to push past him and onto the pages of his journal. With revisions and some convincing, Thoreau achieved that objective, while squandering a much larger chance at establishing himself in the New York literary marketplace.

Emerson's method of managing the placement of "A Winter Walk" indicates his awareness that it could have found a paying venue in the big city. After his urgent solicitation of the piece, Emerson realized upon receiving it that he had not needed it for the July issue after all, and that it would appear in the October number instead. Cognizant of how this might withhold valuable ammunition needed for his assault on the New York periodical market, Emerson offered to return it if Thoreau had found a publisher there. Thus Emerson promised to hold it "subject however to your order if you find a better disposition for it," a suggestion to which Thoreau was rather passively amenable.[45] Both men had been acculturated to serving the needs of *The Dial*, their labor of love, and thus failed to act assertively to serve the needs of Thoreau's professional career instead at this crucial juncture. "The tact, delicacy, and indirectness with which each tried to accommodate the other's wishes"—both seeing the opportunity but neither aggressively seizing it in a charade of mutual deference—"suggest how ill suited both men were for dealing with the *business* of writing," as Fink notes.[46]

Whereas "The Landlord" and "Paradise (to be) Regained" were his only publications (both in the *Democratic Review*) from his venture into the New York magazine market, by 1846 Thoreau would eventually publish his most ambitious periodical piece. "Carlyle" appeared in *Graham's Magazine* under the agency of Greeley, whom he had met three years prior in New York. This work had great potential to become a book, as Greeley, far more sensitive to emerging demand and developing readerships in the literary market than Emerson, conceived a volume of biographical sketches of noteworthy contemporary authors. He offered Thoreau $25 to profile Emerson as his next biographical subject in the series to appear in the *New York Tribune*. More than any other formal offer of his career, Greeley promised economic independence and ongoing financial stability, as the deal would have enabled Thoreau to essentially earn double returns on his writing both as articles and as a book. Once through with the piece on Emerson, Greeley suggested, he might move on to "one about Hawthorne at your leisure, etc., etc. I will pay you the money for each of these articles on delivery, publish them when and how I please, leaving you the copyright expressly." This was tantamount to a multiyear salaried position eventuating in a book deal, as "In a year or two, if you take care not to write faster than you think," never a worry for Thoreau, "you will have the material of a volume worth publishing, and then we will see what can be done" to market it.[47]

In many ways, Greeley had the professional savvy Emerson either lacked or was frankly uninterested in. Greeley was therefore more agent than patron; theirs was far less an aesthetic mentorship in which the young disciple struggled to match the lofty wisdom of his master, than a no-nonsense business relationship. Greeley, sensitive to Thoreau's anti-capitalist bent, carefully assuaged these leanings in the young writer, not so much as a father figure, but as a seasoned career counselor. Ironically, Emerson never matched Greeley's expression of the paradox of pursuing a commercial career in literature as a transcendentalist. Greeley was careful always to couch the sales objective as morally inferior to the literature itself, noting that his essay on Carlyle, initially too long for magazines to be interested in, was "too solidly good, I fear, to be profitable to yourself or attractive to publishers." His logic readily accepts that high literary standards can stand in the way of profitability, and that compromise and flexibility are essential for market success in the literary business. In expressing that truth, which Thoreau so badly needed to hear since Emerson had never uttered it, Greeley reinforced, rather than violated, the transcendental ethos toward excessive materialism in a tone at once damning commercial authorship and confessing complicity with the sinful conditions of the trade: The saying, "'Ye cannot serve God and Mammon' [is] applicable to literature," he wrote, noting that "if any thing is calculated to make a scoundrel of a man, writing to sell is that particular thing."[48]

Despite such a sympathetic agent backing him, the security of a virtually salaried position for the *Tribune*, and a future in book writing firmly in his grasp, Thoreau still shuddered at tending to "the results of other men's living," particularly those of his peers and patron.[49] Thoreau could afford to act on principle in this instance, because a very attractive competing offer had just arisen to publish *A Week on the Concord and Merrimack Rivers,* at that point his magnum opus. The opportunity sprang forth due to the unusually persuasive and rhetorically effective letter Emerson had written Evert Duyckinck on his behalf. Emerson suggested Duyckinck publish *A Week* in the Library of America series he edited for Wiley and Putnam, referencing Charles Dickens's "pictures of Italy" and enumerating the multiple types of "nature lovers" who would take an interest in it. The language is the most ardently commercial of any in Emerson's letters: "This book has many merits. It will be as attractive to *lovers of nature,* in every sense, that is, to naturalists, and to poets, as Isaak Walton. It will be attractive to scholars for its excellent literature, & to all thoughtful persons for its originality & profoundness. The narrative of the little voyage" will appeal to the masses, he implied, while its "big ideas" will speak to the educated elite who will surely appreciate it as "a book of the results of the studies of years."[50]

Duyckinck may very well have rejected even such an eloquent and persuasive appeal had Nathaniel Hawthorne not written him in 1845 about Thoreau's capacity to write a salable book for his series. However crushing Hawthorne's assessment of Thoreau's character as "the most unmalleable fellow alive—the most tedious, tiresome, and intolerable—the narrowest and most notional," he nonetheless describes the most readable subject and genre for him, which, interestingly anticipates that of *A Week*: "The only way in which he could ever approach the popular mind, would be by writing a book of simple observation of nature, somewhat in the vein of White's History of Selborne."[51] On one level, as Emerson's subsequent letter to Duyckinck indicated, *A Week* could appeal to the masses as "a book of simple observation of nature," for "nature lovers." But Thoreau's strength lay in his capacity to wed nature to the "big ideas" Emerson had so deeply cultivated in him, which were now rapidly becoming his own.

Duyckinck received the manuscript with open arms, thrilled at the prospect of publishing it. Refusing Greeley for a Wiley and Putnam imprint on his most ambitious work to date was much more than a business decision. It validated Thoreau's memory of his brother John, with whom he shared that week on those rivers. Further, it promised to fulfill, at last, the expectations of, and repay debts to Emerson, his most loyal patron, who had furnished him with the setting and materials necessary to write the book itself at Walden Pond, as well as mentor him to become the writer that book proudly represented. Concord was in *A Week*, Emerson's land supported it, and two brothers and two rivers ran deeply through it.

Greeley's offer would never have received a second thought if Duyckinck had not been summarily fired from his post for a dispute with publishers Wiley and Putnam. The manuscript for *A Week* then went to John Wiley, who rejected it. The breathless search for another publisher thus began, as Greeley's offer receded into the past. The urgency to print now was overwhelming; Thoreau was all too willing to sacrifice financial interests to see the book materialize. Thus Emerson's naïve financial advice to accept James Munroe and Company's demeaning and damnable offer based on his own experience should be placed into the psychological context of the book's publication for Thoreau, for whom, finally, nothing was ever strictly and only about business. The closure on John's death and gratuity to Emerson thus met with the worst professional advice Emerson ever gave Thoreau, ironically not long after Emerson's winning letter to Duyckinck, the most powerful and commercially efficacious recommendation he had ever written.

Instead of half profits, Monroe had offered in 1849 to publish *A Week* at the author's own expense, payable through the initial profits earned from the book. Such an arrangement was dangerous for an author like Thoreau, whose circulation in the market at the time was limited to *The Dial* and a few other magazines, and nonexistent in the book trade. He had just rejected an offer to publish with Ticknor and Fields under the condition that he pay $450 to cover production expenses; now the lure to sign with Munroe for advance payment for costs was too tempting. His book would be in print, his sins to his literary father atoned, his dead brother resurrected on its pages. Thoreau might have survived such a deal had there been a solid readership awaiting him like the one to which Emerson had grown accustomed. His advice speaks volumes to the distance between his professional experience as an established and salable brand name in the market and that of an unknown like Thoreau, putting his literary son at risk in a deal from which he not only failed to profit, but that drove him into severe debt with the publisher. In an 1846 letter to his brother explaining why he favored Munroe, Emerson wrote, "It is best for me to keep the property of my own book as I have usually done and only employ them as publishers. I have unusually found that in that way, I received at last only a little less than 33 per cent on the retail price of the book or if I cheapen the book to trade say 30 to 25 per cent. There is no risk in doing so, for my books uniformly pay for themselves," a sentiment that clearly could not apply to the fledgling Thoreau. Further, with a provincial publisher like Munroe, Emerson acknowledged the risk of having an isolated market, but his optimism outstripped his wisdom, noting that "if the book is good, the distant trader will have to send for it, & then it will go to him at trade prices."[52] But as Fink observes, not only was such advice dangerous when applied to an unknown writer like Thoreau, who could not be sure his book would sell enough initially to cover costs. It also focused too narrowly on per book royalties, while overlooking how restricted distribution hampered profits, as "the more ambitious and successful houses of New York and Philadelphia willingly sacrificed retail commissions for high volume and wide distribution," signaling the dawn of the cheap mass market paperback that would take over by the 1850s.[53]

Thoreau's own decision "to let it lie" and wait on the publication of *A Week* at what he claimed was Emerson's suggestion came after repeated stalled negotiations with a parade of publishers that included James Munroe and Company, Wiley and Putnam, Crosby and Nichols, and Harper Brothers. Backing off on his enthusiasm for the book expressed in his exuberant first reading of passages to Emerson at Walden Pond, his attitude was now blasé to the point of passive-aggressive. "If I liked the book well enough, I should not delay," he moped, "but for the present I am indifferent," a line of action he listlessly ascribed to his patron: "I believe this is, after all, the course you advised,—to let it lie."[54] Such sentiments reflect a sense of futility, and underlying anger in the process of trying to publish *A Week*. But under the circumstances, waiting was a better option than following Emerson's reckless advice: "I am not of opinion that your book should be delayed a month," he wrote, correcting his protégé's assumption. "I should print it at once, nor do I think that you would incur any risk in doing so that you cannot well afford. It is very certain to have readers and debtors here as well as there."[55]

When *A Week* finally appeared, Emerson refused to review it. Emerson's justification of his withdrawal of support and abandonment of his role as patron at this crucial time did nothing to soften what Thoreau took as a brutal blow. Emerson refused editor Theodore Parker's solicitation of a review for the *Massachusetts Quarterly* because he felt his role as Thoreau's patron would have linked him too closely to a project for which he was rapidly losing faith. His stated reason for not writing it was that he and Thoreau were "of the same clan and parish," and that Parker might do better to find "a good foreigner" for the job.[56] Another reviewer, Emerson urged, would provide more credible and authoritative judgment, especially for readers aware of his patronage of the young author. Parker countered by pointing out that a sympathetic reviewer would improve *A Week*'s popular and critical reception, a truism that applies to any book. Parker was only looking out for Thoreau's best interests, and those of Emerson by association. Reviews attacking Thoreau's pantheistic anti-Christian bias—precisely the reception that tarnished Melville's reputation in the 1840s as well—drove sales down, leaving Thoreau feeling betrayed and abandoned.

"OUR HATE IS STRONGER THAN OUR LOVE"

The wording of Thoreau's journal in late May 1849 reveals his animosity toward his patron, whom he felt supported the book's strengths early on only to point out its flaws after it was too late. "No one appreciates our virtue like our friend, yet methinks that I do not receive from my friend that criticism which is most valuable & indispensable to me until he is estranged from [me]—& then the harmless truth will be shot with a poisoned arrow[,] will have a poisoned barb," he wrote. "Poisoned barb" apparently called to mind William Blake's "A Poison Tree" for Thoreau, as the next few lines echo the 1794 poem's simple declarative statements of parallel repetition accounting for the source of poison in their relationship. Blake's lines also paradoxically straddle tones of open, unselfconscious direct confession and venomous "wrath," relating the events of profoundly complex emotional significance in spare, childlike language. Thoreau takes his keynote and structure from Blake's lines—"I was angry with my friend: / I told my wrath, my wrath did end. / I was angry with my foe: / I told it not, my wrath did grow"—to express the trauma of Emerson's vacillating attitude toward *A Week*. "I had a friend, I wrote a book, I asked my friend's criticism, I never got but praise for what was good in it—my friend became estranged from me," he wrote, concluding his litany of frustration by ironically casting himself as the poisoned "foe outstretched beneath the tree" at the close of Blake's poem, with Emerson's ill-timed criticism, of course, providing the poison: "and then I got blame for all that was bad,—& so I got at last the criticism I wanted."[57]

It took four years for Thoreau to rid himself of the $300 debt incurred from the publication of *A Week*, and much longer to rid himself of his wrath for Emerson. His journal reflects a tortured soul, obsessing over the loss of his closest friend and greatest literary model. One such entry aptly represents the journal's prevailing tone at the time: "Here I have been on what the world would call friendly terms with one [for] fourteen years, have pleased my imagination sometimes with loving him, and yet our hate is stronger than our love."[58] Significantly, Thoreau conceives of the strife with his patron, fourteen years his senior, in the authoritarian patriarchal role: "Why are we related, yet thus unsatisfactorily? We almost are a sore to one and other."[59] Thoreau's failure confirmed Emerson's earlier doubts about his apprentice's wayward vocational identity. In disgust, Emerson recorded his chagrin at Thoreau's return to work, to the exclusion of his literary efforts, at the family pencil factory: "Henry will never be a writer he is active as a shoemaker."[60] As Robert Sattelmeyer notes, Emerson's criticism of *A Week* was a "confirmation of [and] not cause of their rift."[61]

The fallout over *A Week*, indeed, did not represent an abrupt, sudden break, but instead opened old wounds. Emerson openly questioned Thoreau's expressions of his rebellious spirit, the epitome of which was his now iconic poll tax protest that landed him in jail. Emerson denounced the protest as "mean and skulking and in bad taste," a view entirely at odds with twentieth-century civil rights leaders, most notably, Martin Luther King Jr., who found it especially inspiring as a model of civil disobedience.[62] In 1848, Emerson disparaged Thoreau's experiment in deliberate living at Walden Pond,[63] noting how "very seductive the first steps from town to the woods, but the End is want and madness."[64] Thus Emerson denigrated the two most significant actions—his night in jail and his life at Walden Pond—for which Thoreau has been revered. It is not by coincidence that these two events distinguished Thoreau's transcendentalism from Emerson's as lived experience immersed in nature and the "the essential facts of life" to access the ecstatic vibration of its vital core. Thoreau's approach at times complemented, but now very much opposed, Emerson's desire to form laws that described human existence by viewing nature as an abstract entity from a distance.

By 1849, Emerson's and Thoreau's career trajectories were radically divorced. As Thoreau's career was reaching its commercial nadir, Emerson's international renown was reaching new heights, as his journey to Europe in 1847–48 confirmed. While abroad, the technological innovations of the English train system captured his imagination, sparking a new appreciation for efficiency and results. He thus grew impatient with Thoreau's increasing skepticism toward technology. Thoreau's now famous questioning of constructing interstate telegraphs heedless of what might be communicated through them, and his description in *Walden* of the railway behind the pond as lacerating the land combined with his social insularity and lack of professional progress clashed sharply with Emerson's orientation toward these vital issues.

With their personal distance broadening, Emerson confirmed his bitterness toward the younger generation's unfulfilled promise. His slight to that generation is clear in the opening lines of "Experience": "Did our birth fall in some fit of indigence and frugality in nature that she was so sparing of her fire and so liberal of her earth, that it appears to us that we lack the affirmative principle, and though we have no health and reason, yet we have no superfluity of spirit for new creation?"[65] His rhetorical question is rooted in his personal irritation with Thoreau that appears in his journal entry on how, in general, "some unfriendly excess of imbecility neutralizes the promise of genius," which he found particularly repellant in his apprentice, who typifies how "young men who owe us a new world, so readily and lavishly they promise, but they never acquit the debt; they die young and dodge the account: or if they live, they lose themselves in the crowd."[66] Emerson had little to say about Walt Whitman, another of his disappointments, after his oft-cited over-exuberant letter in praise of the poet, snubbing him in 1874 from inclusion in *Parnassus*, in which he named the most significant poets of the century.

This part of Emerson saw Thoreau and his generation not only as an affront to his own accomplishments, but also, as Sattelmeyer has suggested, even his dead son Waldo. The intriguing insight that "the personal tragedy of Waldo's death was inextricably bound up in the death of his literary sons, whose very lives were a reproach to the memory of that promising boy," also sheds light on Emerson's regrets toward his own unfulfilled potential tutelage of Waldo into literary greatness.[67] In this vein, Emerson likely felt bittersweet toward the rising career of his friend Henry James's son. Emerson lived to see James Jr. publish *The Portrait of a Lady* one year prior to his death in 1882, and was painfully aware that Waldo, who died at age six, would have been James Jr.'s contemporary had he lived. To nurture his own biological son into such literary fame as James Sr. had the privilege to do, in some ways was Emerson's ultimate dream. For in that case, patronage would have needed no framing within transcendental theories of friendship, as unadulterated fatherly love, unlike his love for Thoreau, would have driven it. Emerson yearned for precisely this kind of satisfying and gratifying fatherhood, embodied by the rich "sensuous education" James provided for his sons William and Henry Jr. in Europe. Such conditions James provided would turn out two of the most influential writers in the history of American thought. In the next generation, Rebecca Harding Davis would provide indispensible advice to her son Richard, as discussed in the previous chapter. Like James Jr., Richard Harding Davis rose under the tutelage of his famous literary and biological parent, going on to achieve fame of his own significant enough to win him the friendship of President Theodore Roosevelt. Under his father's mentorship, William James became perhaps the most noteworthy American philosopher besides Emerson himself.

Interestingly, Emerson's lament for his literary son's lack of such achievement was met with the equal and opposite force of Thoreau's desperate desire to evolve out of this role as young apprentice. Emerson, Thoreau wrote, "would not meet me on equal terms, but only be to some extent my patron."[68] Like Melville and Duyckinck, the strength of their personal bond outlasted the professional turmoil and controversy that plagued their relationship in the late 1840s and early 1850s. Melville had the utmost reverence for Duyckinck until his dying day. Likewise, it was Emerson who, not with belittling tones, but with the profoundest respect for his disciple, invoked the image of Thoreau as son in the warmest sense of endearment and collective pride, reflecting a sense of the growth of the nation in all his youthful brazen fearlessness: "the country knows not yet, or the least part, how great a son it has lost."[69] It is telling that Emerson, reflecting upon Thoreau's memory shortly after his too early death at forty-four, still marveled at how ill at ease he was with the emergent capitalist ethos, still judging his performance like the patron he was, assessing his investment in him with financial language: "he chose wisely no doubt for himself," rather than his patron, or others who invested in him, "to be the bachelor of thought and nature that he was . . . how near to the old monks in their ascetic religion!" his apprentice's ultimate vocation became. The next sentence, interestingly, meditates on why he drifted so, squaring his account as Thoreau's career guide, wondering out loud how his most promising youth of all his protégés became a monk of nature. "He had no talent for wealth," Emerson finally concludes, releasing himself from liability to Thoreau's career traumas. Emerson came to understand his protégé's professional demise as attributable to "his way of living, without forecasting it much, but approved and confirmed it with later wisdom."[70] Calming his anxiety, and assuaging his guilt over his lack of literary success, Emerson chooses to remember Thoreau as lacking an innate predisposition for success as a professional author, falling unconsciously into his natural way of life. Yet Emerson's comment that Thoreau could only explain his way of life and attendant poverty with "later wisdom" indicates that its onset occurred without such wisdom and "talent," for he knew the Thoreau who struggled and failed in the marketplace. But owning his complicity in this poverty—that he provided Thoreau with the materials and connections to establish a career, but offered guidance that squandered their potential—was too much for Emerson to bear.

Emerson thus reinforced the heroic individualistic persona in *Walden* that resonates with his anti-capitalist transcendentalism. However, Thoreau would never commit a spectacle of self-immolating martyrdom in the marketplace. Instead, behind his minimal successes and monumental struggles was a network of literary intermediaries, activated by Emerson, who supported the management of his career. Thoreau shared the project of winning an audience beyond the narrow circle of Concord and *The Dial* with his most important patron, Emerson, who saw him not only as his disciple but also as his professional apprentice. While Emerson fathered Thoreau's career—he was truly responsible for conditioning its origins—he also guided its growth, and at several crucial junctures played a hand in Thoreau's sense that in New York, "Literature comes to a poor market here, and even the little I write is more than will sell."[71]

6

SIBLING STRIFE

Fanny Fern's Search for a Literary Brother

MOVING FROM Ralph Waldo Emerson and Margaret Fuller's troubled literary parent-child relationship with Henry David Thoreau, we now consider another fraught familial dynamic. The sibling rivalry between Fanny Fern (Sara Payson Willis Parton) and N. P. Willis, like Thoreau's relationship with his literary parents, took on monumental professional consequences. But the results were vastly different. Whereas Emerson's mismanagement of Thoreau's career eventuated in later animosity between the two after his commercial fate as an author had been sealed, Fern exploited early conflicts with literary intermediaries to her professional advantage, transforming herself into a world-famous author. As the previous chapter offers a rare glimpse at the single-minded Thoreau struggling to comply with the often-faulty professional guidance of his literary father figure, this chapter views Fern's search for a literary brother not as passive compromise, but as the establishment of personal and financial independence for increasingly progressive cooperative business partnerships. Indeed, she herself conceived of, and established the parameters for, the ideal literary partnerships in which she flourished throughout her long and successful career. The sheer magnitude and force of Fern's popularity gave her considerable sway in such matters, not only with the anonymous mass audience, but also with key publishers, authors, and promoters in the literary marketplace. *Ruth Hall* is a virtual manifesto of literary partnership, offering the print culture a clear code of ethics governing publication practice. It deftly combines the cultural premium of sympathy, especially as articulated through the dynamics of sibling love, with a strong belief in economic independence promised to the champions of laissez-faire capitalism.[1]

The violation of sympathy erupted in public controversy in Fern's career, which she deftly managed to her commercial advantage. She knew that public controversy—displays of wild unfettered rage and aggression in broad daylight between respected figures otherwise known as proper ladies and gentlemen—was not uncommon in the streets of antebellum New York City. Violence flared, for example, when notable businessman Charles Astor Bristed assumed he could openly keep a mistress according to French custom; Mrs. Bristed broke up the affair herself when she assaulted, or "clapper clawed," as reports had it, her rival in public.[2] Victims of famous author Willis's infidelity in the 1850s likewise openly aired their rage on a national stage, as the most talked about romantic rivalry at the time drew Willis, *Home Journal* editor and fastidious dandy, into the unforgiving glare of the public spotlight. The spectacle occurred in 1850 on a June evening in New York City's Washington Square, where famous actor Edwin Forrest flogged Willis prostrate with a school master's gutta-percha whip (made from natural rubber introduced to the West in 1843) before an astonished crowd of onlookers. Merchants, vagrants, and bystanders rushing to Willis's aid withdrew immediately when Forrest screamed, "This man is the seducer of my wife!"[3] Any potential sympathy for Willis rapidly transformed into voyeuristic Schadenfreude, anticipating the public's prevailing attitude toward him over the next five years, as a messy divorce trial ensued.

To make matters worse for Willis, his sister Fanny Fern would deliver in many ways a more painful and lasting drubbing in her autobiographical rags-to-riches novel *Ruth Hall* (1854). As the novel presents it, Willis's sin against her, like his crime against Forrest, was also infidelity, only of the filial sort, as he coldly spurned her desperate requests for aid in launching a literary career to escape the acute poverty threatening the welfare of her children. *Ruth Hall* indicts Willis for breaching codes of sibling sympathy and succor, loyalty, and protection, virtually unpardonable transgressions by antebellum standards.[4]

If Willis was the wrong literary brother, then Oliver Dyer, editor of the *New York Musical World and Times,* who is John Walter in *Ruth Hall,* was Mr. Right, the capital companion and literary partner she needed to realize her full literary and commercial potential. All the repellent features of Willis were rectified in Dyer, and later in Robert Bonner, editor of the *New York Ledger.* Mr. Walter embodies Dyer's and Bonner's patronage of generous financial protection and investment. Mr. Walter's loyalty is exceeded only by the tender warmth of the sympathetic tears he sheds at several key moments in the novel, the most telling of which is when he first sees Ruth's impoverished living conditions. As the foil to Hyacinth Ellet, Willis's fictional counterpart in *Ruth Hall,* Mr. Walter reflects Fern's code of literary business ethics and practice in the guise of a "real, warm-hearted, brotherly brother such as she had never known."[5] While Hyacinth may wear the clothes and pantomime the manners of a gentleman, he lacks the love and loyalty that Mr. Walter provides.[6]

Sympathy in antebellum narratives of the sort that drives the scene in which Walter selects Ruth as his author "diffuses the inequities of economic dependency through norms of emotional interdependency," as Lori Merish explains. Such "narratives define a psychology of ownership that is both conservative and defensive: the desire for control over, and psychic investment in, domestic possessions."[7] Mr. Walter's possession of Ruth as his exclusive author tellingly is enacted in a domestic scene when he enters her home; his compassion for Ruth not only compensates for the market's prevailing unsympathetic treatment of women authors, as seen in editors like Mr. Lescom and Mr. Tibbetts who characterize the norm, but also, more darkly, bears "an index of a psychic sense of futility in the larger social realm."[8] Significantly, Walter's pledge to Ruth's daughter Netty to be her friend illustrates the "companionate family" Merish identifies as forming the basis of literary constructions of market capitalism, which "inscribe sympathy as the spontaneous emotional faculty that enables the flourishing of both" family and market.[9] (As Cindy Weinstein notes, sympathy works to reconstruct or replace broken consanguine relationships, such as that between Ruth and Hyacinth.) In *Ruth Hall,* this dynamic does not occur only from a consumer perspective—though Mr. Walter identifies, desires, selects, invests in (emotionally and financially), and possesses Ruth—but also constitutes a way of doing business applicable to literary partnerships.

Fern's business ethic borrows liberally from the larger culture's obsession with filial love and sympathy. Within the context of laissez-faire capitalism and its attendant radical individualism taking hold in the young Republic, Fern promotes sympathy as the key to superior business relations.[10] Fern's emphasis on the filial love at the heart of the best business partnerships speaks to her understanding of the limitations of individualism and the power of cooperative teamwork, adding a crucial and complicating dimension to her well-established independence—as portrayed in Joyce Warren's groundbreaking 1992 biography *Fanny Fern: An Independent Woman*—for which she has justifiably become an icon in literary history. What has motivated this critical preoccupation is the desire to reverse the image of antebellum women as passive and dependent through Fern's triumphant example. By adding the dimension of partnership to Fern's independence, we gain a sharper sense of her reform of gender roles in the literary marketplace precisely to aid her professional ascent.

MARKETING SCANDAL

The Willis adultery scandal only gained momentum during the five years between his public beating and the appearance of *Ruth Hall*, as a gory divorce trial during the winter of 1851–52 drew out in lurid detail the full portrait of the affair. The press seized upon the story, endlessly titillating a general public who delighted in the inversion and compression of such an arbiter of moral wisdom, manners, and etiquette they came to know through his editorship of the *Home Journal*. The trial also inverted and compressed accepted understandings of the business of literary celebrity, exposing the culture's latent anxieties about the commercialization of art—in this case literature and theater—and the ephemeral and volatile nature of the construction and dismantling of popular figures for public consumption. Herman Melville's *Pierre* (and by extension Melville himself), as discussed in chapter 2, suffers a similar precipitous fall soon after an abrupt rise in his career. The marketplace is the stage for both attacks on Willis—the literal one of Washington Square and the fictional setting of *Ruth Hall*—especially as it stands in plain view of a shocked and engrossed public audience.

Willis's misdeeds figured prominently in *Ruth Hall*'s call to higher standards for male behavior, fueling its objective to reform modern masculinity. The novel traces Fern's rise to success in spite of her famous brother, whose *Home Journal* (which Fern mockingly calls the *Foam Journal*) enabled Willis to cultivate a public profile that was morally righteous, conservative, and seemingly impeccable. As an arbiter of the nation's fashionable and genteel culture, and the spokesman for a harmonious, comfortable domestic setting, nothing could have been more shameful for Willis than to have his adultery scandal appended by news that his sister despised him for his refusal to publish her writing.

Turmoil in private familial relationships was anathema to the exemplary domestic life his *Home Journal* showcased. If Willis eschewed politics and divisive issues in his journal, they were the main features of attraction in *Ruth Hall*, which centers on the politics of the literary marketplace and the divisive self-interest that drives key figures in it, like Willis. Reviewers castigated *Ruth Hall* for its improper desecration of a respectable public figure and family member, a violation of what they believed was a universal law of unconditional filial love through "a furious bombardment of her own family."[11] What rescued *Ruth Hall* from being received as an "unfilial" novel was Ruth/Fern's discovery of a professional sibling in Mr. Walter, whose liberating, yet supportive business ethic and practice made him better than a genetic brother.

Antebellum literature commonly portrayed the biological family as inadequate to the task of providing the love and support of far more loyal, yet nonrelated friends. Weinstein demonstrates how a preponderance of antebellum novels are "replete with attestations and denials of consanguinity, as if desire rather than DNA were the decisive factor in establishing the proper criteria for kinship."[12] Although nostalgic for families as blood-related, and thus cohesive units, she argues, "novel after novel is engaged in ridding itself of the paternalism of consanguinity by replacing it with a family that is based on affection and organized according to a paradigm of contract," figured in the literal one Ruth signs with the affectionate Mr. Walter. Her own parents and in-laws all reject her requests for aid, whereas Walter's "freely given love rather than blood" functions, in accordance with Weinstein's theory, "as the invincible tie that binds together individuals in family." In the context of *Ruth Hall*, as well as Fern's own career, genetic brother Hyacinth/Willis fails mainly because his style of patronage and business practice are inferior to those of Walter/Dyer, whose "freely given love" is emblematic of the free market's new potential to bind people according to shared capital interests.[13] Indeed, Walter's (and Dyer's by extension) investment in Ruth/Fern is both emotional and economic, so that the domestic sphere is not totally replaced by market relationships, but that its core values of sympathy and compassion can realize their full power in the public context. It is not entirely surprising, therefore, that Fern would marry James Parton, the assistant editor to the *Home Journal*, who first fell in love with her in print (not unlike L. Clarke Davis's evolution from fan to husband and sometime agent of Rebecca Harding Davis discussed in chapter 3) while admiringly scissoring her columns for Willis's paper.

Whereas Weinstein emphasizes how replacement parents reconfigure "the organizational structure of the family and arrive at an expanded definition of what a family is," I focus on Fern's expansion of the definition of "brother" in the context of literary business, especially the economic treatment of women workers by their male employers. Hyacinth/Willis functions as the obstacle and antithesis of her desired sibling, a literary brother, with whom she can unleash her full artistic and commercial potential since he defends and respects her authorial role, her relation to her readers, her quiet pride in fame, and above all her artistic autonomy through ongoing financial security. The root of these core behaviors that make him ideal is "sympathy—also called feeling, sentiment, or affection [which] is the *raison d'etre* of the family," as Weinstein notes.[14]

The antithesis of sympathy is neglect, a subject about which Fern was acutely aware, as she lived in impoverished conditions in the Washington Street boarding houses during the early 1850s following her controversial divorce from her second husband. She thus did not view poverty at a distance, nor solicit it as a subject for literary sentimentality, the way Henry Wadsworth Longfellow does in "The Slave in the Dismal Swamp," a patronizing poem in the worst sense of the word that eschews political causation for maudlin sentimental Christian passivity. The very title, for example, of her June 25, 1864, *New York Ledger* column, "Whose Fault Is It?" bears her focus on causality in her consideration of New York poverty. The controlling image of blood opens the piece, uniting "pigs and children" on "a warm day," as the fetid, rank squalor spreads over the scene: "there were slaughter-houses, with pools of blood in front, round which gamboled pigs and children; there were piles of garbage in the middle of the street, meat-bones, cemented with cinders, and penetrated by the sun's rays, emitting the most beastly odors."[15] The final sentence of the piece nails the culprit and proposes a fiscal solution: "Alas! If some of the money spent on corporation-dinners . . . where rivers of champagne are worse than wasted, were laid aside for the cleanliness and purification of these terrible localities which slay more victims than the war is doing, and whom nobody thinks of numbering," progress might be made. Corporate champagne is behind the pools of blood and grimy little faces of this "*little piece of hell*," representing a gross misallocation of capital seen politically in a lack of social programs and economically in corporate gluttony.[16] The image anticipates government corruption and the rise of the robber barons in the Gilded Age. Fern's reference to the Civil War is also telling; the obsession with tallying war casualties obscures those casualties in our midst, and they are children.

Fern's own situation as an aspiring author fictionalized in *Ruth Hall* rhetorically serves the same function. Her own brother's negligence embodies the broader pattern of corporate corruption behind the neglect of the poor, a major symptom of economic domination. Hyacinth's icy rejection of her request for aid, a fictionalization of Willis's real one, obsessively repeats "you-me" pronouns in a class comparison designed to define her as socially and artistically inferior, and thus unworthy of his aid: "writing can never be *your* forte; you have no talent that way. You may possibly be employed by some inferior newspapers, but be assured your articles never will be heard out of your own little provincial city. For myself I have plenty of contributors, nor do I know any of my literary acquaintances who would employ you," he sneers, associating himself with his elite coterie. Fern dryly undercuts his withering parting advice "to seek some *unobtrusive* employment" elsewhere with the hypocritical salutation, "your brother," exposing his preposterous pretentions to that title.[17]

More than excessive self-love motivated Hyacinth's real counterpart to refuse Fern. According to Willis's biographer Thomas N. Baker, the style and tone of her writing were too tart and saucy for his journal's genteel and refined taste. Willis's sensitive and careful cultivation of the *Home Journal*'s readership was one of the keys to its success, and the introduction of Fern's fearlessly subversive and confrontational columns clearly would have injured it. Willis was judging Fern's younger self as much as her present one with an eye toward his own business, not realizing how much damage he was doing. Indeed, Fern's wild reputation so deeply at odds with his paper was common knowledge long before this correspondence.[18]

Beyond a position with his paper, Fern was also requesting his patronage in general, and perhaps the benefit of his considerable influence in being placed elsewhere. Indeed, Fern's real shock most likely came from his blanket refusal to act as her temporary agent, a task he had done for countless unrelated young female authors before. The scandalous fallout of her second marriage (which I discuss later) threatened to exacerbate his Forrest adultery trial, however, which had just dredged up news of Willis's younger brother's conviction of rape. Thus he suggested she kindly leave town, as New York was the "most overstocked market in the country [and] your writings show talent, but they are in a style that would only do in Boston." Were he to stop here, offense may not have been taken, but his encouragement to try another market rapidly deteriorated into the tone of a man trying to drive her away, as a badly timed toothache inflamed his irritation at the thought of her name further sullying his. A procession of increasingly venomous statements ensued: "You overstrain the pathetic, and your humor runs into dreadful vulgarity sometimes. I am sorry that any editor knows that a sister of mine wrote some of these which you sent me," he sniffed, worrying about her effect on his public profile. His frustration about his current trials in the media colored his command to, "For God's sake, keep clear of that." He implies that if she were to write for God's sake she might find success in the religious papers, and thus forge a pious popular persona to reflect credit upon his image. But such self-preservation was buried in words that appeared only arrogant, prompting Fern to vow eternal revenge against his suggestion that the religious papers accept a "certain easily acquired kind of writing. I see no chance for you—unless, indeed, you can get employed by the editors you write for already." Fern's biographer, Joyce Warren, has taken Willis's underestimation of her talent here as disingenuous, as a sign of his fear that she might outdo him as an author. Willis's biographer, by contrast, has said that under the circumstances of the "vortex of scandal" surrounding him, he had no choice but to refuse her: "he could never puff Sara, as he had so many other deserving and not-so-deserving lady protégés, without risking the taint of her disrepute." Willis blamed his toothache for the letter's curt tone before signing off, fully apologizing (too late indeed) for any inadvertent sting in his words.[19]

Ruth Hall, of course, says nothing of the divorce scandal Willis faced, nor does it mention Fern's second marriage to Samuel P. Farrington. The former would have shifted focus away from Willis's damaging letter and thus robbed it of its dramatic import. The latter would have fully discredited Fern in the eyes of her readership. The absence of both in the novel makes it easier for Fern to attribute Willis's rejection entirely to arrogance. However much condescension is in his letter, removing it from the context of his own divorce trial, his brother's conviction of rape, and Fern's own divorce from Farrington is to distort Willis's villainy as the sheer malice of a sibling rival. Indeed, Fern had begun her attack on Willis in 1853 in her column "Apollo Hyacinth," which took him to task under the name she would use for him in the novel. In the column, she decries the sentimental insincerity of his patronage, noting that "should you die to-morrow, Apollo would write a poetical obituary notice of you, which would raise the price of pocket-handkerchiefs; but should your widow call on him in the course of a month, to solicit his patronage to open a school, she would be told 'he was out of town,' and that it was 'quite uncertain when he would return.'" The comment clearly corresponds to how Willis eulogized Fern's first husband Charles Harrington Eldridge as "a specimen of manly beauty," but was conspicuously absent when Fern needed more practical help, as "he cannot bear trouble . . . that it unfits him for life—for business." She warns in a thinly veiled self-reference that "should you hear that a friend or relative of his, even a brother or a sister, was in distress, or persecuted in any manner, you could not do Apollo a greater injury (in his estimation) than to inform him of the fact."[20] As in the column "Whose Fault Is It?" the target is neglect and a refusal of accountability.

Fern's feminism, in this sense, never begs for patriarchal succor so much as it invokes the virtue of reallocation of scarce resources and a communal, generous sharing of valuable contacts. Hyacinth's pattern of friendship is one-way, with no inclination toward generous patronage; he demands protection from his friends, but offers none himself in return; he seeks "friends who can bear their own troubles and all his."[21] Fern's bitterness continued in this pointedly personal vein as late as 1861 in a column entitled "A Bit of Injustice," in which she assails men who begrudge women at both ends of the professional and domestic spectrum. It is clear that she means her brother when she notes that men who despise women with "a smart business talent or capability" frequently are "also the most intolerant of dependent female relatives."[22] Willis rejected her at her neediest, she suggests, and loathes her at her strongest, after she has achieved fame.

Fern's estrangement from her own family indeed occurred when she was at her neediest, in the wake of her embattled second marriage. Farrington was a successful businessman whom Fern had married three years after the October 1846 death of her first husband ("Harry" in *Ruth Hall*). Eldridge's death left Fern economically desperate, as failed real estate speculations forced the sale of their home in Brighton near Boston. Farrington's financial status seemed a quick panacea to her economic woes, but brought galling unintended consequences, as Fern found herself shackled in sexual slavery under him. Farrington committed what is now called marital rape, not once, but as a habitual condition of their marriage, prompting Fern in January 1851 (two years after the wedding) to flee to the safety of the Marlboro Hotel in Boston and begin proceedings for a divorce. Sadly, no statutory code existed for marital rape in the state of Massachusetts in 1851, thus leaving her with no legal recourse. Not only was Farrington enraged by her escape, he successfully used it as the legal grounds of "desertion" upon which he filed a divorce from her two years later. Farrington also responded by spreading rumors about her infidelity, none of which were ever substantiated. He then moved to Chicago, demanding that the children (from Fern's first marriage) join him there. Fern's refusal in the correspondence provided the written evidence to prove desertion. (The cruel irony here is that Fern's allegations of Farrington's violence against her could lose in a court of law to his claim of desertion immediately after he himself fled the family for Chicago.) Neither Fern's own family, the Willises, nor her former in-laws, the Eldridges, supported her in the dispute, as antebellum gender codes regarding motherhood and loyalty to husbands dictated their unsympathetic reactions.[23]

Her rendition of her troubles, again thinly veiling her own and Farrington's identity, appeared in an 1857 *Ledger* column, "A Word on the Other Side." "While women submit to have their wifely honor insulted," especially in the case of marital rape, "and their lives jeopardized by the legalized or un-legalized brutality of husbands, just so long they will have to suffer it, and I was going to say, just so long they *ought* . . . Does she shrink from self-support?" Given the meager pay for women's work available at the time, many women did indeed shrink from self-support, abetting an economy of sexual exchange in which marriage becomes a form of prostitution rooted in the gross imbalance of legal and economic power. She nonetheless inspires such victims to face financial risk as she herself did. "What toil," she asks rhetorically, "could be more hopeless, more endless, *more degrading* than that from which she turns away?" Her controlling image turns to murder, an apt metaphor for the living death of her marriage to Farrington. With his abuse figured in "the glittering knife at her throat," she points to "aggravated cases" such as marital rape "for which the law provides no remedy," fully justifying a woman's decision to "leave her husband and family."[24]

The embittered William Moulton of the *True Flag,* who had lost Fern to rival publisher Dyer, rushed in to supply readers with the news of her failed second marriage, attempting to injure her by disclosing precisely what she strategically omitted from *Ruth Hall.* (The source of Moulton's vengeance was his own unflattering portrait in *Ruth Hall* as Mr. Lescom, a target of satire for his unsympathetic, exploitative business practice.) *The Life and Beauties of Fanny Fern* finally revealed the identity of Fern along with her most satirical and unconventional columns which, the author noted, had been left out of *Fern Leaves from Fanny Fern's Portfolio,* a compendium of her column published in June 1853. The book was also filled with quoted and paraphrased hearsay designed to cast doubt on her moral integrity, specifically supporting Farrington's allegations of desertion and infidelity. As one can imagine, the attempt to impugn her character with an unauthorized edition of works actually only stimulated interest in Fern, while doing little damage to her reputation. Her frank, bold, and unsentimental expressions of often-subversive views specializing in exposing phonies had firmly established her fame well before the appearance of *Fern Leaves.*

Moulton's account of the Farrington divorce predictably also hinges on the issue of wifely propriety, arguing that her husband's role in the debacle was unassailable. "A man of energy and upright character," Farrington comes off as the harried and harassed husband of a wildcat wife whom Moulton blames for expecting all husbands to be "equally fond and indulgent." The issue of sympathy is paramount in the debate; where Fern would find Farrington beneath contempt in this area, Moulton finds him "well qualified to sympathize with the young widow" due to his own prior experience as a husband and father. Moulton then legitimates Farrington's travel west in order to attain the sober, quiet reflection his uncontrollable wife would not allow, depicting his judgment as brutal, yet correct in this case: "The contrast was, in fact, so vast and amazing, that it seemed to require solitude and quiet, to consider it in all its bearings. Accordingly, Mr. Farrington resorted to travel and a change of scene; journeyed westward; and has not since been seen on the down-east slope of the continent." Moulton portrays Farrington serving Fern her just deserts, as he "legally knocked down his wife with the hammer of divorce" to make her "once more a widow."[25]

Readers familiar with Fern's column, now in the widely circulated *New York Ledger*, likely saw Farrington as a villain, although Moulton did not intend to present him that way. Since Moulton's sketch of Farrington fit the mold of *Ruth Hall*'s malicious males in general, and Mr. Skiddy in particular, readers would have enjoyed connecting the dots between the two works, sparking a fascination that likely only escalated sales of *Ruth Hall* to a stupendous 70,000 copies in its first year. On the heels of Moulton's *Life and Beauties*, Fern's own testimony of the Farrington episode appeared in her semiautobiographical second novel *Rose Clark* (1856). It sets the record straight, while also pointing back to the centrality of Fern's failed relationships with Farrington and Willis in *Ruth Hall*. Farrington's reprehensible actions supplied not only her most salient points against misogynistic exploitation in the legal system at the time. They also provided Fern with a template against which to characterize ideal patronage worth supporting. (This code of ethics guiding effective male literary partnership is codified in Mr. Walter's sensitive yet aggressively commercial business practice, which I discuss later.) In *Rose Clark*, Gertrude Dean marries John Stahle upon the death of her first husband to provide her child with a good home; the circumstance of the marriage instantly puts her in a dependent and thus vulnerable economic relationship with Stahle. He is exposed shortly thereafter as "a hypocrite, and a gross sensualist. That was his passion, not love, which he felt for me, and that marriage was only the stepping stone to an else impossible gratification." As in Fern's marriage to Farrington, Gertrude has no legal recourse, and is so intimidated that she performs her domestic duties as flawlessly as possible to protect herself from any charges he might level against her for violating her wifely role. "The more my heart recoiled the more strict was my observance" of such duties, she says. Stahle devises an assortment of schemes whereby he can establish grounds for divorce, from deceiving her into appearing to be having an affair, to taking control of her possessions. He claims correctly, though viciously, that "the law says you can have nothing that is not mine," to which she inwardly laments, "O, how many crushed and bleeding hearts all over our land can endorse the truth of his brutal answer."[26]

The method by which Stahle cinches the grounds for divorce based on desertion replicates Farrington's. He leaves her and sends letters requesting that she join him in another city, without her child, spreading rumors about her infidelity to justify *his* desertion. Her letters refusing to join him provide the evidence for desertion, especially in light of his own letters requesting her presence. Stahle is astonished that Gertrude does not marry immediately out of economic necessity, but responds by developing her own artistic career through an unstoppable resolve to "shut herself up, work night and day, and give the lie to every one of" his false allegations of her wayward immoral lifestyle. John Perry then intervenes to protect her in a gesture of patronage that echoes Mr. Walter's of *Ruth Hall* and Dyer's in Fern's own career. Gertrude does not marry Perry because she believes men who marry widows only really want housekeepers or nurses for their children, a sentiment shared in spirit, if not voiced, by Ruth Hall.

Leaving Gertrude and Ruth unmarried in both novels testifies to Fern's sensitivity to Farrington's effort to tarnish her public image by associating her with promiscuity. The absence of marital strife from Ruth's life only adds to the significance of brotherly affection as the key to successful literary partnerships. Fern places her marital strife in the margins of the story in the secondary narratives of Mrs. Skiddy and Mary Leon. Both tales emphasize the importance of economic independence for women in troubled marriages. The first is a happy, even comic, retelling of the Farrington debacle, as it begins with Mrs. Skiddy leaving to escape her husband and returning to reclaim her children, whereupon her husband departs. Skiddy, unlike the litigious Farrington, fails in business while his wife succeeds in her business. She capitalizes on the space he vacated and "filled" their home "with *lodgers;* who paid her good prices." Thus Skiddy's letter is a radical departure from Farrington's manipulative correspondence from Chicago that would lead to his legal victory. Skiddy pathetically and "' 'umbly' requested his dear Maria Matilda to send him the 'passage money to return home,'" to which she "hissed out, like ten thousand serpents, the word 'N—e—v—e—r!'" Mrs. Skiddy's own business success dominates his high-risk capital speculation that leaves him bitterly blaming ill fortune (and never himself) for his losses: "He was 'disgusted' with ill-luck at gold-digging, and ill luck everywhere else; he had been 'burnt out,' and 'robbed,' and everything else but murdered."[27] Mr. Skiddy's just deserts foreshadow and reinforce the main narrative's focus on Ruth's defeat of Hyacinth in the literary marketplace.

Mary Leon's shocking and horrifying story immediately follows the humorous, entertaining tale of Mr. and Mrs. Skiddy. Fern abruptly swings from a light, boisterous tone to a style that anticipates Rebecca

Harding Davis's grim social realism, with its exposure of the imbalanced power at the heart of woman's economic dependence that leads to exploitation, incarceration, madness, and death. Whereas Mrs. Skiddy triumphs in her hissing vow, Mary marries for money. Growing tired of her as if she were a purchase that had lost its novelty, Mary's husband puts her out of the way by committing her to a mental hospital though she is perfectly sane. Ruth visits her, only to discover she has died a most miserable death there. The environment makes Ruth "shudder, as the gibbering screams of the maniacs over head echoed through the stillness of that cold, gloomy vault."[28]

Ruth and Gertrude shun marriage to take a stand against the abuses legally condoned within the institution of marriage. Their hollow spousal love is now replaced by fulfilling filial affection for Mr. Walter and Mr. Perry, who are not only brotherly confidants, but also professional advocates. While this sort of love fosters economic independence, it significantly refigures promiscuity in the successful forms of literary popularity, promotion, and publicity. Melissa Homestead astutely notes that the frequent poaching of Fern's columns early in her career made her appear a "woman of easy virtue" and a "hot commodity."[29] In *Ruth Hall*, this association of popular female authorship with sexual accessibility is illustrated by the situation of Ruth's residence in the boarding house across from the brothel. Thus Ruth's (and Gertrude's) apparent desexualization through their swearing off of male lovers and husbands—the ministerial Walter and Perry are portrayed with little or no erotic appeal—is replaced in part by adoring male fans.[30] Such fans are interested in her physicality, as reflected in Fern's oft-cited 1870 *New York Ledger* column "How I Look" and in the epistolary solicitations of Ruth's bust and hand in marriage in *Ruth Hall*.

The placement of a female identity in the marketplace as an in-demand public good (and entertainment service) takes on these "working woman" connotations, ironically enough, while portraying the protagonists as so chaste as to be beyond remarriage. Ruth cites her dead first husband as her reason never to remarry, invoking in a romantic context the commercial language of trade courtesy—recognition of and respect for a publisher's exclusive right to an author upon establishing a prior claim to her writing—that Fern's own popularity in the market was rapidly eroding.[31] "'My *husband* has the *first* claim,' said Ruth, resuming her place by his bedside," and thus she remains not only unwilling to hire a nurse to watch over his dying days, but also refuses a replacement husband for herself. She is "married" to his memory, which is invoked on the last page of the novel. Here she solemnly broods over his tombstone, with the understanding Mr. Walter looking on: "There was a vacant place left by the side of Harry—Ruth's eye rested on it—then on her children—then on Mr. Walter."[32] Fern delineates rather bluntly for her conservative readers the moral hierarchy of Ruth's life that places her wifely domestic role above all. The gesture is far more complex than it appears, however, since it is carefully designed to temper the triumphant image of her wielding the $10,000 check two pages before. Fern's sleight of hand here is remarkable: while paying homage to the institution of marriage, Ruth still appears very much reverent toward marriage and devoted to her husband. But, as in the case of St. John at the end of *Jane Eyre*, with whom antebellum readers were quite familiar, Harry is conveniently dead, clearing space for her marriage to her readership, managed and officiated by Mr. Walter.[33] The scene suggests Mr. Walter, thankfully, will never fill Harry's role, which is a great benefit to Ruth, as husbands hamper, stymie, badger, and drive women insane in this novel and much of Fern's other writing.[34] Mr. Walter's embodied presence in the final scene speaks to his real involvement with and support for Ruth's life in contrast to Harry's metonymic tombstone. Further, Mr. Walter is an emotionally and financially available man who makes no sexual demands upon her, unlike the overwhelming majority of husbands in Fern's fiction, most notably, Mr. Leon, Mr. Skiddy, and Mr. Stahle. Harry's idealization allows Fern to maintain a pious position toward marriage in the novel to placate a significant portion of her readership.[35] (Fern was more financially savvy than spiritually devout in her own life, however, as she insisted on a prenuptial agreement prior to marrying third husband James Parton.)

The limitation of Ruth's marriage to inner piety and devotion to Harry's memory opens up considerable space to allow for her development as a popular author. Specifically, it removes a key obstacle to her full market potential wherein she may consummate her relationship with the mass audience. When Ruth's celebrity begins to bloom earlier in the novel, the editorial practice of reprinting—cutting and printing the best of other papers' columns in exchange for the promotion (i.e., "puff") of that paper in advertising or editorial notices—is a sign of her popularity, associated with promiscuity in the broader culture. For example, the

French opera singer Celine Varens, who besets Rochester's honor in *Jane Eyre* is one such figure, yet Ruth differs from her crucially by remaining unsoiled by fame's tawdry connotations for popular female entertainers. Thus protected, "scissoring" increases publicity as integral to the antebellum process of the development of literary fame, refiguring her "easy virtue" (she merely laughs off a flood of epistolary marriage proposals) as paradoxically both celibate *and* a "hot commodity." Hyacinth senses this heat rising and diabolically commits the unpardonable sin of an intermediary blocking an author from her desirous readers. His attempt to stymie her popularity brings new meaning to Henry James's quip that "there is nothing so debasing as to become an agent in between the supply and demand of a commodity," a line originally intended to denigrate the development of editors into publicists, but which in this case aptly explains the danger of a malicious intermediary's power to wreck a career.[36]

Hyacinth's lackey, who represents Fern's third husband, assumes this directive must have been motivated by a personal grudge, as it so obviously reverses a growing relationship that seems so natural. No nepotism inspired Parton's clippings, as he recalled his "post of assistant-at-work upon *The Home Journal*" and "finding these Fern leaves afloat in the papers, and having no suspicion that the author was in any way related to my chief, I used to clip them diligently, and scarcely a week passed without one being published in the paper."[37] In *Ruth Hall*, Hyacinth's refusal to scissor and thus promote her in *Irving Magazine* thwarts a courtship that is at once romantic (with Parton) and commercial (with her mass audience). Piracy is beside the point, as scissoring was such common practice in the antebellum periodical press.

Hyacinth is crucial to the function of the scene both dramatically not only as the villainous foil to her publicity, but also in terms of Fern's overall strategy to market the novel. It is rarely noted, for example, "that the publicity resulting from Fern's obvious caricature of N. P. Willis . . . accomplished the same ends that his promotion of her would have affected."[38] Thus she would make use of Willis's celebrity, even without his consent. The satirical inversion of this reality appears in *Ruth Hall*, as an editor of an English paper, "disgusted with Hyacinth's toadyisms, fopperies, and impudence while abroad, took occasion to cut up [Ruth's] book . . . because the writer was said to be [Hyacinth's] sister. That is the way *his* reputation has helped her."[39] The tables are turned, as Ruth's novel is cut up because of its association with *him*, his figurative punishment for halting scissoring out of personal animosity, a sin that violates the market culture of reprinting in the system of periodical exchange and thus becomes an allegory of failed promotion, patronage, and brotherhood.

LOVING PROMOTION

Ruth succeeds in spite of Hyacinth's failure to carry out his supporting sibling role. But this does not automatically make hers a tale of "a self-made woman who succeeded without paternal assistance," according to Nicole Tonkovich, who cites how "Sara Willis was distanced from her father's scrutiny and patronage."[40] On the contrary, Ruth's (and by extension Fern's) own use of male patronage and support, and indeed the vital companionship and friendship it provided, are crucial components to her own career. Parton's memoir speaks to the importance of Dyer's entrance into Fern's life, the timing of which could not have been better. "Mr. Oliver Dyer of New York visited Boston for the purpose of seeing this new light," he recalled, and "became warmly interested in her affairs; told her how she was throwing herself away; secured engagements upon two New York publications at rates about twenty times that paid in Boston; and in many other ways cheered her mind and advanced her interests." Sensitive to the way Fern's social criticism drew material from the surrounding culture, Dyer promised "the pavements of New York would be fertile in subjects for her pen."[41] Unlike Hyacinth, Dyer truly encouraged and inspired her, "cheered her mind and advanced her interests" in a filial way that courted personal intimacy, as he was "warmly interested in her affairs." Writing for Dyer's *New York Musical World and Times* sprung her career, opening up a lucrative opportunity with J. C. Derby to publish a volume of her collected sketches. Dyer was instrumental in her decision to accept royalty payments of ten cents on each copy sold, a wise one indeed, since it "sold over 80 thousand copies in less than a year's time from date of publication," as Derby reports in his memoir. From there, Fern would find even greater success, accepting a deal with Bonner's *New York Ledger* at $100 per column.[42]

Dyer entered Fern's life as she was writing for Boston's *Olive Branch* and *True Flag* on a salary of $6 per week to support herself and her child. The collusive editors of those weeklies conspired to keep her wage low, a maneuver she justifiably vilifies in *Ruth Hall*. The Boston papers held fast to Fern, as Moulton in particular was sour about Dyer's theft, demanding she stay and write with him based on his prior claim. Dyer allowed her to write for them for a limited time before she moved to New York, and only on the condition that they raise her salary. Dyer was motivated as much by compassion as commerce, blending techniques of literary partnership anticipating those of modern literary agents to bestselling authors, only with considerably more care and attention due to her vulnerability as a professional single mother. Derby refers to Dyer as "her good friend" who "doubled the amount she was receiving" to rid her of the stingy Boston editors.[43]

Dyer's style of dealing with authors is echoed in Derby's, whom Fern specifically thanked for blending friendship with business. Clearly moved by "Yours and Mrs. Derby's kind and cordial invitation [that] touched my heart," Fern emphatically showed her pleasure with the New York publishing world's method of doing business. Of course, her star had already risen, and these men were brokering her talent for profit, yet their kindness and compassion was a welcome relief from Willis's condescension and Moulton's stinginess. Dyer, Derby, and Bonner respected her, paid her what she deserved, and cared to blend business with pleasure. "I wonder if you *know* how pleasant it is, this personal interest my publishers take in me? I like it; and I like *you*," she gushed in her letter to Derby. Her praise for Dyer ends the letter, as she lauds his latest editorial in the *Musical World and Times*, telling Derby to "see what Dyer has written. Isn't he keen? He says more original things in half an hour than I could get off in a year, and then he's good and sincere and independent and dare say what he thinks," words that describe her own style, and indeed set up Dyer as something of a literary model she emulated in sharp contrast to Willis. "I like that," she exclaimed, referring to Dyer's sincere and independent daring, as opposed to her ever obfuscating and precious brother whom the letter's last line targets, intoning what also serves as a kind of keynote for *Ruth Hall*: "I hate *pussy cats*."[44] Cats and dogs constitute the controlling image and conceptual binary of the letter, as she intertwines reminisces about a friendly dog she and Derby had both known with praise for both Derby's and Dyer's forthcoming, approachable demeanors. Whereas such disapproving feline dandies as Willis (who is implicitly if not overtly referenced in the letter) rankle Fern, she prefers a more approachable, friendly, and indeed loyal canine disposition, as it were, in her publishers.

Fern's admiration of Dyer reached ecstatic heights in *Fern Leaves for Fanny Fern's Portfolio* (1853), which enabled her to realize her true value both commercially and artistically. The volume of collected weekly columns was crucial to her establishment in the book market prior to the release of her magnum opus, *Ruth Hall*, a year and a half later. "To my truest friend," the superlative dedication of *Fern Leaves* begins, "Oliver Dyer, whose friendship never faltered, in adversity; whose sympathy and encouragement cheered me, when no bow of promise was set in my sky; this book is gratefully dedicated by the author."[45] Dyer's role as new brother—sympathetic, loyal, encouraging—to replace Willis found expression in the volume in a sketch called "Barnum's Museum." Her commentary on one of the museum's displays particularly challenges and refigures the cultural assumption that blood relations are naturally congenial and harmonious. She marvels at "animals and birds which are the natural prey of each other, living together in such pleasant harmony as would make a quarrelsome person blush to look upon." Her relationship with Dyer as it is dramatized through Mr. Walter of *Ruth Hall* resonates with her admiration of "the many striking instances of fraternization among creatures which have been considered each other's irreconcilable foes." Indeed, Ruth making an editor such a close confidant and significant personal and professional partner comes as a surprise in the novel given the abuse she suffers at the hands of the editors prior to his sympathetic entrance. Before Mr. Walter's entrance, editors and other businessmen appear as the natural foes of aspiring women authors, prone as Tibbetts and Lescom are to colluding to limit her wages and exploit her popularity for their own profit.[46] Thus the Mr. Walter-Ruth relationship is something of a Barnumesque freak show pairing two "naturally" hostile creatures (a woman in the public sphere doing business with a man) in blissful harmony. She leaves the museum, significantly, "with a most distinct impression that the 'getting up' of Creation was no ordinary affair," puzzling not at how Barnum assembled his tricks, but at the range and diversity within nature that could accommodate for such counterintuitive pairings, much like her own hatred of her consanguine brother and love of her editor. Interestingly, this view organicizes both Barnum and her own commercial expression for sale in the marketplace, praising "the only man who has ever made money by the operation of [displaying] such a state of harmonic antagonisms."[47] Finding a brother in an employer was just such a harmonic antagonism, a mismatch of the commercial and the filial, of the public and private. Like the tough-talking persona she loved in Dyer and came to embody in her own writing, her voice was that of a woman borrowing fully from the male discourse that condoned confrontation with an unlikely rival, like a brother. Such paradoxes liberate her from the stultifying domestically defined "lady" from which her writing so assertively departs.[48]

Barnum catered to the masses in an aggressive style, and as an entrepreneur entertainer he was no pussycat. Willis's finicky class bias was totally at odds with Barnum's shocking style. For this reason, Fern may have also taken to Walt Whitman, whose frank depictions of sexuality and the erotic power of the human body struck her as admirable in their democratic leveling of gender. To Fern, Whitman's pen "paints not nude Nature, but stealing Virtue's veil, with artful artlessness now conceals, now exposes, the ripe and swelling proportions."[49] Whitman's revolutionary approach to poetry was also couched in bold gestures of self-promotion and market appeal, much like Fern's own. Her praise for Barnum similarly embraces a popular commercial venture perhaps the most visible in culture at the time, as Bluford Adams notes.[50]

Chapter 67 of *Ruth Hall*, entitled, "Mr. John Walter," also extols this bold, energetic commercial spirit. What complicates the editor's portrait is that his strongest suit is his capacity to channel his sympathy and powers of reflection upon human character and conditions into cold cash. Indeed, the first image of him in the chapter is of man thinking, "his right finger pressed against the right lobe of his organ of causality . . . and the fingers of his left had been beating a sort of tattoo on a fresh copy of The Standard, which lay upon the table by his side," in an attitude "of profound meditation." The pose is reflective, sophisticated, and sensitive here, as he almost appears to be channeling Ruth's column through his fingertips into his mind. His powers of perception lead to sympathy, as he notes that she "did not draw upon her imagination for this article," which he read as a "wail from her inmost soul." He moves from pity to respect, "what powers of endurance!" and then to adoration that reads like the sort of advertising copy he would eventually use to promote her. "What an elastic, strong, brave, loving, fiery, yet soft and winning nature!" he effuses, with Fern's own self-promotional machinery revving at Whitmanian levels. The right hand of thought, perception, and sympathy so accurately characterizing her condition immediately transfers to the business his fingers are drumming up ("beating a tattoo") on the paper.

His rumination thus moves directly into a consideration of "whether she gets paid for her writing," and how to acquire her for his publication. Fern is careful not to present him as a greedy poacher, but as interested in securing a just wage for Ruth. "I wish I were rich, that I might give her such a price as she really deserves," he laments. His compassion for her situation thus transforms not into charity, but a business prospect. "If I could secure her pen all to myself," he muses, "the advertising that such a connection would give The Messenger would be worth something," namely, a chance to personally profit from her talent. The sympathetic and the commercial cohere in his desire to make "my purse commensurate with my feelings." Mr. Walter's "man thinking" pose at the beginning of the chapter translates directly into the active, vigorous "man selling."[51]

Herein lies a key to Fern's definition of the ideal literary partner. Mr. Walter's sympathy for Ruth as a reader and thinker seamlessly, even naturally, flows into his sales mentality, his form of articulating her value in the market, which will then command her salary. His energy funnels into advertising, his penultimate expression of support for her. Ruth (and Fern by extension) suffers a "history of wrongs" primarily because no professional has extended sympathy to her, which if sincere and vital, leads to promotion and publicity in the literary market. If you love me, so the logic goes, you will promote me with all your heart and soul. Mr. Walter has the "mercantile honor" to do this, while Hyacinth does not.

Mr. Walter's tears speak to his capacity for sympathy and attendant robust business support conspicuously absent in Hyacinth and the stingy Moulton figure, Mr. Lescom. Lescom's exploitation of Ruth is cast as villainous and evil precisely because he fails to live up to the part of Fern's ideal for literary partnership that demands him to be congenial and companionable with his author. His sins are not merely economic. What legitimates Mr. Walter's victory over Lescom is the latter's uncaring approach toward his woman writer. Lescom asserts that "*friendship* has nothing to do with business." Indeed, his biggest flaw lies in his refusal to love his writer/worker like a sibling, while instead unemotionally dealing with her in a cold and "business-like logical way."[52]

Mr. Walter responds to Lescom's protests against the stealing of his prize author by upbraiding him for pretending to be the architect of Ruth's success, when in fact *The Standard*'s success has ridden solely on her writings. But we know what Mr. Walter's success will ride on once he signs Ruth to his publication. Why is he so aggressive about signing Ruth if he could do without her? His aggression, finally, is not portrayed as that of a profiteer looking to line his pockets from the work of the latest literary sensation. Instead of material extravagance, Walter's objective is portrayed as economic necessity played out in the melodramatic key of a gentleman publisher (rather than a genteel one like Hyacinth) rushing to the aid of a lady writer. He wells up in tears at first sight of Ruth's impoverished living conditions, with the signs of her struggle to feed her children triggering his sympathetic overflow of sentiment: "Mr. Walter's keen eye glanced about the room, noting its general comfortless appearance, and the little bowl of bread and milk that stood waiting their supper . . . his eyes were glistening with tears."[53] The ensuing conversation speaks volumes of Walter's contrast to Lescom, as little Nettie innocently approaches and says, "I don't know you," to which Walter replies: "But you will, my dear, because I am your mamma's friend."[54]

Friend indeed, as he escorts Ruth about town and even to the phrenologist, a visit both personal and professional because it confirms her genius for writing as well as her "capacity for unusual sympathy and tenderness of feeling," especially when it comes to her choice of friends, to whom she is very "devoted and attached." Her filial love for Mr. Walter is explicit: "you have a high regard for chivalry, manliness, and intellectuality in man, but you also demand goodness, and religious devotion." Several chapters later, Mr. Walter's intimacy with Ruth's children emerges as they begin calling him "uncle," keeping secrets with him, "their best friend, and the impersonation of all that was manly and chivalrous."[55] According to this articulation of the ideal literary partnership, business has everything to do with friendship and sympathy.

Fern harshly criticizes the unsympathetic business practice of shopkeepers toward their female workers, for example, in "Tyrants of the Shop," a *Ledger* piece from 1867. She admonishes these tyrants for verbal abuse, described as "brutal language," reflecting their "bad policy of such an exhibition of unmanliness." Fern draws sentiment out of the futility of the situation, as Merish's theory predicts, yet ends by advocating the civilizing effect of entrepreneurial self-interest. She enlists the forces of capitalism for gender activism: "if it would deter even one employer from such brutality to the shop-girls in his employ, not because of the brutality, perhaps, but because by such a short-sighted policy," Fern writes, shifting emphasis to lost profits, "he might often drive away from his store, ladies who would otherwise be profitable and steady customers."[56] The column's exposure of shopkeepers' reprehensible business practice puts them at financial risk if their abuse persists. Fern made men literally pay the price for unethical behavior toward women in the market, much in the way her exposure of her brother's neglect toward her cost him considerable credibility and threatened his income. This is precisely the tactic Fern used to eclipse her brother's popular appeal. She unveils the cold, neglectful self-interest behind the "mastery of the bewitching techniques," in Baker's words, "of what we might call a *sentimental commerce* with adoring readers."[57] In order to reform sexist working conditions for women and defend her own just advocacy in the market, Fern manipulates consumer preferences against both "tyrants of the shop" and Willis's literary tyranny. The profit motive, as we have seen, certainly brings out the gentleman in Mr. Walter as it did in Dyer, his real counterpart. Without a legal apparatus to protect women during this time, the next most powerful mechanism for such social reform was through the market, which continues to our present day to team with the legal system to give corporate disincentives—the threat of fines, lost reputation—for illegal labor practices.

"Tyrants of the Shop" suggests that men should heed women's new earning and spending powers (represented by Fern's success and the column itself), not out of principles of sympathy and social justice divorced from economic concerns, but as wedded to the ripe earnings awaiting businessmen who treat their women workers respectfully. Fern uses the market's profit motive as a powerful mechanism to alter male behavior and thus gender relations under the assumption that sympathy alone often fails to motivate men, not because they lack that phrenological development on their craniums. Instead, she believes that profound sympathy exists buried in the hearts of all men, and that coaxing it out often requires that it be conjoined with their own economic self-interest, a corollary she knew too well from the responses of Willis and Dyer. The former stood only to be hurt financially by his association with his sister, whereas the latter had abundant self-interest behind his investment in Fern's authorial stock. Indeed, even in the sentimental sketch "Something to Come Home To" Fern praises displays of male sympathy and love—"a man never looks so grand, as when he bends his ear patiently and lovingly, to the lisping of a little child. I admire that man whom I see with a baby in his arms"—and "self-abnegation," not for their own sake, but in terms of their professional consequences. He now has "something to work for," and a new inspiration to increase his income not for "his own selfish ease and wants," but to provide for his expanding family.[58]

Economy and sympathy are thus fundamental to Fern's notion of the ideal literary partner in such a way that warns against the limitations of extreme individualism as heartless as well as economically limiting. She even makes this point in terms of statecraft, noting that the worst governments, lacking compassion for their people, "may settle questions to their liking, or leave them unsettled. What to them is the future of others, if *their selfish present* be undisturbed?"[59] But more frequently, she emphasizes the fiscal rewards for men who follow a code of "mercantile honor." This code places female labor, whether domestic or professional, on more equal grounds, recognizing the right "to what she so laboriously earns," just as "the money that her husband receives from his customers is *his*, instead of his next-door—drygoods—neighbors." Again, her rhetorical appeal is to provide a perspective of women's experience through an economic lens to conjure male empathy. In this way, her 1869 column "Women's Salaries" advocates sympathetic domestic male behavior toward women as much as it does laissez-faire capitalism. She supports cooperative collaboration, as in her ideal literary partnerships, but staunchly advocates a laissez-faire approach to the earners' allocation of their wages. True love means husbands will never ask how wives spend their money: "never, never be mean enough to charge a woman of this kind 'to spend it carefully' [if you] 'love' your wives," she asserts. Put more sternly and with more dire consequences, Fern couches economic exploitation in terms of the grim reality that "Our insane asylums are full of women, who, leaning on some human heart for love and sympathy, and meeting only apprehension, have gone there, past the Cross, where alone they could have laid down the burdens too heavy to bear unshared. A great book is unwritten on this theme."[60]

First Dyer, and eventually, Bonner shared those burdens with Fern, who in a variety of forms, and especially when viewed through the perspective of literary partnerships, indeed wrote that "great book . . . on this theme." Fern's story of economic survival always already was about literary partnerships and forms of male patronage, given the context of the male-dominated market in which she was operating. Her active transformation of those partnerships assailed the sins of her own brother and touted the virtues of an unrelated businessman. But she knew that literary production[61] began with her, as she reflected on the essential differences between authors and editors, who did not produce so much as "light a cigar, draw up a chair, stick their feet up twice as high as their heads, and—proceed to business(?)." Calling into question the true nature of their "business," they merely "tell excruciatingly funny stories, poke each other in the ribs . . . retail all the 'wire pulling' behind the scenes, calculate which way the political cat is going to jump and shape the paragraph accordingly, shake hands, keep their intellects sharpened by a collision with the bright and gifted—in short live in one perpetual clover field," receiving lavish tokens of gratitude for such "work"—"the handkerchiefs they get perfumed, and gloves mended—for nothing!"[62]

If she could laugh at the idiosyncrasies inherent in the supportive role editors play, she also knew they were indispensible to an author's success. It was more than the "wire pulling" or political paragraph shaping that she admired in her best editors, it was their capacity to understand her as she herself wished to have been understood, to know, for example, that after fourteen years of writing for the *Ledger*, compensation was due out of the mutual respect of a successful business partner: "I enclose a check as a present to remind you of the event," Bonner wrote, quickly catching himself in the awareness of his audience's pointed views on the power dynamics of payment. "No, not exactly as a present, for you might not like to receive it in that way; but as compensation for some anonymous paragraphs which I want you to write for the *Ledger* whenever you feel like it."[63] Initially presenting the check gratuitously (perhaps out of habit), Bonner was careful to reframe the money as a business proposition, extending their partnership for a new phase of production.

So Bonner brought the companionship and stewardship necessary for Fern to settle into a long and protected career in the market, like that of popular *Ledger* author Sylvanus Cobb. Like Fern, Cobb had a long and fruitful partnership with Bonner, and he addressed him with filial endearment. "Brother Cobb," he wrote, "thirty years is a long time. When we made our first contract, had we looked ahead, 30 years would have appeared a fearful way in the distance." Careful to avoid a melancholy tone, he ends on a note of optimism inherent in his brave, enterprising spirit: "evenings are sometimes bright. Let us do our best to make ours so."[64] Whereas Cobb and Bonner have gone down in literary history as "the magnificent partnership" on the basis of their friendship and lucrative enterprising, Fern's attack on Willis and independent rise to success have taken over the master narrative of her career.[65] Her partnerships with Dyer and Bonner were even more magnificent than that of Cobb and Bonner, however, especially in light of how, unlike Cobb, she turned the turbulent waters of public controversy to her advantage early in her career precisely by defining her ideal publisher-editor in her writings, thereby intimating the very conventions through which she would interact in the business world. Dyer and Bonner were happy to serve her based on the terms laid out in her columns that critiqued husbands for their faulty home economics, for example, and demanded dignity and proper compensation for women's work. Fern returned Dyer's and Bonner's compliance to these guidelines for business practice with warmth, loyalty, and one of the most powerful products on the literary market. Free from the perils of gender in antebellum professional culture, the resulting partnerships enabled Fern to sail serenely into the sunset of her career with all the grace and ease of Cobb's and Bonner's retirements. The security of those partnerships would provide the tranquility that characterized Fern's final years.

The opposite might be said for Willis, who ominously forecasted in his 1848 poem "The Wife's Appeal" his own fame's function as a lightning rod for controversy, wreaking havoc on his domestic tranquility. The poem portrays a famous author whose "wife—his spotless wife—had been assail'd / By slander, and his child had grown afraid / to come to him—his manner was so stern / He could not speak by his own hearth freely."[66] These lines anticipate the turmoil Willis suffered only two years later in his first public beating in broad daylight on the streets of New York City, and in the second public beating in the pages of *Ruth Hall*. Fern was never spotless, but her management of scandal to her professional advantage—especially in her early attack on Willis, the suppression of the Farrington divorce from *Ruth Hall*, and later peripheral placement of it in *Rose Clark*—surpassed that of her victimized brother, as her prenuptial agreement enabled her to speak her mind freely at her hearth while married to Parton.

Much of Fern's career and attendant feminist attitudes grew out of her personal grudges against Farrington and Willis, inspiring her to cultivate her trademark commentary on gender roles within the broader culture. Her writings rank among the century's most masterful achievements of both social criticism and commercial cunning. She spent decades transforming received notions of domestic and professional codes of behavior to forge an understanding of literary partnerships that weds sentimental culture's most potent theme of sympathy to the forces of market culture. The best literary partnerships, her writings suggest, more than replace dysfunctional sibling relationships, especially between brothers and sisters. Tremendous emotional and financial success awaits those who heed the warnings of Fern's cautionary tales at the heart of her ethos of professionalism. For women, this means not assuming the role of passive recipient of patronage like Mary Leon and Gertrude Dean, but aggressively taking a productive stance as a vital literary partner; for men like Mr. Tibbetts (for whom the list of pitfalls is much longer), this means not exploiting and disrespecting female authors financially and personally, but emotionally sympathizing with them and imaginatively promoting their careers. Mutual capital interests deepen the sympathetic investment, and vice versa. Virginia Woolf may have asserted in the next century that economic independence was a necessity of female authorship in *A Room of One's Own*, but Fern demonstrated a hundred years earlier that every woman writer needs an open channel to her readership, the management and maintenance of which ideally to be carried out by a partner, as near as kin—yet nearer still—guided by the genuine affection and sympathy of personal and commercial shared interests.

CONCLUSION

"JUST LIKE BROTHERS"

Ernest Hemingway and Gertrude Stein

IN THE TWENTIETH CENTURY, literary partnerships would take on an entirely new significance, especially in terms of gender. The half-century from 1870 to the 1920 represented the sharpest rise in the number of professional women writers in the history of literature. This development meant more women became role models for young aspiring male writers, serving as mentors, friends, and collaborators. Margaret Fuller and Henry David Thoreau's relationship in this regard was rare indeed, and suffered primarily from its triangulation with Ralph Waldo Emerson, Thoreau's primary patron. Thoreau may have very well flourished under Fuller had Emerson not taken ownership of him; she had much to teach him, and he was eager to learn, especially with regard to realizing the full rhetorical potential of pastiche narrative form. On the surface, it might appear that the author of *Woman in the Nineteenth Century* (1845), who directly challenged the essentialist gender politics of Catharine Beecher's wildly popular *Treatise on Domestic Economy* (1842), may have been a volatile match for Thoreau, who voiced his vitriolic distaste for women's literature in the chapter "Reading" of *Walden*. Yet Fuller's response to Beecher also excoriates sentimental serial fiction in such venues as *Godey's Ladies Book;* they in fact shared the desire to elevate literature, and Thoreau had the utmost respect for her work, especially her nature writing, which served him as a model worth emulating. Whereas gender or cultural barriers clearly may have hampered their partnership in the absence of Emerson—could Thoreau have maintained his independent man-of-the-woods persona under a female mentor?—many signs also point to its potential success.

The male-female partnerships I have discussed in the nineteenth century—from Rebecca Harding Davis's familial collaboration with her husband and tutelage of her son's career, to Fanny Fern's surrogate family of male editors, to E. D. E. N. Southworth's business "marriage" to Robert Bonner—would branch out in the next century to include the sort of disconnected newcomers, indeed foreigners, to literary scenes that Ernest Hemingway was in Paris in 1922. This conclusion discusses Hemingway's transnational apprenticeship under Gertrude Stein in the early years of his career as a case study of the transition into twentieth-century literary partnerships. The legacy of nineteenth-century partnerships and their codes of behavior that specifically recast women into greater positions of managerial significance now comes full circle in the Hemingway-Stein relationship. Gender categories are immediately reversed in Hemingway's own description of Stein in a letter he wrote two months after meeting her. He says, "Gertrude Stein and me are just like brothers and we see a lot of her," in a curious line that could have cast her just as easily as literary mother or sister.[1] Indeed, Stein would inspire Hemingway to "write like a man" and achieve the direct style for which he would become famous. Ironically, the extremely masculine prose style he would forever be associated with he learned from a woman. Stein's influence stamped the uniqueness upon Hemingway that made him "Hemingway," a distinct brand name in literary culture. This relationship has larger implications for gender role inversions that reach into the twenty-first century as well. The *Journal of Vocational Behavior*, for example, notes that "androgynous sex role orientation reported more mentoring functions than did those with masculine or feminine orientations." The implications in such a relationship range not only into the twenty-first-century literary scene, but also into vocational settings other than professional authorship.[2] This pattern is corroborated by how Stein held sway over Hemingway as mentor, guide, and patron through her belief in "the notions put forth in a book called *Sex and Character* (1906), by the Viennese psychologist Otto Weininger, who maintained that completely female women were devoid of imagination and that the only ones who possessed it were those who were part male," as Kenneth Lynn notes.[3]

The simultaneously emotive and commercially savvy Mr. Walter of *Ruth Hall* also fits this gender description of the ideal mentor, as he bears distinct elements commonly associated with both genders in Fern's novel. Unlike with Mr. Walter (and Oliver Dyer by extension), however, the early professional training ground Stein created and conditioned for Hemingway was fraught with sexual tension. The complexity of the sexual dynamics of their literary relationship was so highly charged as to prompt Stein's jealous partner Alice B. Toklas to drive him away. (Hemingway was married to his first wife at the time.) "You know, I made Gertrude get rid of him," she told a friend later; "it reached the proportions of, 'You give up the friendship of Hemingstein or you give up me,'" Hemingway later recalled.[4] The roles Stein played are dizzying. Having established herself first as his chum and "brother," the relationship rapidly complicated as they grew more intimate. Stein would become the godmother to his firstborn child "Bumby" (John), as well, donning a maternal role. A 1924 photograph, for example, captures her bathing the baby with maternal tenderness.[5] Yet Toklas was not insensitive to the wide range of roles and variations played out in their relationship. Stein's long talks with Hemingway about sexuality aroused him, ironically enough, as he reported to a friend that he "wanted to fuck her and she knew it and it was a good healthy feeling and made more sense than some of the talk." Instead of acting on the impulse, Hemingway, "so sold on her theory" of the superiority of lesbian sexuality, "went out that night and fucked a lesbian with magnificent results; i.e., we slept well afterwards."[6]

Hemingway's crass bombast was designed to amuse his readers, as are many of his humorous yet sharp barbs at Stein in *A Moveable Feast*, his 1964 memoir of the Paris years. Yet the truth remains that there was a deep attraction that sprang from their literary relationship. In the nineteenth century, Dyer and Fern similarly expressed admiration and fondness with pitched compassion that never veered toward the erotic, as in Southworth and Bonner's relationship. The most fluent literary partnership in this regard was that of the Davises, whose marital bond sanctioned the physical expression of their mutual love. Sexual attraction, depending on the context, can problematize or reinforce successful literary partnerships; it tended to do both, as it certainly drove Hemingway's early adoration of Stein. The telling tableau is of Hemingway enraptured as Stein held forth in all her queenly presence, leaning on her knees like a hard-bitten CEO before him discoursing on the art of composition. "He comes and sits at my feet and praises me," she wrote. Stein assumes the male role of sage Emerson-like authority here to Hemingway's role of young apprentice. Not only great writing, but also great literary partnerships transcend the limitations of gender, particularly separate spheres and heterosexual normativity. The nineteenth-century woman author always already inverts dominant gender roles by her sheer presence in the marketplace commanding capital and profits. But she rarely, if ever, plays mentor or patron to an aspiring male author as Stein does here, except in the rare case of a mother-son partnership like that of Rebecca Harding Davis and her son Richard.

The Stein-Hemingway partnership anticipated the almost infinite variations of literary business relations to come in the twenty-first century. The innovative aspects of their partnership have been obscured by Hemingway's monumental reputation in American letters and attendant mainstreaming into American commercial culture that would have him deliberately distancing himself from her and ridiculing her homosexuality. Yet, as Loren Glass astutely observes, "Stein's development of a public persona that screened out her private sexuality in *The Autobiography* was not all that different from Hemingway's own construction of the tough-guy alter ego in the 1930s." Both methods aimed for greater appeal in the U.S. literary market, deliberately downplaying whatever innovative gender roles they thrived upon during the heyday of "the experimentation with sexuality and gender boundaries characteristic of bohemian Paris of the 1920s," Glass notes.[7] Their estrangement toward the end of the decade thus overshadowed much of what was new, promising, and fruitful about their work together. Their relationship tells a new story indeed, but it is well leavened with ingredients of the old, bringing together the various strands of the partnerships that animate this book. Stein's *Autobiography of Alice B. Toklas* (1933) has been remembered for its assault on Hemingway, from his manhood to his writing, just as *A Moveable Feast* is viewed primarily as his counterpunch.[8] His running joke about the *Autobiography* is reflected in his blurb on the cover of James Thurber's *My Life and Hard Times:* "Even in the earliest days when Thurber was writing under the name of Alice B. Toklas we knew he had it in him if he could get it out," he quips.[9] But veiled under this public literary brawl was Hemingway's genuine desire to learn, and Stein's invaluable generosity not only in teaching him, but in putting him in contact with the best minds of 1920s France. Evert Duyckinck similarly connected Herman Melville to the Knickerbockers and beyond; their relationship also ruptured, yet healed under a solid foundation. Stein and Hemingway may have cut ties more conclusively than Duyckinck and Melville, but their initial respect and admiration for each other positively boosted their careers and nurtured their creativity.

FIRST LESSONS

Some of the first literary advice Stein offered Hemingway was apparently to censor his story "Up in Michigan" for its sexually explicit detail. It rankled him enough to have (mis)remembered it thirty years later when he wrote his memoir. Melville similarly resented Duyckinck's early distaste for his anti-missionary stance in *Typee* and later attempt to repress the publication of *Pierre,* which inspired Melville's cruel parody of him in the new material he subsequently added to the novel. Stein found Hemingway's story too racy in "trying to use words that people actually use"; it was "*inaccrochable* . . . like a picture that a painter paints and then he cannot hang it when he has a show and nobody will buy it." Neither painter nor promoter can hang it, so to speak, as it is not for public viewing. Hemingway, like Melville, wanted darkness revealed, while Stein, like Duyckinck, allegedly wanted "to know the gay part of how the world was going; never the real, never the bad."[10] But Stein's instruction to keep explicit sexuality out of view did not mean that she fully disapproved of those energies, but rather that they would be more powerful if kept nascent much in the way their own relationship was made more powerful without physical sex. "*Inaccrochable,*" like so many reminiscences of Hemingway's, came to sound like the punch line of an anecdotal joke told at her expense. In fact, it was a crucial part of his concept of writing that would become indispensible to the formation of his distinctive style and thus his authorial brand name.

Hemingway took Stein's advice so seriously in fact, that he held up publication of "Up in Michigan" "because she said it was *inaccrochable.* It had been in a drawer somewhere" before it appeared in his first book *Three Stories and Ten Poems* (1923). He initially left it in the drawer not because he passively succumbed to her pressure, but because he believed she was right in ways that reached far deeper than censorship. He ardently applied her theories, promising her in a 1923 letter, "I've thought a lot about the things you said about working and am starting that way at the beginning," hoping she might have more advice for him, so "If you think of anything else I wish you'd write it to me."[11] The depth of her teaching is evident when Hemingway tips his hand in his memoir to reveal his application of Stein's advice against excessive detail, which was not obtuse Victorian prudery so much as a metonym for her overall campaign to teach him the virtue of modernist omission. Indeed, leaving key incidents out, like the adverbs in his very own sentences, led to his overall narrative signature of submerged experience left off the page. In his story "Out of Season" he says, "I had omitted the real end of it which was that the old man hanged himself." He attributes his decision to "my new theory," which he hardly created in isolation, but instead smacks of removing the "*inaccrochable*" element from the narrative to enhance its suggestive power. Indeed, Hemingway likely misrepresented her concept in his memoir, obscuring its resonance in his own writing, denying that he learned from her that "the omitted part would strengthen the story and make people feel something more than they understood." He even echoed Stein's own rally cry against the charge of incoherence often leveled against her work. What people did not immediately apprehend in this new style, he (and Stein) had faith that "they will understand the same way that they always do in painting. It only takes time and it only needs confidence."[12]

In Hemingway's letter to W. G. Rogers, author of one of the first books on Stein, Hemingway emphasized the mutually beneficial nature of their relationship. His softer tones indicate that he is telling the truth and not grandstanding when he confesses personally "I always loved her very much," and professionally "she learned to write dialogue from me just as I learned the wonderful rhythms in prose from her." Two years before her death in the fall of 1944, he saw her and "told her I always loved her and she said she loved me too which was, I think, the truth from both of us." He thanked Rogers for explicating a passage from *A Farewell to Arms* to reveal "how much I learned from her." Stein's death had left him hollow, stuck in a "lonesome trade" and missing conversation with her, as there is "no good talk anymore . . . I certainly hate for Gertrude to be dead." Interestingly, he uses a masculine baseball metaphor to praise her confidence and nonconformity: "She discovered a way of writing she could do and be happy every day. She could never fail; nor strike out; nor be knocked out of the box because she made the rules and played under her own rules."[13] He admires her despite himself in *A Moveable Feast*, as he portrays her as sturdy and mannish, yet *vital*, "heavily built like a peasant woman [with] her lovely, thick, alive immigrant hair." Likewise, her love for him leaks onto the pages of the *Autobiography*, as she confesses, "whatever I say [against him] . . . I always have a weakness for Hemingway."[14]

Stein's personality was irresistible, and spoke to her well-connected status in the art and literary scene, equipping her with the ideal credentials to promote the young author. Critics had "enthusiasm for her as a person," placing "confidence in her judgment" since she had "discovered many truths about rhythms and the uses of words in repetition that were valid and valuable and she talked well about them."[15] Stein directly influenced "Up in Michigan"; Hemingway's use of "shifting points of view, patterned repetition, qualitative progression and, in some cases, the identical syntax and diction of [Stein's] *Three Lives*," as Dennis Ryan observes, "was not accidental."[16] Bringing a terse, direct style from his newspaper days with him to Paris, he "found in Gertrude's writing an authority for the repetitions and prolixity that only emphasized the weaknesses of his own style," as James Mellow comments. Likewise, "Gertrude seems to have blossomed under the attentions of the young writer."[17] The mutual stylistic borrowings and influences echo the Davis collaboration on *Put Out of the Way*, in which L. Clarke would deliberately employ his wife's signature proto-social realism blended with gothic effects to support his didactic purpose. In that case, as in Stein-Hemingway's, love was shared as much as literary method.

Just as important as Stein's aesthetic counsel was the companionship she provided. Hemingway arrived in Paris specifically to work with her, bearing a letter of introduction from Sherwood Anderson, making her his sole contact in the entire city. From there, she showered him with patronage and friendship, allowing him to visit any time he pleased, with instructions to the maid to let him in even in her absence. "Hemingway, you have the run of the place. Don't you know that? I mean it truly. Come in any time and the maidservant will look after you and you must make yourself at home until I come."[18] He took advantage of this on several occasions, leaving behind warm notes for her. Opening her house to him was akin to Bonner's gestures of support and communion toward Fern and Southworth. Stein's human touch in sending Hemingway "an enormous candied casaba melon . . . pretty nearly as big as a pumpkin" betokened the imaginative wit and intimacy between them, much as the thermometer Duyckinck sent Melville metaphorically expressed his appreciation for the rarified country air of Pittsfield. One particularly telling occasion reveals how Stein and Hemingway's professional bond was driven by compassion and open expressions of sentimentality. Hemingway "came to the house about ten o'clock in the morning," as Stein recalled in her *Autobiography,* "and he stayed, he stayed for lunch, he stayed all afternoon, he stayed for dinner and he stayed until about ten o'clock at night," clearly with something on his mind he needed to share. "And then all of a sudden he announced that his wife was enceinte and then with great bitterness, and I, I am too young to be a father. We consoled him as best we could and sent him on his way."[19]

The emotional support of this passage evokes Southworth's emphasis on sympathy and love, especially in *The Artist's Love,* her novel about a woman whose artistic endeavors are fueled by the love she channels from her lost infant, and the love she finds in the caring guidance, both personal and professional, of Ishmael Worth. Stein was a shoulder to cry on in Hemingway's most fearful hours, as well as his most important literary guide. In return he completed "the small jobs, made the necessary appearances, brought people that were asked for"; this was the functional equivalent of Thoreau tending Emerson's garden, fixing broken items, tutoring his nephew, a list of tasks that grew into the more significant burdens of burying Emerson's retarded brother and searching for the drowned remains of Fuller. Just as Thoreau repaid Emerson's generosity through these odd jobs, Hemingway's assistance to Stein consisted of "a number of practical things for her such as getting her long book started as a serial with Ford and helping type the manuscript and reading her proof." The economy of such patronage was not beyond either Thoreau's or Hemingway's grasp. Thoreau was acutely aware of his pressure to succeed in the New York market, and the very real limitations he faced in it as a transcendental writer, just as Hemingway understood the limitations of female patronage in the male-dominated publishing industry. "There is not much future in men being friends with great women although it can be pleasant enough before it gets better or worse, and there is usually even less future with truly ambitious women writers."

Hemingway's praise for Stein in the early days of their relationship echoed Thoreau's zeal for Emerson, a relationship that often operated outside of and even against commercial concerns. Like Thoreau, Hemingway was a wide-eyed literary disciple, viewing his mentor as nothing less than a revolutionary taking on "a rebuilding, an entire new recasting of life in the city of words." In tones more like a giddy fan than a serious student of her craft, he gushes in a letter to his friend Bill Smith, "She's the best head I know. Never wrong. Geest she can pick them—painters, etc. when nobody can see it. Never picked a loser . . . She's sure given me straight dope." Stein's language experiment and powers of perception left him awestruck, much as Emerson's did for Thoreau, as his hero worship took on the juvenile form of combing his hair like Emerson's and mimicking his speech and manner. "She's trying to get at the mechanics of language. Take it apart and see what makes it go . . . But she ain't no fool."[20] Stein's meticulous stylistic tutelage of Hemingway bears a striking resemblance to Thoreau's poetic apprenticeship under Emerson, as each instilled a work ethic for unusually rigorous rituals of revision that lasted the duration of their careers.

Such hero worship did not happen between the Davises, Irving and Murray, or Melville and Duyckinck. But Southworth and Fern certainly considered Bonner to be a hero of sorts, especially because of his commercial genius and companionable demeanor. Thoreau had not only a literary model in Emerson, as Hemingway did in Stein. He also had a financial investor in his career and thus a figure, like Stein, bearing the burden of a wild assortment of frequently contradictory roles. Hemingway and Thoreau gained early models and muses from their mentors, points of reference into which they could pour their youthful exuberance and dare to build their own styles, find their own voices, new, bold, and brave enough to inspire the courage to launch their authorial careers, a decision otherwise frightening and fiscally unsound.

Fiction writing was the romantic choice for Hemingway; journalism initially kept him fed. Literature was the romantic choice for Thoreau; his family's pencil factory initially kept him fed. Abandoning these sure sources of income brought risk, which placed Irving, Southworth, and Fern into precarious positions of writing hungry early in their careers. Winning a patron is the obsession of Paul Poitier of John Guare's contemporary play *Six Degrees of Separation*, as well as Hugh Wolfe of Rebecca Harding Davis's "Life in the Iron-Mills"—both deliriously idealistic pursuits end in spectacular failure. The rude awakening for these characters, created more than a century apart, is the realization that patrons of the sort they envision do not exist anymore. They discover, instead, an economy of exchange far more demanding and unprotected. Arthur Miller elevated to the heights of modern tragedy the opposite misread of market realities in *Death of a Salesman*'s cautionary tale about the dangers of excessive self-reliant ambition and bloated individualism in the free market. These misperceptions of market intermediaries—either idealizing the patron as an impossible panacea, as Paul and Hugh pray for the prospect of a patron to deliver them from their impoverished lives, or egotistically shunning readily available aid, as Willy refuses his neighbor's loans and job offer—beg the question of which, if any, alternative models work given the demands and risks inherent to laissez-faire capitalism. The antebellum market economy that would turn corporate by the twentieth century opened up new opportunities for group ventures that threatened to all but make the myth of the autonomous entrepreneur obsolete, or at least as preposterous as Ayn Rand's theory of Objectivism embodied by the impossibly self-reliant architect of *The Fountainhead*, Howard Roark. Melville and Thoreau fell prey to this thinking at key moments in their careers. Irving, Southworth, Davis, and Fern successfully managed their literary partnerships from fraught power struggles with publishers to the complex intertwining of marriage, family, and friendship with authorial commercial and aesthetic ambition. Their effective blend of literary collaboration and business partnership anticipates the proliferation of joint, and even corporate, ventures of later decades.

By 1926, Hemingway had moved on from Stein, finding her *Composition as Explanation* laughable. Her adverse reactions to his early stories exposed their fundamentally different conceptions of authorship, particularly as literary production into a market for a buying audience. Stein held fast to her individualistic notion of authorship that should not bend to accommodate the masses, much as Thoreau refused to write a series of works for Horace Greeley on notable men of the time, including Emerson. Note the trust Hemingway places in the audience and its judgment of quality, a position a successful commercial author, like Southworth, is more likely to take: "she was too lazy to write for other people because writing for other people is very hard because other people know when the things do not come out right and are failures, at least always some of them do," he wrote, mimicking her repetitious style and criticizing her tendency to "eliminate the need for [her writing] to mean anything and simply write and sometimes it will mean something and sometimes it will not."[21] That sort of approach, to Hemingway, was ironically too nonconformist and solipsistic for what he believed were the discipline, strictures, and craft of writing demanded by a discriminating readership.

The instinct to parody Stein in the above quoted scribblings of his notebook eventuated in the more deliberate publication of the story "My Own Life" in the *New Yorker.* Playing up what he would call her "Roman Emperor" rigidity, Hemingway again made her gender the butt of his joke, as she comes off here as the stereotypically brusque dyke to his timid, quavering neophyte: "'I am trying to form my style on yours Miss Stein . . . I want to write like you, like Henry James, like the Old Testament and—'I added, like that great Irishman, James Joyce,'" to which she replies, "All you men are alike." Hemingway's narrator is inconsolable: "Frankly I was hurt." The humor again downplays the significance of Stein's influence by overemphasizing his eagerness to learn in the early days of his career. He is also poking fun at the critical establishment's scramble to find a literary lineage, to which he might be related, embodied by an antecedent who could be demarcated as his "source" of technique and method.

While Stein's increasing disapproval of Hemingway's writing ("Hemingway, remarks are not literature," she said) and Toklas's growing jealousy weakened their friendship, Ford Maddox Ford all but shattered it. Ford's request to dedicate his latest book to Stein signaled that the patron now had a new protégé, spurring Hemingway to vent his anger in his satirical novel *The Torrents of Spring.* Ezra Pound rapidly became Hemingway's new confidant and literary partner, as described in *A Moveable Feast.* Hemingway praised Pound's style of patronage, which was just as generous and brotherly as Stein's, exuding warmth that would have lived up to even Fern's high standards. The difference, however, was that Pound formalized his patronage into a communal system that gathered financial resources from the members of his studio, Bel Esprit, to help artists and writers in need. Pound founded Bel Esprit with the capital of "Miss Natalie Barney who was a rich American woman and a patroness of the arts," whom Hemingway mocked for her in-house art salon and small Greek temple in her garden. Though she was the true fiscal force behind Bel Esprit, Hemingway disrespected her pretentious association with the arts, biting the hand that fed him and voicing his clear preference for friendships with practitioners. Elsewhere in his memoir, Hemingway's aversion to wealthy patrons who were not artists themselves emerges as he tells of the "system of not visiting people. I had to learn it. Much later Picasso told me that he always promised the rich to come when they asked him because it made them so happy and then something would happen and he would be unable to appear." Instead, Hemingway preferred the company and direct patronage of Pound, "the most disinterested" and "generous writer I have ever known," for providing monetary aid to "poets, painters, sculptors and prose writers that he believed in and he would help anyone whether he believed in them or not if they were in trouble. He worried about everyone and in the time when I first knew him he was most worried about T. S. Eliot," a source of extreme jealousy for Hemingway. Thus he was not fully sympathetic to Eliot's plight when "Ezra told me, [Eliot] had to work in a bank in London and so had insufficient time and bad hours to function as a poet."[22]

So began a charity drive among the artists and writers of Bel Esprit to help pull Eliot out of his dilemma. Hemingway pokes fun at the project by comparing it to a drive to support a war veteran, calling Eliot "Major Eliot" and satirically invoking nationalism. Hemingway enjoyed annoying Pound in this way, soliciting funds "to get Major Eliot out of the bank," telling potential donors "either you had Bel Esprit or you did not," either you could "understand the significance of the small Greek temple" or you did not, either you were on our side or you were with the enemy, and if so "keep your money. We wouldn't touch it." Despite Hemingway's skepticism and thanks to the solicitations of the others in the circle, the method worked to outfit Eliot with enough resources to abandon his bank job and apply himself fully to his craft. The result of this patronage was the production of his magnum opus *The Waste Land*.

Such communal patronage is reminiscent of the vigorous pooling of resources by Emerson, Fuller, Ellery Channing, and other denizens of Concord to support Thoreau's wayward career in letters. Unlike the Eliot example, Thoreau's material support mainly came from those with a direct stake in the project of transcendentalism. As the founder of the transcendental movement, Emerson of course was no Barney, an outsider only pretending to be on the inside of the 1920s modernist Paris art scene for the sake of social status. But money nonetheless there was, and money there had to be for Thoreau to have forged the career he did. Its indirect source was, interestingly, wealth from the estate of Emerson's first wife, not unlike the financial buffer Melville enjoyed by marrying Elizabeth Shaw, a prominent judge's daughter. Neither the Shaws nor Emerson's first wife could be described as insiders in any identifiable antebellum literary coterie. The lines of financial support trace back to sources totally unconnected to literary circles. Fascinatingly, Pound appeared to reverse this trend with his organized pledge drive to save the flagging Eliot from the soul-killing bureaucratic grind that threatened his career as a poet. But Pound really drew his funds not from the authors and artists of Bel Esprit themselves, but from their contacts with deep pockets, the very wealthy patrons whom Hemingway had studiously avoided through the "system of not visiting people" he learned from Pablo Picasso. Thus money still came from elite non-producing patrons, only the writers directly solicited it in a concerted effort of economic and aesthetic ("you either had Bel Esprit or you did not") solidarity.

This sort of rescue mission was precisely what Fern had hoped for from her own family, especially her brother N. P. Willis, who could turn unknown authors into successes at will, not unlike what Sir Walter Scott intended for Washington Irving. Were it not for Irving's enterprising decision to angle for an even bigger payoff by bidding for the imprint of celebrity publisher John Murray, Scott would have easily accommodated him. Fern's great expectations were thwarted, and unlike Eliot, she was forced out into "the business streets" to market her writing unprotected from patronage. Her self-reliance to forge her product in the face of this breakdown of communal support makes her story remarkable. But what I emphasize is that her success, signified by the $10,000 bank note she brandishes at the novel's conclusion, still required intermediaries to unlock her full market potential. Dyer and Bonner thus proved essential in removing the persistent editorial gender bias that stymied her early efforts in the market.

Dyer and Bonner respected Fern's principle that a man should pay a woman without questions and demands regarding her allocation of the funds. They never told her how to manage her funds, functioning instead as business partners on more equal footing. Herein lies a key difference between the economies of exchange of earned salary versus charitable donation. "Friends of the arts" of the sort supporting Eliot, for example, frequently felt at liberty to inquire into the allocation of their money, and even dispense with business directives of their own. Financial supporters of the arts frequently assumed the position of business advisors, as in the case of Emerson directing Thoreau's venture in the New York City market. Compared to Thoreau, Hemingway did not receive nearly as much direct monetary aid from Stein, but certainly was fed by her, even if her advice to buy paintings instead of clothes was obtuse and impractical for the hungry young author. Paradoxically, her advice to quit journalism drove him into severe poverty, as he often went without eating until late in the afternoon and frequently could afford only bread. Stein had told him "if you keep on doing your newspaper work, you will never see things, you will only see words and that will not do, that is of course if you intend to be a writer."[23] Hemingway followed her advice, as he found hunger integral to the development of his artistic vision. "All the paintings were sharpened and clearer and more beautiful if you were belly-empty, hollow-hungry," he wrote. "I learned to understand Cezanne much better and to see truly how he made landscapes when I was hungry." Thinking of his own work of writing, he "used to wonder if [Cezanne] were hungry too when he painted." Convinced this was the way to mastery, he proceeded with the confidence of a zealot, turning his mentor's advice into the self-fulfilling prophecy of established truth. Bonner's aesthetic guidance, unlike Stein's, always served the highest priority of their joint commercial objective of winning and sustaining the faith of the widest mass audience possible. His style of patronage assumed that writers wrote best when handsomely compensated for their work, producing in a well-fed condition, as it were.

Writing hungry is thus a metaphor for desiring to replace isolation with the companionship, partnership, and patronage of an ideal reader. Southworth, Fern, and Irving hungered for the recognition of value in their work, for an ideal reader to be their muse for future projects, and an agent to help secure a material reward. Such contact and companionship were essential to establishing their names in the literary market, whose stock is authorial talent brokered on the writer's association with celebrated names, from informal associates to the supporters who provide blurbs and commercial promotion. This commodification of authors' names prompted Boston's Roberts Brothers to publish a "No Name Series" of volumes. The concept was lauded in the *New York Graphic* in 1876 as a balm for "the name business in literature," which they claimed was "terribly overdone." Without names as shorthand to guide consumption patterns, readers would be "forced to trust more to their own taste and judgment, and rely less on reputations" made larger than life by the literary commercial apparatus, now mounting into a formidable mechanism of fame. *Harper's* also liked the premise because "it will pique the curiosity of the reader," thereby enhancing sales and stimulating the economy of the literary market. They hoped it would encourage a deeper appreciation of the texts themselves and thus deter the fetishization of the star authors behind them. It would also work as a disincentive for famous authors to fall into complacency by leaning on the appeal of their names. "It will put the writers on their mettle to do their best, and absolutely prevent that trading on reputation which is the greatest vice of American *litterateurs*."[24]

PARTNERSHIP AND THE AUTHORIAL NAME BRAND

It is fitting that this book on the history of nineteenth-century U.S. literary partnerships end with Hemingway-Stein, because it points to the formation of an aesthetic and economic orientation toward the craft that occurred not in the snows of Kilimanjaro, on the lion hunt in Africa, or in the bull ring in Madrid, but in the studio apartment at 29 rue de Fleurus where Gertrude and Alice lived. This is a Hemingway we do not usually see—sentimental domestic and engaged in fully inverted gender dynamics—because his name has been traded on reputation more than any other author, besides Melville, in the history of American literature. Having survived feminism, deconstruction, and poststructuralism, he remains the most recognizable twentieth-century American author. "Hemingway was famous for being famous," Matthew J. Bruccoli observes. "He deliberately cultivated and manipulated his public images" originally in order to disaffiliate himself from Stein. Indeed, he was careful to parody or trivialize the true significance of their relationship in the formation of his career in order to create his best fictional character of "Ernest Hemingway" entirely apart from and even at odds with her. Bruccoli aptly describes the authorial persona Hemingway created as "really a cluster of characters: hunter, fisherman, soldier, aesthetician, philosopher, naturalist, intellectual, anti-intellectual, traveler, war correspondent, boxer, big-game hunter—and author," but not the confidant, collaborator, and aesthetic partner in their revolutionary experiment to "get at the mechanics of language. Take it apart and see what makes it go" for an "entire new recasting of life in the city of words."[25] Hemingway's obsession with crafting his public image as the consummate professional in all these extra-literary pursuits was a reaction to authorship's association with mere amusement, the amateurish pursuit of a dilettante or hobbyist. Interestingly, Thoreau courted precisely the latter associations—however ironically humorous they appear in his writing—for the majority of his career, which understandably appalled Emerson and left him feeling like an exasperated parent whose painstaking guidance was wantonly jettisoned.

The authors examined in this book based their professional identities on and against those who were closest to them as they practiced their craft and interfaced with the market. The history of literary partnership shows how the real commercial entity of the author—as real as Melville's spotted reputation in the early 1850s, and as real as the rising star of Fern and attendant descent of her brother's fame—took shape in relation to these literary partners. From the earliest days of the market revolution, authors' reputations were the collaborative derivative products of a network of intermediaries in the publishing industry. Because authorial reputations were created, fabricated, and carefully managed to sell does not make the concept of "author" somehow disappear into an illusory postmodern vapor. The author's commodification as a brand name in the market, no matter how reprehensible *Harper's* found its habit of "trading on reputation," is production into a specific literary market for sale. An entire social network supports that process of production. At Bonner's *Ledger*, for example, the network comprised the full range of editors, typesetters, proofreaders, printers, ghostwriters, and authors; within Emerson's Concord circle, the network consisted of myriad poets, teachers, reformers, and philosophers. Partners provided access to a group affiliation, whether a publishing firm or a literary circle. In the last years of his life, for example, Melville paid homage to his Knickerbocker roots in his tribute to Irving, "Rip Van Winkle's Lilacs," a token of gratitude for his debts toward, and regret for his disaffiliation from, that circle.

This tendency to form groups in and around the publishing industry through a literary partner points to how "professional groups arose" sporadically in the antebellum era and widespread in the Gilded Age "to manage new corporate and bureaucratic structures of power, and in the process attained a more powerful economic social status," as T. J. Jackson Lears explains. Such partnerships and group affiliations gave authors the "authority achieved by professionals, limited by their complicity with the structures of [market and later] corporate capitalism."[26] Irving, the Melville of *Typee*, and the women authors of this study, however, were not "limited by their complicity with" commercial structures, but were indeed *inspired* by the opportunity the market held for them. Gravitation toward an associate for safety in that enterprise, paradoxically enough, was a reaction to the professionalization of the trade. The professionalization of authorship, which threatened the writer's very humanity and artistic integrity (he would become a "mere shopman of literature," Davis warned)[27] according to the broader culture, prompted the anti-commercial themes in so much of the literature this book has examined. The literary intermediaries, particularly editors, functioned "as supposedly expert guides to new and disorienting social structures," to assuage how professionals in the publishing industry "were themselves subject to widespread fears of a 'weightless' existence," as Lears pinpoints it.[28] The partnerships were formed out of compensatory sympathy to counter market savagery, while at the same time forging an alliance to make a profit. "Sentimental materialism," as Lori Merish calls the pattern of literary consumption of the era, is thus a phrase equally applicable to literary producers. The aggressive free market enterprise of authors and their publishers was routinely justified as mutual friendship, loyalty, and even love. Love ironically justified the will to power and economically dominate competitors; it was the oil that lubricated the machinery of profiteering in the markets for sentimental fiction and romantic literature, genres ironically embedded in market conditions by their very "natural" orientation against them. In Southworth's case, the profit motive could not have been more consonant with sentimentality, as it fostered the longest lasting and deepest friendship of her life with Bonner. Their relationship was representative rather than exceptional; other careers would follow a similar course. Ann S. Stephens's successful New York career with *Peterson's Magazine* was attended by a friendship so close with the journal's owner Charles Peterson that she elected to live her final years at his home, dying there contentedly at the age of seventy-six.

While this book's interest in literary criticism and authors' careers has emphasized writers, there is yet another one to be written specifically on the intermediaries, focusing on their histories, with authors in supporting roles. Ezra Greenspan's fine biography of George Palmer Putnam moves in this direction. The formation of the publisher's career is brilliantly presented with authors, true to the perspective of a representative antebellum publisher, as their stock in trade. Putnam's success in business, like that of Murray and Duyckinck of chapters 1 and 2 of this book, hinged on his ability to select, and develop literary renown. My book has attempted to put a human face on that industry, looking at the warmth and compassion possible in such an enterprise, as the capital bonds of a business that is at once humanitarian and commercial.

Bette London in her study of British women's literary partnerships remarks that "the enduring afterlife of certain cherished images of the [autonomous] author . . . appear all the more powerful as they cease to correspond to any material practice."[29] Her debunking of the myth of autonomous literary production is well taken, but those enduring "cherished images" were realized in key dimensions of the authors' lives I have described. That is, London, like many others, is still working out of the old mutually exclusive binary of individualism versus collectivism. Independence—never in totality, for such absolute autonomy in any market pursuit is impossible—was indeed visible in the material practice of Fern and Southworth as they persevered through their alienating early work for cold and exploitative employers. The binary threatens to minimize the importance of their early struggle in an unsupportive male-dominated antebellum literary market. London's feminist perspective is well taken in the anecdotal cases she provides of the collaborative partnership of the Brontë sisters, for example. But no female colleagues were so readily available to befriend and support antebellum women writers in the United States like Southworth and Fern, who thus turned to their editors as sounding boards and confidants, transforming them into brother and (platonic) husband figures. Even when Bonner merged with their lives, they pointedly, and in the case of Fern, fiercely defended their economic autonomy. Ironically, Fern criticism has moved in the opposite direction of London and others by rallying behind the author's revolutionary independence from separate spheres gender codes to the neglect of partnerships and alliances in her career.

Fern and Southworth, like all the authors of this study, relied on themselves and others to succeed. Economically vulnerable conditions often stimulated production, yet it is equally true that authors rarely succeeded without an agent or advocate. Production thus became a function of that advocacy. Authors produced to attract an advocate like Scott, Bonner, or Duyckinck. They also created the ideal advocate in the fiction itself as gratuitous flattering portrait, as Fern had done, or as mocking the search for a patron as an end in itself as in Irving's Ichabod Crane. The profound shaping presence of partnerships in American literature speaks not only to anxieties about the professionalization of authorship, but also to the unprecedented demands and pressures placed on author advocates. The increasingly complex business world demanded that editors also be marketing representatives, advertising agents, and stockbrokers of literary talent, anticipating the multifaceted nature of today's publicists and literary agents. These were the new patrons, aggressively engaging the free market rather than smugly sitting outside of it. Yet the personal nature of patronage in the early Republic persisted even into the twentieth century, and continues to characterize literary collaboration and author-publisher relations today. Patronage's legacy of personalizing, even sentimentalizing, literary business significantly shaped each partnership examined in this book. Stein's gifts, open-door policy, and warmth toward Hemingway outlived the quarrel reflected in their memoirs and persisted to Stein's death. A genial spirit endured between Melville and Duyckinck despite their humiliating debacle over *Pierre.* Thoreau thrived on the domestic, filial quality of his friendship with Emerson, though Emerson's tutelage and hospitality failed to nurture Thoreau into a professional success. Happiest in Concord in Emerson's house, and on his property at Walden Pond, Thoreau had active *disincentives* to succeed in the New York market under the easily accessible and highly lucrative path Greeley laid for him.

TWENTY-FIRST-CENTURY IMPLICATIONS

The Stein-Hemingway partnership ties together many of the strands of this book. Early on, Stein played a maternal role, a godmother in so many ways, reminiscent of Emerson's literary adoption of Thoreau. Like Emerson, Stein would teach Hemingway the finer theoretical and syntactical points of writing. She also offered brotherly warm-hearted protection and emotional support like that of Dyer and Bonner. Stein and Hemingway shared a sexually charged intimacy at the height of their aesthetic intercourse, echoing the marital bond of the Davises. They dueled against one another in fraught negotiation prompting public slights as in the Irving-Murray and Melville-Duyckinck partnerships. While braiding together these strands of nineteenth-century U.S. literary partnership, they also pointed toward the twenty-first century in entirely new ways. The chameleonic Stein-Hemingway relationship's transnational setting (two Americans in France) and complex gender and ethnic fluidity (a straight, lapsed Catholic, midwestern, bourgeois American male and a minority ethnic, Jewish lesbian) anticipate the present global condition of literary enterprise and the formation of international renown. In this context, furthermore, to be a "partner" has taken on entirely new meaning in the cultural lexicon since the mid-1990s. Whereas it once alluded to a business associate, "partner" now also means spouse, a lexical convergence of monumental importance to this book. Today, "partner" reflects the cultural awakening to increasingly complex gender identities and orientations and the political adoption of same-sex marriage in the form of civil unions. Further, the rise in same-sex partnerships as a more widely accepted social phenomenon beyond the curiosity that Stein and Toklas were in 1920s France (Hemingway called them "the gargoyles of my youth") has coincided with a rise in dual-career couples in general. Gay couples, it should be noted, have also been dual-career couples at higher rates than straight ones, and generally more affluent in their double incomes as they emerged in greater numbers in the 1990s.[30] They were therefore at the forefront of the new postmodern understanding and growing acceptance of the various work and domestic arrangements available to couples.[31] Now more than ever couples in diverse gender roles work in similar professional fields. Significantly, "partner" connotes not only life companion, but also one who shares a commercial interest and financial stake. Thus loyalty, love, and business—with roots dating back to the fall of formalized patronage in the nineteenth century—have come to resonate with the notion of the literary associate as precisely this sort of capital companion.

In addition to this sociocultural transformation of vocation through gender and coupling, this book has implications for the profound transformation of the editorial profession initiated by the evaporation of print media. In particular, the development of online information sources in the twenty-first century has threatened to make the job of editor extinct in some previously lucrative venues. President of the American Society of Newspaper Editors Gilbert Bailon laments that "the halcyon days in which printed newspapers dominated with highly profitable classified advertising in employment, real estate and automotive are history . . . Dollars in those categories will never return to past levels, nor will circulation return to past levels for the printed edition. Audiences will continue to grow, but chiefly through online and niche products." It is telling that the interpersonal dimension of the trade so apparent in all of the literary liaisons of this book, particularly in the human touch of Bonner and Duyckinck, is precisely what will outlive the passing of this print culture staple, as "top-ranking editors have morphed into life coaches and career-guidance counselors," according to Bailon.[32] Indeed, the best literary partners I have surveyed were also the best life coaches and career-guidance counselors with the best intentions if not results, as in the case of Emerson's professional advice to Thoreau. The market is currently changing faster than our vocational lexicon, and the industry has responded by falling back on the elemental job of personal support inherent in the best editors who loyally fight for their staff.

This book's commercial history of literary partnership points toward inviting new avenues in research, including the interconnectedness of key figures in the antebellum literary market. One could readily identify six degrees of separation (apologies to Kevin Bacon) between Duyckinck and any major figure in the publishing industry at the time. Duyckinck figures into the careers of Melville (his editor), Emerson, Thoreau (nearly Thoreau's publisher upon Emerson's good word), and Irving (his first biographer). The same could be said of Bonner, who worked with Southworth and Fern, and intersected with Davis. Such histories are waiting to be told; biographies of Duyckinck, Bonner, and Southworth have yet to be written, although inroads are being made in group-biographies, such as Megan Marshall's *The Peabody Sisters: Three Women Who Ignited American Romanticism* (2005). Marshall gives us a convincing look at the particularly overwhelming significance and influence of Elizabeth Peabody, bringing to light advocacy, patronage, agency, and support for rising authors in interconnected circles. Connections between major literary circles in antebellum U.S. literature as well as any culturally significant "achievement in art or in letters grows more interesting," as Henry James said, "when we begin to perceive its connections; and, indeed, it may be said that the study of connections is the recognized function of literary criticism."[33] Melville's meditation on connections in his monkey-rope metaphor from *Moby-Dick*, the controlling image at the opening of this book, rings true here, for in a free market economy in which authors operated, compassion, faith, trust, and love are good business, and prove that nothing can be accomplished alone.

Notes

INTRODUCTION

1. Herman Melville, *Moby-Dick; or, The Whale,* ed. Harrison Hayford, Hershel Parker, and G. Thomas Tanselle (Evanston, Ill.: Northwestern University Press, 1988), 72.

2. William Charvat, quoted in Steven Fink and Susan S. Williams, eds., *Reciprocal Influences: Literary Production, Distribution and Consumption in America* (Columbus: Ohio State University Press, 1999), 24.

3. Leon Jackson points out that throughout the nineteenth century, exchange became increasingly characterized by "various mediatory individuals and agencies who stood between an author and his or her readers." *The Business of Letters: Authorial Economies in Antebellum America* (Stanford: Stanford University Press, 2008), 3.

4. Henry James, *Hawthorne* (London: Macmillan, 1967), 45.

5. Informing my method is Richard Brodhead's definition of the history of authorship as a series of "acts—successful, failed, and partially achieved—by which potential authors have made themselves into authors within the opportunities and obstructions of particular social situations." *Cultures of Letters: Scenes of Reading and Writing in Nineteenth-Century America* (Chicago: University of Chicago Press, 1993), 115.

6. Susan Coultrap-McQuin, *Doing Literary Business: American Women Writers in the Nineteenth Century* (Chapel Hill: University of North Carolina Press, 1990), 32.

7. My approach to publishing history puts into sharper relief John Tebbel's insight that "it became a question of two businessmen, agent and publisher, negotiating, while the editor-and-author relationship, with the publisher more and more removed, went on in the way now familiar with our time." *Between Covers: The Rise and Transformation of Book Publishing in America* (New York: Oxford University Press, 1987), 147.

8. Particularly relevant here is Susan S. Williams's assertion that authors "understood that relating to that market was not always a simple choice between resistance and collusion. Instead, they increasingly adopted authorial strategies that enabled them to succeed in the literary market on their own terms." "Authors and Literary Authorship," in *A History of the Book in America, Vol. 3: The Industrial Book, 1840–1880* (Chapel Hill: University of North Carolina Press, 2007), 91.

9. Like Gustavus Stadler, I am "less concerned with revealing a truth lurking underneath ideology—something on the order of say, 'an author is really just a laborer'—than with the processes by which cultural production *becomes apparent,* in particular forms." *Troubling Minds: The Cultural Politics of Genius in the United States, 1840–1890* (Minneapolis: University of Minnesota Press, 2006), xviii. While Stadler outlines a genealogy of genius as an ideologically produced cultural type often cloaked in the guise of the solitary romantic author, and with an eye to its capacity to subvert conventional middle-class beliefs in steady labor and commensurate reward, I see the author more as marketing executive in the business of promoting his or her career with a trusted associate.

10. William Charvat, *The Profession of Authorship in America, 1800–1870,* ed. Matthew J. Bruccoli (New York: Columbia University Press, 1992 [rpt. 1968 ed.]), 3.

11. Henry James, Review of *Waiting for the Verdict,* by Rebecca Harding Davis, *The Nation,* November 21, 1867, rpt. in *Literary Criticism: Essays on Literature, American Writers; English Writers,* ed. Leon Edel (New York: Library of America, 1984), 220.

12. Roland Barthes, "The Death of the Author," in *Image, Music, Text* (New York: Hill and Wang, 1977), 147, 148.

13. For more on literary partnerships and the sociology of authorial support, see Jack Stiller, *Multiple Authorship and the Myth of the Solitary Genius* (Oxford: Oxford University Press, 1991); Susanna Ashton, *Collaborators in Literary America, 1870–1920* (New York: Palgrave, 2003); Bette London, *Writing Double: Women's Literary Partnerships* (Ithaca, N.Y.: Cornell University Press, 1999); Katie Roiphe, *Uncommon Arrangements: Seven Portraits of Married Life in London Literary Circles, 1910–1939* (New York: Dial Press, 2007); Shirley Marchalonis, ed., *Patrons and Protégées: Gender, Friendship, and Writing in Nineteenth-Century America* (New Brunswick, N.J.: Rutgers University Press, 1988); David Laskin, *A Common Life: Four Generations of American Literary Friendship and Influence* (New York: Simon and Schuster, 1994); and Irene C. Goldman-Price and Melissa McFarland Pennell, eds., *American Literary Mentors* (Gainesville: University Press of Florida, 1999).

14. Ed Folsom, *Whitman Making Books, Books Making Whitman: A Catalog and Commentary* (Iowa City: Obermann Center for Advanced Studies, 2005).

15. David Blake's question about Whitman bears special significance to my study: "Is celebrity a form of exalted individualism, or does it signify a broader communal identity?" *Walt Whitman and the Culture of American Celebrity* (New Haven, Conn.: Yale University Press, 2006), 5.

16. Recent studies contextualizing the collaborative aspects of authorship include Ronald and Mary Saracino Zboray, *Literary Dollars and Social Sense: A People's History of the Mass Market Book* (New York: Routledge, 2005); Jackson's *The Business of Letters*; and Stadler's *Troubling Minds.* David Lazar notes that such approaches "intrude on the Promethean myth of creativity. What Creator needs a boost over the wire fence of ignorance, of political, logistical or neurotic obstacles?" Among such obstacles, I would add, are the commercial Scylla and Charybdis of the literary marketplace against whom author and agent do battle. Although Lazar misses the economic implications inherent in the notion of the literary collaborative enterprise, he rightly notes that discussing such relationships "center stage may invoke feelings—to invoke another myth—that one's rugged individualism is neither so rugged, nor so individual." "On Mentorship," *Ohio Review* 5 (1994): 28.

17. Eudora Welty, "The House of Willa Cather," in *The Eye of the Story: Selected Essays and Reviews* (New York: Vintage, 1979), 48.

18. This book seeks to answer Ronald J. and Mary Saracino Zboray's call to expand beyond exclusive treatment of "canonical writers, their coteries, and their publishers—a tiny group compared to the unsung armies contributing most copy to the press," an approach that leaves little room "for virtual collaborators who, by hatching ideas, offering encouragement, or disseminating writings fostered authors' literary development," xv.

19. Quoted in Michael D. Sharp, *Contemporary Popular Writers* (Tarrytown, N.Y.: Marshall Cavendish, 2005), 1367.

20. Walter Benjamin, *The Arcades Project* (Cambridge, Mass.: Harvard University Press, 2002), 23. Rosalind Remer, *Printers and Men of Capital: Philadelphia Book Publishers in the New Republic* (Philadelphia: University of Pennsylvania Press, 1996), details the

transition from printing to publishing that would develop into the more commercial model of the antebellum market revolution, which Charles Sellers defines in *The Market Revolution: Jacksonian America, 1815–1846* (Oxford: Oxford University Press, 1996). S. Grantland Rice's *The Transformation of Authorship in America* (Chicago: University of Chicago Press, 1997) also treats the revolutionary and early national period in terms of civic conceptions of authorship that led toward professionalization of letters.

21. David Laskin, *A Common Life: Four Generations of American Literary Friendship and Influence* (New York: Simon and Schuster, 1994), 17.

1. "THE ROMANCE OF TRADE"

1. For more on how Irving found his way to Murray, see David Pancost, "How Washington Irving Published *The Sketch Book* in England," *Studies in American Fiction* 14.1 (1986): 81; Stanley T. Williams, *The Life of Washington Irving*, vol. 1 (New York: Oxford University Press, 1935), 176; and Irving's own rendition in "The Author's Account of Himself," in *The Sketch Book*, ed. Haskell Springer (Boston: Twayne, 1978), 9–10.

2. Williams accounts for *The Sketch Book*'s publication in England by saying it was all the work of Scott, 176; Ralph M. Aderman, "Introduction," in *Critical Essays on Washington Irving* (Boston: G. K. Hill and Company, 1990), 1–29, does not mention Constable and concludes that Murray rejected *The Sketch Book* simply because "he could not secure the copyright," 4; and Mary Weatherspoon Bowden, *Washington Irving* (Boston: Twayne, 1981), does not mention Constable's or Miller's role in the process. See also Ben Harris McClary, ed., *Washington Irving and the House of Murray: Geoffrey Crayon Charms the British, 1817–1856* (Knoxville: University of Tennessee Press, 1969), 19; Andrew Burstein, *The Original Knickerbocker: The Life of Washington Irving* (New York: Basic Books, 2007), 150; William L. Hedges, *Washington Irving: An American Study, 1802–1832* (Baltimore: Johns Hopkins University Press, 1965); Robert Weisbuch, *Atlantic Doublecross: American Literature and British Influence in the Age of Emerson* (Chicago: University of Chicago Press, 1986), 17; Pierre M. Irving, *The Life and Letters of Washington Irving, Vol. I* (New York: Oxford University Press, 1935), 445.

3. Herbert L. Kleinfield, "Irving: As Seen Through His Letters," in *Washington Irving: A Tribute* (Tarrytown, N.Y.: Sleepy Hollow Restorations, 1972), 61. Cooper received advice from Irving on copyrighting *The Spy* in England to protect it from pirates, while Melville was given the unique privilege of breaking into the book trade with his first publication, *Typee, or a Peep at Polynesian Life*, on Irving's recommendation to his own publisher, G. P. Putnam, which eventually published it. Andrew Delbanco, *Melville: His World and Work* (New York: Knopf, 2006), 67; Ezra Greenspan, *George Palmer Putnam: Representative American Publisher* (State College: Pennsylvania State University Press, 2000), 181.

4. Burstein usefully points out that in 1819 "the literary marketplace mattered more to society than it had before," as "it was where one sought out new insights and new freedoms, and discovered new genius," 336. That rich cultural context means today's critics are not "'distressed over the fact that [Irving] was not Herman Melville or Ernest Hemingway'" as they had been in prior generations. Edward Wagenknecht, *Washington Irving: Moderation Displayed* (New York: Oxford University Press, 1962), 188.

5. Burstein, 150.

6. Pancost, 81.

7. Terry Eagleton, "Buried in the Life: Thomas Hardy and the Limits of Biographies," *Harper's* 315.1890 (2007): 89–94, has complained of a trend in recent literary biography that I hope to avoid here. "We are interested in what Jane Austen had for breakfast because we are interested in her fiction; but what she had for breakfast throws exceedingly little light on the fiction," 89. Conversely, "a good biographer works like a realist novelist, delicately touching on stray details to generate what Henry James called the air of reality." Eagleton, 89.

8. Michael Denning, *Culture in the Age of Three Worlds* (London: Verso, 2004), 95.

9. McClary, 184.

10. Greenspan, 387–88, 217.

11. McClary, 188.

12. Washington Irving, *Scribner's Magazine* 40.8 (1848): 609, 614, quoted in McClary, 188.

13. Pancost, 77.

14. Walter Sondey, "From Nation of Virtue to Virtual Nation: Washington Irving and American Nationalism," in *Narratives of Nostalgia, Gender, and Nationalism*, ed. Jean Pickering and Suzanne Kehde (Washington Square: New York University Press, 1997), 54. Sondey has made Irving out to be a paternalistic enemy of nothing less than Jeffersonian representative democracy, class mobility, and opportunity through a "genteel nationalism that has contributed to the oppressive exclusions of divisions that characterize class, gender and race relationships in the United States," 68. He accurately defines Geoffrey Crayon's politics, but to the neglect of its dynamic relationship with Irving's own innovative business practice.

15. Herman Melville, "Hawthorne and His Mosses," in *The Piazza Tales and Other Prose Pieces*, ed. Harrison Hayford, Alma A. MacDougall, and G. Thomas Tanselle (Evanston, Ill.: Northwestern University Press, 1987), 248.

16. Washington Irving, *Journals and Notebooks, Vol. III, 1819–1827*, ed. Walter A. Reichart (Madison: University of Wisconsin Press, 1970), 663.

17. Quoted in Henry A. Pochman, "Washington Irving: Amateur or Professional?" in *A Century of Commentary on the Works of Washington Irving*, ed. Andrew B. Meyers (Tarrytown, N.Y.: Sleepy Hollow Restorations, 1976), 429.

18. The British had built a veritable wall of criticism deploring American literature by this time, putting Melville's and others' "claims for cultural superiority . . . embarrassedly into the future tense," according to Robert Weisbuch, 26. The bias against American literature that Irving successfully broke through was pervasive, as Weisbuch explains: "Sydney Smith's famous 1820 query, 'In the four quarters of the globe, who reads an American book?' is only one example of a tradition of blunt insult stretching before and after. *The Quarterly*, probably Southey, 1809: 'No work of distinguished merit in any branch has yet been produced among them; . . . ' *The British Critic*, 1818: 'The Americans have no national literature, and no learned men.' *Colburn's New Monthly Magazine*, 1827: 'To talk of literature in America is to talk of that which has no existence.' *The Athenaeum*, 1831: 'this want of originality in American literature is, we think, likely long to continue . . . ' *The Westminster Review*, 1860: 'For almost every work of note which has been produced there, the mother nation can show a better counterpart,'" 16.

19. Burstein, 397.

20. R. H. Dana, "Review of *The Sketch Book*," *North American Review* 9 (1819): 322–56. Quotations on 348. It is important to note here that even the English could perceive strain in his attempts at "suavity," as one British reviewer, like Melville, found him to be imitating "Mackenzie's manner" in his *Man of Feeling*, which they regretted and hoped in the future he might take "a more manly line of composition." *British Critic* 14 (1820): 514–25. Quotation on 514.

21. Washington Irving, *Journals and Notebooks: Vol. V, 1832–1859*, ed. Walter A. Reichart and Lilian Schlissel (Boston: Twayne, 1981), 311.

22. Peter Antelyes, *Tales of Adventurous Enterprise: Washington Irving and the Poetics of Western Expansion* (New York: Columbia University Press, 1990), 23.

23. McClary, 20.

24. Sondey, 65.

25. The terms are from Washington Irving, *Journals and Notebooks: Vol. V*, 311, 317.

26. McClary, xliii.

27. *The Letters of Richard Ford, 1797–1858*, ed. Rowland E. Prothero (New York: E. P. Dutton & Co., 1905), 165, quoted in McClary, xliv.

28. *Jane Austen's Letters to Her Sister Cassandra and Others*, ed. R. W. Chapman (Oxford: The Clarendon Press, 1932), II, 425, quoted in McClary, xliv.

29. Rice, 73.

30. Washington Irving, *Journals and Notebooks, Vol. II, 1807–1822*, ed. Walter A. Reichart and Lillian Schlissel (Boston: Twayne, 1981), 58.

31. McClary, 25.

32. Pierre M. Irving, *The Life and Letters of Washington Irving, Vol. I*, 437.

33. For more on *The Sketch Book* and the origin of the literary sketch as a genre, see Jeffrey Rubin-Dorsky, "Washington Irving and the Genesis of the Fictional Sketch," *Early American Literature* 21 (1987): 226–47.

34. Pancost, 81.

35. Washington Irving, *Letters I*, ed. Ralph M. Aderman, Herbert L. Kleinfield, and Jennifer S. Banks (Boston: Twayne, 1978), 577. Several weeks later, he writes to his brother Ebenezer that he would not have signed with Miller "had there not been a likelihood of these works being republished here from incorrect American numbers," 578. Significantly, he never addresses why he chose Miller over Constable to achieve this objective.

36. Ibid., 577.

37. Pierre M. Irving, *I*, 442–43.

38. Pancost, 80.

39. Hedges notes that "*The Sketch Book* was a gamble for literary success taken by a man who felt that in the ordinary concerns of this world he had been something of a failure," 13. Aderman et al., in *Letters, I*, similarly describe Irving's decision to stay in England rather than return to the United States to work with the Navy Board: "But Irving declined the position, saying that he preferred to remain in England and gamble on the literary project he had under way," xxxiii.

40. Irving understood American culture's unwillingness to support literature as a profession, a situation aptly described in *Analectic Magazine*: "Unqualified for business, in a nation where every one is busy; devoted to literature, where literary leisure is confounded

with idleness; the man of letters is almost an insulated being, with few to understand, less to value, and scarcely any to encourage his pursuits." Quoted in Hedges, 14.

41. McClary, xli. The argument that 1817 marked a sea change in British publishing thanks to the tremendous price Byron and Scott were capable of commanding for copyright was first made by A. S. Collins, *The Profession of Letters: A Study of the Relation of Author to Patron, Publisher, and Public, 1780–1832* (London: George Routledge and Sons, 1928), 155–70, and later by Royal A. Gettmann, *A Victorian Publisher: A Study of the Bentley Papers* (Cambridge: Cambridge University Press, 1960), 1–7. Since then, it has become almost common knowledge that "booksellers" distinguished themselves from dealers unable to pay for the production of books on their own at this time and hence began to function more like prototypes of today's publishers.

42. Burstein, 156.

43. Pierre M. Irving, *II*, 22.

44. Pierre M. Irving, *I*, 455, my emphasis.

45. Washington Irving, *Journals and Notebooks: Vol. II*, 95.

46. Ibid., 11.

47. Washington Irving, *Journals and Notebooks, Vol. III*, 76. Portrait sittings: 153, 180, 316, 318, 320, 321, 322, 323, 434, 481. *Letters I*, 461; Pierre M. Irving, *I*, 359; Washington Irving, *Journals and Notebooks, Vol. III*, 81, 96.

48. Washington Irving, *Journals and Notebooks: Vol. II*, 384.

49. Washington Irving, *Journals and Notebooks: Vol. V*, 317.

50. David Castronovo, *The English Gentleman: Images and Ideals in Literature and Society* (New York: Ungar, 1987), 21.

51. Washington Irving, *Journals and Notebooks, Vol. III*, 659.

52. Ibid., 658.

53. C. R. Leslie, *Autobiographical Recollections, Vol. II*, ed. Tom Taylor (London: John Murray, 1860), 105, quoted in McClary, 24.

54. Pierre M. Irving, *II*, 461–62.

55. Washington Irving, *Letters, I*, 398.

56. I want to avoid what Louis Menand in "The Lives of Others: The Biography Business," *New Yorker* (August 6, 2007): 64–66, calls "the Rosebud assumption that the real truth about a person involves the thing that is least known about them," 65. Instead I look at Irving's public image as a reworked manifestation of his private affinities, such that the binary itself can be read not in one direction only—"that the 'real' person is the private person, and the public person is mostly a performance"—but in the sense that the public image is just as revealing as the private self. Thus my understanding of Irving here is based as much upon Geoffrey Crayon's construction and reception as it is upon the letters and diaries, the latter of which are habitually seen as the "real materials upon which biographies are built," 65.

57. Byron, quoted in Pochman, 428.

58. Washington Irving, *Letters, I*, 570.

59. Ibid., 515.

60. Washington Irving, *Journals and Notebooks, Vol. II*, 10.

61. Ibid., 343.

62. Ibid., 190.

63. Ibid., 659.

64. Ibid., 658.

65. Castronovo, 41.

66. Washington Irving, *Letters, I*, 570.

67. Washington Irving, "The Country Church," in *Sketch Book*, 102.

68. Ibid., 103.

69. Washington Irving, "The Legend of Sleepy Hollow," in *Sketch Book*, 332.

70. Ibid., 345.

71. Ibid., 354.

72. Washington Irving, "The Country Church," in *Sketch Book*, 103.

73. Washington Irving, *Journals and Notebooks: Vol. V*, 311, 317.

74. Pancost, 81.

2. "DEAR DUYCKINCK"

1. Hershel Parker links Gansevoort's efforts on behalf of Melville to his sudden decline: "No one ever said it, but everyone could reflect privately that if Gansevoort had not driven himself in the last months to launch Herman's career, he might have recuperated in some pleasant village outside London and survived his illness, which had attacked, the doctors said, so many organs of his body." *Herman Melville: A Biography, 1819–1851* (Baltimore: Johns Hopkins University Press, 1996), 430.

2. Herman Melville, *Correspondence*, ed. Lynn Horth (Evanston, Ill.: Northwestern University Press, 1993), 50.

3. Melville, *Correspondence*, 50.

4. Ibid., 54.

5. Robert Milder, "Herman Melville, 1819–1891: A Brief Biography," in *A Historical Guide to Herman Melville*, ed. Giles Gunn (New York: Oxford University Press, 2005), 25. Andrew Delbanco insinuates that the relationship ceased entirely by citing the vitriolic Book XVII of *Pierre* and Duyckinck's suavely condemning review. Delbanco flatly casts Melville as rebellious truth-speaker to Duyckinck's conservative ninny. *Melville: His World and Work* (New York: Knopf, 2005), 94, 205. Theirs was a public, boisterous brawl but it did not end their relationship. Hershel Parker and Sheila Post-Lauria also underestimate the depth and endurance of the Melville-Duyckinck bond. While Milder and Delbanco assume the relationship virtually ended in 1852 with the publication of *Pierre*, Parker suggests Cornelius Mathews was the major cause of the rift, 606. In *Correspondent Colorings: Melville in the Marketplace* (Amherst: University of Massachusetts Press, 1996), Post-Lauria notes only that Duyckinck inexplicably recanted his earlier support for mixed-genre fiction and condemned formal experimentation upon the emergence of *Moby-Dick*, 125–26.

6. Daniel A. Wells represents the critical exaggeration of Melville's renunciation of the Duyckinck circle. He cites Duyckinck's negative reviews of *Moby-Dick* and *Pierre* as the "clean break" from which "the critical and philosophical split had become a personal one" signaled by Melville's cancellation of his subscription to the *Literary World*. "'Bartleby the Scrivener,' Poe, and the Duyckinck Circle," *ESQ: A Journal of the American Renaissance* 21 (1975): 35. Delbanco's portrait of Duyckinck is painted largely from the template of Whit-

man's caricature—"very clerical looking—thin—wanting in body: men of truly proper style, God help 'em!"—an image flavored largely by the distinct tang of sour grapes Whitman tasted upon noticing his omission from Duyckinck's *Cyclopedia of American Authors.* Horace Traubel, *With Walt Whitman in Camden* (Boston: Small, Maynard, 1906), I, 39. Donald Kay comes closer to the truth, arguing that Duyckinck "was at first only a business connection, but gradually a truly personal relationship developed: a literary relationship which affected the art of Melville's fiction and poetry." "Herman Melville's Literary Relationship with Evert Duyckinck," *College Language Association Journal* 18 (1975): 339. He does not define those effects, such as Melville's connection to the Knickerbocker circle, as I do here.

7. Quoted in Weisbuch, 16.

8. Edgar Allan Poe, "The Literati of New York City," *Godey's Magazine and Ladies Book* (July 1846), quoted in Parker, *Herman Melville,* 433.

9. Donald Yanella, *Dictionary of Literary Biography, Vol. 250: Antebellum Writers in New York, Second Series,* ed. Kent P. Ljungquist (Worcester: The Gale Group, 2001), 135.

10. Donald Yanella and Kathleen Malone Yanella, "Evert A. Duyckinck's Diary: May 29–November 8, 1847," in *Studies in the American Renaissance,* ed. Joel Myerson (Boston: Twayne Publishers, 1978), 230.

11. William M. Gibson, "The American Literary Scene, 1815–1860," in *Washington Irving: A Tribute* (Tarrytown, N.Y.: Sleepy Hollow Restorations, 1972), 81.

12. Parker, *Herman Melville,* 640.

13. Yanella and Yanella, 208.

14. John Evelev, *Tolerable Entertainment: Herman Melville and Professionalism in Antebellum New York* (Amherst: University of Massachusetts Press, 2006), 83–84.

15. Parker, *Herman Melville,* 540.

16. Herman Melville, "Rip Van Winkle's Lilac," in *A Century of Commentary on the Works of Washington Irving, 1860–1974* (Tarrytown, N.Y.: Sleepy Hollow Restorations, 1976), 76.

17. Melville, "Rip," 84.

18. Oakey Hall, "Review of *White Jacket,*" *Commercial Bulletin,* April 9, 1850, quoted in Parker, *Herman Melville,* 730.

19. Henry T. Tuckerman, "Introduction," in *Old New York* by Dr. John W. Francis (New York: W. J. Widdleton, 1865), quoted in Parker, *Herman Melville,* 572.

20. Evert Duyckinck, "Review," *Literary World,* November 10, 1850, quoted in Parker, *Herman Melville,* 709.

21. The reviewer called *Mardi* a "transcendental *Gulliver,* or *Robinson Crusoe* run mad" in the *London Examiner,* March 31, 1849, quoted in Parker, *Herman Melville,* 628.

22. Melville, *Correspondence,* 78.

23. Evert Duyckinck, "Review of *Omoo,*" *Morning News* (1847), quoted in Parker, *Herman Melville,* 482.

24. Evert Duyckinck, May 14, 1847, quoted in Merrell R. Davis, *Melville's Mardi, a Chartless Voyage* (New Haven, Conn.: Yale University Press, 1952), 35.

25. Yanella and Yanella, 241.

26. Ibid., 241.

27. Ibid.

28. James T. Fields, *Yesterdays with Authors* (Boston: J. R. Osgood, 1872), quoted in Jay Leyda, ed., *The Melville Log, vol. I* (New York: Gordian Press, 1969), 384.

29. Melville, *Correspondence,* 165.

30. Duyckinck, quoted in Parker, *Herman Melville,* 564.

31. Melville, *Correspondence,* 204.

32. Duyckinck, quoted in Parker, *Herman Melville,* 855.

33. Melville, *White Jacket,* quoted in Parker, *Herman Melville,* 562.

34. Melville, *Correspondence,* 167.

35. Ibid., 168.

36. Ibid.

37. Ibid., 176.

38. Ibid.

39. Ibid., 201.

40. Ibid., 124.

41. Melville, *Moby-Dick,* 21.

42. Melville, *Correspondence,* 124.

43. Parker, *Herman Melville,* 855.

44. Greenspan, 182.

45. George Haven Putnam, George Haven Putnam Collection, Special Collections, Butler Library, Columbia University, quoted in Greenspan, 182.

46. Delbanco, 196.

47. Herman Melville, *Pierre; or, The Ambiguities,* ed. Harrison Hayford, Hershel Parker, and G. Thomas Tanselle (Evanston, Ill.: Northwestern University Press, 1992), 260.

48. Ibid., 261.

49. Ibid., 376.

50. Quoted in Laurie Robertson-Lorant, *Melville: A Biography* (Amherst: University of Massachusetts Press, 1996), 250.

51. Ibid., 355.

52. Ibid.

53. Such confinement takes the shape of unsympathetic and neglectful readers blind to (what Melville perceived as) his lofty literary methods. Paul Lyons, "Melville and his Precursors: Style as Metastyle and Allusion," *American Literature* 62 (1990): 450.

54. Robert Milder emphasizes the Freudian rather than the professional and biographical implications of such self-mockery: "Melville turned against himself early in *Pierre* through the mocking self-reference of the Glendinning/Gansevoort parallels and the giddy delight his narrator takes in promising to topple Pierre from his 'noble pedestal' and strip him of all inward and outward complacencies." *Exiled Royalties: Melville and the Life We Imagine* (New York: Oxford University Press, 2007), 130. Such evidence can situate Melville as a "Freudian melancholic," but it also points to his well-known complaint to Hawthorne: "What I feel most moved to write, that is banned,—it will not pay. Yet, altogether, write the *other* way I cannot. So the product is a final hash and all my books are botches." Melville, *Correspondence,* 191.

55. Melville, *Pierre,* 247.

56. Melville rebelled against the popular dandy style preferred by Duyckinck: "Give me my grandfather's . . . cane," he exhorts in a passage from *White Jacket,* "a cane that . . .

would break down the back of the switch-carrying dandies of these spindle-shank days; give me his broad-breasted vest . . . furnished with two strong boxes of pockets to keep guineas in; toss this toppling cylinder of a beaver overboard, and give me my grandfather's gallant, gable-ended, cocked hat." *White Jacket*, ed. Harrison Hayford, Hershel Parker, and G. Thomas Tanselle (Evanston, Ill.: Northwestern University Press, 1970), 325. Style is an emblem of expression here and in an image tied to authorship as Ishmael exclaims, "Give me a condor's quill!" "The Fossil Whale," in *Moby-Dick*, 439.

57. Melville, *Pierre*, 283.

58. Emory Elliot, "'Wandering To-and-Fro': Melville and Religion," in *A Historical Guide to Herman Melville*, ed. Giles Gunn (Oxford: Oxford University Press, 2005), 194.

59. Melville, *Correspondence*, 192.

60. Melville, *Pierre*, 333.

61. Ibid., 420.

62. Melville, *Correspondence*, 618.

63. Ibid., 226.

64. Ibid., 227.

65. Ibid., 228.

66. Ibid., 620.

67. Post-Lauria asserts that *Pierre* was not a botched domestic novel so much as a fully realized version of the sensational French romances popular at the time, 129–40. If the work is to be considered a "popular" success for effectively drawing on such popular forms, one must overlook the overwhelming evidence of its commercial and critical failure documented by Brian Higgins and Hershel Parker, eds., *Herman Melville: The Contemporary Reviews* (Cambridge: Cambridge University Press, 1995), 419–52.

68. Quoted in Parker, *Herman Melville*, 376.

69. Hart's book may have annoyed Melville to no end, but it certainly appears to have inspired him on to a similar project in *Moby-Dick*. Perry Miller substantiates the link with quotes from Hart such as, "Oh Shakespeare—Immortal bard—Mighty genius—Swan of Avon—thou Unapproachable! Are there no more fish, no more krakens in that wondrous sea from which thou wert taken? Shall there be no more cakes and ale?" *The Raven and the Whale* (New York: Harcourt, Brace & World, 1956), 241–42.

70. Melville, *Correspondence*, 179, 113.

71. Brian Higgins and Hershel Parker, *Reading Melville's Pierre; or, The Ambiguities* (Baton Rouge: Louisiana State University Press, 2006), 151.

72. Ibid., 151.

73. Melville, *Correspondence*, 218.

74. Melville, *Pierre*, 253–54.

75. Hershel Parker, "*The Isle of the Cross* and *Poems*: Lost Melville Books and the Indefinite Afterlife of Error," *Nineteenth-Century Literature* 62.1 (2007): 29–47. Parker justly indicts Delbanco for suggesting that *Poetry* and *Isle of the Cross* do not exist. Delbanco later acknowledged their existence in his biography.

76. Melville, *Correspondence*, 342.

77. Parker, *Isle*, 39.

78. Melville, *Correspondence*, 121; Leyda, *Log II*, 523.

79. Quoted in Parker, *Herman Melville: The Making of the Poet* (Evanston, Ill.: Northwestern University Press, 2008), 134.

80. Robert D. Putnam, *Bowling Alone: The Collapse and Revival of American Community* (New York: Simon and Schuster, 2000).

81. Jay Leyda, *The Melville Log, vol. II* (New York: Gordian Press, 1969), 607.

82. Ibid., 608.

83. Ibid., 613.

84. Ibid., 641.

85. Ibid., 645.

86. Ibid., 662.

87. Edward L. Widmer, *Young America: The Flowering of Democracy in New York City* (Oxford: Oxford University Press, 1999), 119.

88. Leyda, *Log II*, 665.

89. Ibid., 769.

3. DAVIS, INC.

1. Gerald Langford's 1961 claim that "as a husband, Clarke was all that Rebecca could have hoped for," but because of his association with *Peterson's*, "as a literary influence he could hardly have been less desirable," has corrupted nearly a half-century of scholarship on Clarke's literary influence on Rebecca. *The Richard Harding Davis Years: A Biography of a Mother and Son* (New York: Holt, Rinehart, and Winston, 1961), 85. His sweeping denigration of such writing as meaningless "sentimental and melodramatic potboilers" is fully blind to its reform potential, especially on issues such as mental illness, gender, and economic injustice in which Davis held a deep personal stake, 58. Echoes of Langford's verdict that *Peterson's* "began at once to corrupt her serious work" can be heard nearly twenty-five years later in Tillie Olsen's only slightly mollified damnation of Clarke. In her brief 1985 biography, Olsen characterizes Davis's Clarke-inspired *Peterson's* work as "a different kind of writing—entertainment, not literature." "A Biographical Interpretation," in *Life in the Iron Mills and Other Stories*, ed. Tillie Olsen (Old Westbury, N.Y.: Feminist Press, 1985), 90. Following in line with this portrait throughout the 1990s are Sharon M. Harris, *Rebecca Harding Davis and American Realism* (Philadelphia: University of Pennsylvania Press, 1991), 71–72, 116; and Jane Atteridge Rose, "The Artist Manque in the Fiction of Rebecca Harding Davis," in *Writing the Woman Artist*, ed. Suzanne W. Jones (Philadelphia: University of Pennsylvania Press, 1991), 37. Jean Pfaelzer's 1996 biography continued to condemn Clarke for "encouraging her to write for popular journals," allowing the significant fact, however parenthetically stated, that "Despite recurrent images in Davis's fiction of husbands thwarting women's creative ambitions, there seems to be no evidence, however, that Clarke Davis tried to impede Rebecca's career . . . In fact, he frequently acted as an agent, as a broker, and at least once as a collaborator; never, according to their son Richard Harding Davis, did Clarke edit Rebecca's writing." *Parlor Radical: Rebecca Harding Davis and the Origins of American Social Realism* (Pittsburgh: University of Pittsburgh Press, 1997), 11. Patricia Okker's stellar 2003 *Social Stories* breaks down Langford's false binary, noting it is "unwise to make too sharp a distinction between these two [popular and liter-

ary] careers" since "she would continue to publish in both literary and popular periodicals throughout her lifetime . . . presenting instead a more unified image of her career." *Social Stories: The Magazine Novel in Nineteenth-Century America* (Charlottesville: University of Virginia Press, 2003), 116. Still more recently and in tune with my approach is Michele Mock, who offers the most accurate depiction yet (however, buried in a footnote) of their relationship. She hails their efforts to reform asylum abuse as an "interanimating" wedding of art and law that showcases the "dialogic activity between the Davises" in a model of literary collaboration with socially efficacious results. "'An Ardor That Was Human, and a Power That Was Art': Rebecca Harding Davis and the Art of the Periodical," in *The Only Efficient Instrument: American Women Writers and the Periodical, 1837–1916*, ed. Aleta Feinsod Cane and Susan Alves (Iowa City: University of Iowa Press, 2001), 146.

2. Charles J. Peterson founded the *Ladies' National Magazine* in January 1842 in direct competition with *Godey's Lady's Book* with its large octavo size; hand-colored fashion plates; three sentimental engravings per issue; and mix of essays, poetry, and fiction, much of it serialized. Stephens was closely associated with the magazine (soon to be renamed *Peterson's*) as a contributor and co-editor up until the 1850s. For more on Stephens's use of fashion in her fiction, see the chapter, "Fashion and the Magazine Novelist: The Case of Anne Stephens," in Okker's *Social Stories*, 55–78. The production of the journal both by and for women distinguished it from its competitors, as its editorial policy made clear: "we shall rely chiefly, if not altogether, on female pens." *Ladies' National Magazine* 3 (April 1843): 128. It enjoyed the status of being the most popular women's magazine in the United States during the 1860s and 1870s, with a circulation of 140,000 in 1869 rising 2 years later to 165,000, as Frank Luther Mott reports in *A History of American Magazines, Vol. II: 1850–1865* (Cambridge, Mass.: Harvard University Press, 1938), 309. Davis shared space in *Peterson's* with authors like Caroline Kirkland, Frances S. Osgood, and Lydia Sigourney.

3. Prior to the French Revolution, the king and his ministers signed *lettres de cachet* to sentence subjects without trial to prisons, hospitals, or exile. The wealthy routinely purchased such *lettres* to remove unwanted individuals. Clarke uses the *lettre de cachet* as an icon of unilateral monarchical tyranny and thus a profane heresy against the sacred American principles of democracy and individual rights. What makes the *lettre* "modern" is the distinctly American antebellum capitalist liability to avaricious graft that abets the purchase of asylum sentences.

4. Harris, *Rebecca Harding Davis*, 104, 72.

5. Rose, 37.

6. Lisa A. Long, "The Postbellum Reform Writings of Rebecca Harding Davis and Elizabeth Stuart Phelps," in *The Cambridge Companion to Nineteenth-Century Women's Writing*, ed. Dale M. Bauer and Philip Gould (New York: Cambridge University Press, 2001), reports that Davis's "The Curse of Education" was included in the 1899 U.S. Congressional Report to argue on behalf of education as an integral part of prison reform. This exemplifies how Davis's didactic critical realism of the 1860s in such works as *Put Out of the Way* anticipated Progressive-era social reform toward the turn of the century, 272.

7. Rose, 37.

8. Rebecca Harding Davis, "The Wife's Story," in *Life in the Iron Mills and Other Stories*, ed. Tillie Olsen (Old Westbury, N.Y.: Feminist Press, 1985), 150.

9. Charles Belmont Davis, ed., *The Adventures and Letters of Richard Harding Davis* (New York: Scribner's Sons, 1917), 55.

10. The exception is Ruth Stoner, "Rebecca Harding Davis's 'Second Life'; or 'Her Hands could be Trained as Well as His,'" *Legacy* 19.1 (2002): 44–52, who recently reclaims both Davis's financial savvy and the status of her *Peterson's* tales as art. Although such tales were "embedded within very conventional imagery and sentimental plots," Stoner argues, they contained subversive thinking about women's sexual repression, 44. Marriage endings and antimaterialist sentiment, I argue, were staples not only of Davis's popular fiction, but her didactic reform tales as well.

11. Pfaelzer, 226–27.

12. Quoted in Harris, *Rebecca Harding Davis*, 68.

13. David S. Reynolds, *Beneath the American Renaissance: The Subversive Imagination in the Age of Emerson and Melville* (Cambridge, Mass.: Harvard University Press, 1989), 65, 68.

14. Evelev, 61.

15. Catherine C. Mitchell, ed., *Margaret Fuller's New York Journalism: A Biographical Essay and Key Writings* (Knoxville: University of Tennessee Press, 1995), 179.

16. Harris claims that many of Davis's stories, "perhaps unwittingly," leave their heroines "rooted in a highly patriarchal world," especially in "The Wife's Story," which ultimately "is a very dissatisfying ending for twentieth-century [as well as twenty-first-century] audiences." *Rebecca Harding Davis*, 114. I argue later that such stories intentionally supported domestic work, for the alternative was not the realistic sort of authorship/artistry that Davis herself practiced, but transcendentalism. Further, Harris tends to overemphasize how after the birth of her son, Davis "now found balancing her marriage and career even more exhausting with the addition of motherhood" and how "the inequities of responsibilities" were a common complaint, for she had "little time for celebrations and none to think of her own career." *Rebecca Harding Davis*, 115–16. Davis was still engaged in a political and literary sense, as seen in her letters to Annie Fields. Such engagement is not so much evidence of literary paralysis, a sort of professional death by domesticity, but testament to her resourcefulness and grit. Such attributes are underestimated by Rose, whose focus on Davis's victimization and unfulfilled, frustrated vision at the hands of S. Weir Mitchell's rest cure, which I discuss later, misses how her production in spite of it is nothing short of inspirational.

17. Melissa Homestead has convincingly argued that "weak copyright laws" were not a disincentive for women to write, but to "wholeheartedly exploit, and even help invent, the structures of commodity capitalism" while also "maintaining an emotional detachment from the market," one that she says was not so much an affective decision as a legal fact since "the law effectively created a distance by refusing to grant most women the legal status of proprietors," 3.

18. Quoted in Rose, 38.

19. Anne E. Boyd, *Writing for Immortality: Women and the Emergence of High Literary Culture in America* (Baltimore: Johns Hopkins University Press, 2004), 211. Pfaelzer's insight qualifies this point. She argues that much of Davis's "portraits of daily life and domestic power" attributed to realism really derived from the domestic sentimental novels, 17. Realism, and its association with literary fiction, was nonetheless coded male, as it remained the driving force behind "the percentage of contributions by women [which]

dropped significantly from 90–100 percent of the total fiction featured in the first seven years of the magazine to only 30–40 percent," as Boyd notes, 210. Such a precipitous drop, Boyd rightly concludes, unmasked the editorial agenda of the *Atlantic* to return to its original identity as a men's magazine, a fact that is crushingly obvious in light of Fields's willingness to drop Davis from the list of contributors in 1868, right as her star was rising as the new face of realism. He did not want that face to be female, as the writing staff by 1871 was mostly male. Such critics as Richard Brodhead have been blind to the institutional sexism of such editorial business practice. His assumption that Fields was operating a meritocracy as the magazine "underwent a palpable stiffening of its selection criteria" is painfully wrong (along with his unfortunate phallocentric imagery to express it), quoted in Boyd, 209. Fields did not raise the bar of his selection criteria so much as he shut out women.

20. Helen Woodward Shaffer, "Rebecca Harding Davis: Pioneer Realist" (Ph.D. dissertation, University of Pennsylvania, 1947), 117.

21. Such a display of Davis's business skill shows a full engagement with and manipulation of the market, a dynamic at odds with the predominant pattern of emotional and psychological detachment from the market described in Ann Douglas, *The Feminization of American Culture* (New York: Knopf, 1977); Lori Merish, *Sentimental Materialism: Gender, Commodity Culture, and Nineteenth-Century American Literature* (Durham, N.C.: Duke University Press, 2000); Mary Kelly, *Private Woman, Public Stage: Literary Domesticity in Nineteenth-Century America* (New York: Oxford University Press, 1984). My perspective derives from Susan Coutrap-McQuinn, *Doing Literary Business: American Women Writers in the Nineteenth Century* (Chapel Hill: University of North Carolina Press, 1990), who demonstrates that antebellum gender codes of conduct governing the publishing industry were not always in conflict with, but in many ways supported professional women writers.

22. Olsen, 135.

23. Quoted in Rose, 58.

24. Ibid.

25. Quoted in Olsen, 128.

26. *Peterson's*, January–June 1863, 350.

27. *Peterson's*, July–December 1865, 291.

28. Rebecca Harding Davis, "The Wife's Story," 197.

29. Kristin Bordeau, "'The Woman's Flesh of Me': Rebecca Harding Davis's Response to Self-Reliance," *American Transcendental Quarterly* 6.2 (June 1992): 132–40, has noted that "The Wife's Story" is a "powerful working class critique of Emerson" in which the protagonist rejects self-reliance for not only domesticity but also the body, 132. Her focus on the maternal and the physical aspects of identity complements my emphasis on realistic images of authorship. Davis equally embraced motherhood and writing with the same realistic ethos.

30. Review of "A Modern Lettre de Cachet," *Medical and Surgical Reporter* (May 30, 1868): 18. Hereafter *Reporter.*

31. Fanny Fern, *Ruth Hall and Other Writings*, ed. Joyce Warren (New Brunswick, N.J.: Rutgers University Press, 1986 [rpt. 1855 ed.]), 111.

32. Ibid.

33. Mock, 135.

34. Davis appears to have modeled Dick Wortley after her own son. Like the fictional artist devoted to the care of his aging mother, Dick Harding was an author whose intense dedication to his mother inspired their joint biography, *The Richard Harding Davis Years: A Biography of a Mother and Son*, by Langford. Tellingly, the first person Wortley asks for upon his liberation from the asylum is not his lover Lotty, but his mother.

35. Davis indeed fictionalized her husband's anecdote of Morgan Hinchman in her novel. However, Mock's claim that Clarke "describes legal injustices perpetuated against women in his essay's conclusion" is less convincing. He only parenthetically references men who use asylums as a way of ridding themselves of wives to avert a costly divorce, 146. Textual evidence does not support a perfect exchange of Clarke's legal case history for his wife's feminist sensibility. Neither of Clarke's other references to women makes light of gender injustice. One illustrates the lack of consensus of a panel of psychiatrists who judged "Mrs. Cumming ('Journal of Psychological Medicine') . . . swearing to their opinions in the most positive terms, one half for her sanity and the other moiety against it." L. Clarke Davis, "A Modern Lettre de Cachet," *Atlantic Monthly Magazine* 21 (1868): 602. The other illustrates the sexual deviance inherent in the living arrangements of many asylums in which "'males and females are found in adjoining, and often in opposite rooms, even in that state of excitement when they will wear no clothing." Ibid., 599–600.

36. Pfaelzer astutely observes that "images of silence and confinement return us to Davis's vocabulary of female repression, while the references to the immobilizing pain of Dick's 'brain fever,' technically a form of meningitis but also a nineteenth-century catchall term for various experiences of depression, suggest the neurasthenia Rebecca suffered during her pregnancy," 234.

37. *Reporter*, 18.

38. Ibid.

39. See David S. Reynolds, *Beneath the American Renaissance: The Subversive Imagination in the Age of Emerson and Melville* (Cambridge, Mass.: Harvard University Press, 1989), 54–91, on the pervasive darkening of moral discourse. Reynolds calls "didactic rhetoric . . . a protective shield for highly unconventional explorations of tabooed psychological and spiritual areas." In the Davises' hands, didactic rhetoric also legitimates their rendition of the horrifying details of asylum life in such a way that is not decadent but progressive in its focus on the stigmatization of the mentally ill and the disproportionate number of women committed to asylums at the time, 55. These were more sobering, yet equally taboo, social problems.

40. *Reporter*, 19.

41. L. Clarke Davis, "Lettre," 588.

42. Ibid., 588.

43. Ibid., 589.

44. L. Clarke Davis, *A Stranded Ship: A Story of Sea and Shore* (New York: G. P. Putnam, 1869), 40; 55.

45. Ibid., 57.

46. Ibid., 70.

47. Ibid., 110, 123.

48. Ibid., 110, 123, 144.

49. L. Clarke Davis, "Lettre," 589.

50. Bertolt Brecht argues that "the concern of the epic theatre," like Davis's didactic purpose, "is thus eminently practical. Human behavior is shown as alterable; man himself as dependent on certain political and economic factors and at the same time as capable of altering them." *Brecht on Theatre,* ed. John Willett (New York: Hill and Wang, 1964), 86. Davis shares Brecht's aim "to portray social processes as seen in their causal relationships" by exposing the exploitation in those relationships, thus alienating the audience from their sense of them as familiar and thus natural, Brecht, 121. "The goal is to enable the audience to recognize its subject," such as begging, "but at the same time make it seem unfamiliar" by portraying the beggars as professionals who practice their technique, complete with costumes and managers, as he does in *Three Penny Opera,* 192. Similarly, a sane man's commitment to an asylum renders the familiar subject of the institutionalization of the mentally ill shockingly unnatural.

51. L. Clarke Davis, "Lettre," 590.

52. Ibid., 590–91, my emphasis.

53. Rebecca Harding Davis, *Put Out of the Way, Peterson's Magazine* 57–58 (1870): 436.

54. L. Clarke Davis, "Lettre," 593, 590, 593.

55. Ibid., 595.

56. Rebecca Harding Davis, *Put Out of the Way,* 437.

57. Ibid., 32.

58. Ibid., 32, 114.

59. Okker, 69.

60. Rebecca Harding Davis, *Put Out of the Way,* 355, 356.

61. Ibid., 436, 41.

62. Ibid., 113.

63. Ibid., 115, 117.

64. Rebecca Harding Davis, "The Disease of Money-Getting," *The Independent* 54.2794 (1902): 1457.

65. L. Clarke Davis, "Lettre," 600.

4. CAPITAL BONDS

1. E. D. E. N. Southworth, *The Hidden Hand; or, Capitola the Madcap* (New York: G. W. Dillingham, 1888 [rpt. 1859 ed.]), 388. Hereafter *Hidden* cited in text.

2. David S. Reynolds, in *Beneath the American Renaissance: The Subversive Imagination in the Age of Emerson and Melville* (Cambridge, Mass.: Harvard University Press, 1989), notes that this fusion of criminality and goodness is at the core of the popular nineteenth-century stereotype of the likeable criminal. The paradox is instructive to how in *The Hidden Hand* "the Conventional, when exaggerated," changes to its opposite, expressing "unsettling truth about antebellum moral culture: The Conventional itself carried the seeds of the Subversive," as Reynolds describes of Melville's *Pierre,* 159. Southworth's oscillation between piety and subversion parallels Melville's in "Hawthorne and His Mosses." In it, Melville exhorts American authors to "breathe that unshackled democratic spirit of Christianity in all things," espousing shortly thereafter the less than Christian solution that "we must turn bullies, else the day is lost.'" "Hawthorne and His Moses," in *The Piazza*

Tales and Other Prose Pieces, ed. Harrison Hayford, Alma A. MacDougall, and G. Thomas Tanselle (Evanston, Ill.: Northwestern University Press, 1987), 248.

3. See Christopher Looby, "Southworth and Seriality: *The Hidden Hand* in the *New York Ledger*," *Nineteenth-Century Literature* 59.2 (2004): 183; Susan Coultrap-McQuin, *Doing Literary Business: American Women Writers in the Nineteenth Century* (Chapel Hill: University of North Carolina Press, 1990), 50–78; Mary Kelley, *Private Woman, Public Stage: Literary Domesticity in Nineteenth-Century America* (Oxford: Oxford University Press, 1984), 21–23, 161–63, 198, 220, 321–23. Older works also documenting Southworth's relationship with Bonner include Ralph Admari, "Bonner and 'The Ledger,'" *American Book Collector* 6 (1935): 176–39, and Frank Luther Mott, *A History of American Magazines, 1850–1865* (Cambridge, Mass.: Belknap Press of Harvard University Press, 1938), 10–11, 15–17, 23–24, 38, 356–63.

4. Mary Noel, *Villains Galore: The Hey-Day of the Popular Story Weekly* (New York: Macmillan, 1954), 89.

5. Quoted in Noel, 88–89.

6. In 1860, Robert Bonner had amassed a $350,000 annual profit from the *New York Ledger*. Noel, 74.

7. J. C. Derby, *Fifty Years Among Authors, Books, and Publishers* (New York: G. W. Carleton and Company, 1884), 205.

8. Bonner's advertisement in *Harper's Weekly* boasted the circulation figure of 400,000 in the January 7, 1860, issue. Frank Luther Mott, *A History of American Magazines, Vol. II: 1850–1865* (Cambridge, Mass.: Harvard University Press, 1938), 359. By comparison, the *Weekly Tribune Circular* had the next largest circulation of 167,000. Bonner heralded reaching a circulation of 100,000 with a 100-gun salute in New York City on June 12, 1856, perhaps the most outrageous display of economic power in the history of U.S. print culture. The salute attracted readers and intimidated competitors with the news of his paper's rapid rise to dominance of the market. Noel, 70.

9. In addition to Fern and Southworth, Bonner outbid competitors with lucrative contracts for popular authors Sylvanus Cobb and Ward Beecher, as Helen Waite Papashvily notes in *All the Happy Endings: A Study of the Domestic Novel in America, the Women who Wrote it, the Women who Read it, in the Nineteenth Century* (New York: Harper Brothers, 1956), 125, 122.

10. Susan Coultrap-McQuin has argued in *Doing Literary Business: American Women Writers in the Nineteenth Century* (Chapel Hill: University of North Carolina Press, 1990) that women's domestic and professional roles were not in the debilitating conflict assumed by many critics, particularly Ann Douglas, *The Feminization of American Culture* (New York: Avon, 1977) and Mary Kelley. Coultrap-McQuin argues that the role of a lady to his gentleman conformed to Southworth's traditional sensibility and "worked for her" because Bonner's commercialism afforded her economic independence, 78. Her aggressively commercial work, further, was not fueled by greed in her mind, but was "entirely compatible with the woman's sphere: she would generously provide support for those whom she loved," 60. I extend these findings further by suggesting that Southworth's role was on more equal footing with Bonner in terms of executive business decisions and thus clearly at odds with that of a traditional nineteenth-century lady. Such a productive,

proactive role, however, augmented rather than contradicted her sense of herself as a nineteenth-century lady, anticipating modern definitions of professional womanhood. The values of that satisfying relationship—both traditional and progressive, both reactionary and innovative—were encoded and/or sublimated into her fiction. Whereas Coultrap-McQuin offers a cursory look at Bonner's business practice and ethic, I examine it more closely in the letters and in the broader and deeper terrain of Southworth's lesser-known fiction.

11. Southworth frequently wrote through severe illness; at one point, she was stricken with smallpox and continued writing nonetheless to meet deadlines. Regis Boyle reports that "from 1852 to 1854, Mrs. Southworth endured so many trials, worked so steadily and had such ill health that in 1855 she suffered a breakdown." *Mrs. E. D. E. N. Southworth, Novelist* (Washington, D.C.: Catholic University Press, 1939), 11. She wrote up to three novels a year in the early stage of her career, and from 1862 to 1890 averaged one a year. In 1881, Southworth reflected back on her routine: "On Monday, Tuesday, Wednesday, and Thursday, *both day and night, until midnight,* I sit at my desk and write, seldom leaving it except for meals—until about half past seven o'clock on Thursday evening when I usually send off my number for the week. It takes me four days and three long evenings to write a number." Quoted in Donald Gallup, "More Letters of American Writers," *Yale University Gazette* (July 1962): 30. Her work ethic through her most impoverished years increased her appreciation of the privileges built into writing for Bonner, as she marveled at how much "trouble visited our home during those two successive years, in which 'The Lost Heiress' and 'Miriam' were written. It is a marvel to me yet, how either of those works were ever completed." Southworth, quoted in Papashvily, 188–89.

12. Herman Melville, *Moby-Dick; or, The Whale,* ed. Harrison Hayford, Hershel Parker, and G. Thomas Tanselle (Evanston, Ill.: Northwestern University Press, 1988), 72.

13. See, for example, Joyce Warren, *Women, Money, and the Law: Nineteenth-Century Fiction, Gender, and the Courts* (Iowa City: University of Iowa Press, 2005), 90–96; Coultrap-McQuin, 53, 64–65; Joanne Dobson, "Introduction," in *The Hidden Hand; or, Capitola the Madcap,* ed. Dobson (New Brunswick, N.J.: Rutgers University Press, 1988), xxiv; Noel, 270–73; Papashvily, 113, 115–16; and Boyle, 28, 37, 47, 52, 53, 57, 62.

14. Joanne Dobson's selective bibliography (labeled "Works") of Southworth novels in the authoritative Rutgers University Press edition of *The Hidden Hand* only lists a fraction of Southworth's novels, and does not include the work I examine in this study, *The Artist's Love* (1872), published by T. B. Peterson in an edition that included several stories by her sister (xliii). No reference to *The Artist's Love* is in the most recent Southworth criticism represented by Coultrap-McQuin and Looby. *The Artist's Love* is only listed in the appendices of Boyle, 159, 164. Southworth's voluminous literary corpus remains untapped, as only a fraction of her ninety-one novels has received critical attention.

15. The standard wage for authors of weekly publications was $2 to $10 per page. Bonner paid Fern $25 per page to lure her away from Moulton. Mott, 20. Bonner also paid the husband-and-wife team of Harriet and Leon Lewis $150 weekly for their writing. Arlene Moore, "The Letters of Harriet and Leon Lewis to Robert Bonner," *Dime Novel Roundup* 61.1 (1992): 2–7.

16. Henry Peterson to E. D. E. N. Southworth, Philadelphia, September 10, 1849, Duke University, William R. Perkins Library, Durham, N.C., quoted in Coultrap-McQuin, 64.

17. Henry Peterson to E. D. E. N. Southworth, Philadelphia, December 24, 1854, Duke University, quoted in Coultrap-McQuin, 65.

18. Coultrap-McQuin, 70.

19. Immediately after signing Southworth to an exclusive contract in 1857, Bonner spent $7,000 in one week on advertising—an unprecedented sum at the time for print publicity—trumpeting his prize to the world, filling entire columns in plain black print so bizarre and stunning in their layout as to be almost impossible to ignore. Noel, 75.

20. Henry James represented the anti-commercial sentiment of the nineteenth century when he quipped, "There is nothing so debasing as to become an agent between the supply and demand of the commodity." Quoted in June Howard, "What Is Sentimentality?" *American Literary History* 11.1 (1999): 74.

21. Noel, 58.

22. Southworth, quoted in Noel, 94.

23. Ibid., 95.

24. Ibid.

25. Coultrap-McQuin, 60.

26. E. D. E. N. Southworth to Robert Bonner, December 26, 1869, quoted in Dobson, xviii.

27. Ibid.

28. Southworth, quoted in Coultrap-McQuin, 72. For more on this temping offer, see Noel, 117.

29. Sarah Robbins, "Gendering Gilded Age Periodical Professionalism: Reading Harriet Beecher Stowe's *Hearth and Home* Prescriptions for Women's Writing," in *The Only Efficient Instrument: American Women Writers and the Periodical, 1837–1916,* ed. Aleta Feinsod Cane and Susan Alves (Iowa City: University of Iowa Press, 2001), 49.

30. Looby, 181.

31. Warren, 70.

32. Robert Bonner, "Woman's True Sphere," *New York Ledger*, May 14, 1859.

33. Warren, 96.

34. Papashvily, 132.

35. Dobson, xviii.

36. Susan Albertine, "Introduction," in *A Living of Words: American Women in Print Culture* (Knoxville: University of Tennessee Press, 1995), xiv.

37. Southworth to Bonner, Prospect Cottage, 1862, Duke University, quoted in Coultrap-McQuin, 72.

38. Howard, 74.

39. Herbert Ross Brown offers a broad view of the intellectual historical origins of the sentimental novel, as well as a chapter of "Popular Isms and Ologies" that is particularly helpful in framing Southworth's notorious dabblings in spiritualism and mesmerism, which I take up later, as they overtly drive much of the narrative of *The Artist's Love.* See *The Sentimental Novel in America, 1789–1860* (Durham, N.C.: Duke University Press, 1940), 181–200.

40. Joanne Dobson, "Reclaiming Sentimental Literature," *American Literature* 69 (1997): 263–88.

41. Jean-Christophe Agnew, *Worlds Apart: The Market and the Theatre in Anglo-American Thought, 1550–1750* (New York: Cambridge University Press, 1986). Quoted in Howard, 72.

42. Thomas L. Haskell finds that "the rise of capitalism . . . had a more telling influence on humanitarianism through changes the market wrought in *perception* or *cognitive style*." Particularly useful for my argument is his sense that a "change in the perception of causal connection" triggered a "shift in the conventions of moral responsibility." "Capitalism and the Origins of the Humanitarian Sensibility, Part I," *American Historical Review* 90.2 (1985): 342. This economic and ethical transformation in the culture helps explain how immoral economic self-interest, such as Southworth's husband's leaving his family in search of employment, would be such a major concern in Southworth's letters embracing Bonner over Peterson as well as her foregrounding such concerns in her fiction. Indeed, the very nature of the intimacy between her and Bonner illustrates "the expansion of the market, the intensification of market discipline, and the penetration of that discipline into spheres of life previously untouched by it." Haskell, 342. This suggests that the prominence of sentimentalism in the popular literary market is not attributable so much to the rise of the middle class as it is to the market revolution of the 1850s.

43. Peter Hulme, *Colonial Encounters: Europe and the Native Caribbean, 1492–1797* (New York: Methuen, 1986), 229.

44. Mary Louise Pratt, *Travel Writing and Transculturation* (New York: Routledge, 1992).

45. Noel, 272. Popularity of individual authors was measured by critical reception as well as sales figures for bound volumes of serialized novels. Editors often aggressively promoted their star contributors, much in the way Horace Greeley had touted Margaret Fuller in the *New York Tribune*. Other indicators of popularity included fan mail (which Fern delightfully satirizes in *Ruth Hall*), authors' salaries, their appearance in advertisements, and their ability to command lucrative contracts throughout the periodical press and book market. Bestsellers were not ranked and reported in top ten lists until the mid-twentieth century.

46. Mott, 19–20.

47. Albertine, xiv.

48. E. D. E. N. Southworth, *The Lost Heiress* (Philadelphia: T. B. Peterson, 1854), 19. Hereafter *Heiress* cited in text.

49. Amy E. Hudock, "No Mere Mercenary: E. D. E. N. Southworth" (Ph.D. dissertation, University of South Carolina, 1993), 108.

50. Marianne Noble, *The Masochistic Pleasures of Sentimental Literature* (Princeton, N.J.: Princeton University Press, 2000), 74.

51. Ann M. Ingram's comments on *The Deserted Wife* apply here: "The novel's many economic metaphors reinforce the conditions of the moral economies at stake and in turn reflect a concern with other economic issues: in particular, a discomfort with the sociocultural effects of a burgeoning capitalist economy. Southworth engages these anxieties through melodrama, a formula particularly appropriate for addressing morality and exploring the parameters of a moral economy." "Melodrama and the Moral Economy of E. D. E. N. Southworth's *The Deserted Wife*," *American Transcendental Quarterly* 13.4 (1999): 271. In this scene the economy of morality is pitched closer to an emotional transaction in an interpersonal affective relationship, specifically extolling the virtues of mutual investment from disparate, even transnational sources. Falconer's capital is his labor, as he is from common stock, and Maud's is land, as she is nobility. The trope, indeed, echoes the

transnational economics and even politics of an ideal union of aristocratic English wealth with hard-earned (however artistic and driven by compassion) American capital.

52. E. D. E. N. Southworth, *The Artist's Love* (Philadelphia: T. B. Peterson, 1872), 56. Hereafter *Love* cited in text.

53. Brown, 187.

54. Papashvily, 120.

55. Southworth, quoted in Papashvily, 121.

56. Ingram, 285.

57. E. D. E. N. Southworth, *The Deserted Wife* (Philadelphia: T. B. Peterson and Brothers, 1855), 25.

58. Thomas Merton, quoted in *Sierra* 93.1(January–February 2008): 24.

5. OUR WAYWARD SON

1. Henry David Thoreau, *The Correspondence of Henry David Thoreau*, ed. Carl Bode (Baltimore: Johns Hopkins University Press, 1958), 654.

2. Ralph Waldo Emerson, *The Journals and Miscellaneous Notebooks of Ralph Waldo Emerson*, ed. William H. Gilman et al., 16 vols. (Cambridge, Mass.: Harvard University Press, 1960), 9: 103.

3. The chapter "Into the World," in Harmon Smith, *My Friend, My Friend: The Story of Thoreau's Relationship with Emerson* (Amherst: University of Massachusetts Press, 1999), 80–94, and the chapter "Now Goes Our Brave Youth," in Steven Fink, *Prophet in the Marketplace: Thoreau's Development as a Professional Writer* (Princeton, N.J.: Princeton University Press, 1992), 86–124, are among the most recent and effective efforts to cast Thoreau's career in a more collaborative social light, moving away from the myth of author as autonomous genius. Culturally constructed relationships—of mentor-pupil, master-apprentice, father-son, prophet-disciple—conditioned in large part by the forces of the business world shape my understanding of Emerson's function as Thoreau's literary parent in this chapter. Smith, however, approaches the relationship from a more psychological perspective, whereas Fink's concern is strictly with Thoreau's business. Jeffrey Steele, "Transcendental Friendship: Emerson, Fuller, and Thoreau," in *The Cambridge Companion to Ralph Waldo Emerson* (New York: Cambridge University Press, 1999), 121–36, offers yet another perspective, addressing their relationship's strain under the idealistic terms of the transcendental theory of friendship. Robert Sattelmeyer, "'When He Became My Enemy': Emerson and Thoreau, 1848–49," *New England Quarterly* 62.2 (1989): 187–204, and Joel Porte, *Emerson and Thoreau: Transcendentalists in Conflict* (Middletown, Conn.: Wesleyan University Press, 1965), both divulge the sources of their rift in the late 1840s, the former tying it directly to Thoreau's passion that merged dangerously close to romantic love for Emerson's wife Lidian while he was touring Europe. The latter investigates the philosophical divergence separating the two during the late 1840s and early 1850s, which Smith has updated with his fine narrative of their emotional lives together. The most recent assessment is in John T. Lysaker and William Rossi, eds., *Emerson and Thoreau: Figures of Friendship* (Bloomington: University of Indiana Press, 2010).

4. Fink, 5.

5. Emerson's string of failed projects, all involving promising young New England au-

thors, included Jones Very, Henry David Thoreau, William Ellery Channing (the younger), Christopher Pearse Cranch, and Charles King Newcomb. As William Moss notes, "He discovered all five within four years, 1838–1842. Each has an air of the transcendental about him. Each initially inspired Emerson to enthusiasm, and each later brought disappointment." "'So Many Promising Youths': Emerson's Disappointing Discoveries of New England Poet-Seers," *New England Quarterly* 49.1 (1976): 47.

6. Ralph Waldo Emerson, "The Editors to the Reader," *The Dial* 1 (July 1840): 2.

7. For more on the economy of exchange animating Irving's style of patronage, see the unfortunately titled "Irving's Literary Pimpery" by Ben H. McClary, in *American Notes and Queries* 10 (1972): 150–51.

8. Emerson, *Journals and Miscellaneous Notebooks*, 5: 294.

9. Ralph Waldo Emerson, *The Selected Letters of Ralph Waldo Emerson*, ed. Joel Meyerson (New York: Columbia University Press, 1997), 289.

10. Margaret Fuller, quoted in Margaret Bell, *Margaret Fuller* (New York: Charles Boni, 1930), 122–23.

11. Walter Harding, *The Days of Henry David Thoreau* (New York: Alfred A. Knopf, 1970), 157–59.

12. Paula Blanchard, *Margaret Fuller: From Transcendentalism to Revolution* (New York: Dell, 1979), 142.

13. Ralph Waldo Emerson, *Letters of Ralph Waldo Emerson*, vols. 1–6, ed. Ralph L. Rusk; vols. 7–10, ed. Eleanor M. Tilton (New York: Columbia University Press, 1939–95), 2: 290, 293.

14. Henry David Thoreau, *Journal*, vols. 1–6, ed. John C. Broderick et al. (Princeton, N.J.: Princeton University Press, 1981–2000), 4: 420.

15. Henry David Thoreau, *A Week on the Concord and Merrimack Rivers*, ed. Carl F. Hovde (Princeton, N.J.: Princeton University Press, 1980), 296.

16. Marie Urbanski, "Henry David Thoreau and Margaret Fuller," *Thoreau Journal Quarterly* 8.4 (1976): 24–29.

17. Margaret Fuller, quoted in Milton Metzler and Walter Harding, *A Thoreau Profile* (New York: Thomas Y. Crowell Co., 1962), 118.

18. Thomas Wentworth Higginson, *Margaret Fuller Ossoli* (Boston: Houghton, 1899), 154.

19. Emerson, *Letters*, 3: 75.

20. Emerson, *Selected Letters*, 303.

21. Ibid., 338.

22. Thoreau, *Correspondence*, 139.

23. In "Thoreau's Declaration of Independence from Emerson in *Walden*," *Nineteenth-Century Prose* 33.1 (2006): 133–65, John Ronan convincingly argues that, unlike Emerson, Thoreau advocated hospitality as more of an unconditional form of giving with no expectations of reciprocation. Thoreau loathes the pressure to compensate for Emerson's patronage with tangible commercial success that might spread his mentor's influence. This is particularly evident in Thoreau's rejection of Greeley's solicitation of a biographical sketch of Emerson for the *New York Tribune*. The exchange of professional favors and puffs between transcendentalists and its corrosive effect on friendships is detailed in Barbara

Packer, "Forgiving the Giver: Emerson, Carlyle, Thoreau," in *Figures of Friendship: Emerson and Thoreau*, ed. John T. Lysaker and William Rossi (Bloomington: University of Indiana Press, 2010), 33–52.

24. Emerson, *Letters*, 3: 158–59.

25. Ibid., 3: 20.

26. Thoreau, *Correspondence*, 89.

27. Ibid., 114.

28. Emerson, *Journals and Miscellaneous Notebooks*, 11: 400.

29. Henry David Thoreau, *Walden*, ed. J. Lyndon Shanley (Princeton, N.J.: Princeton University Press, 1971), 60.

30. Henry David Thoreau, *Huckleberries*, ed. Leo Stoller (Iowa City: Windover Press, 1970), 26.

31. Ibid.

32. Ibid.

33. Thoreau, *Walden*, 249.

34. Thoreau, *Huckleberries*, 27.

35. Raymond R. Borst, *The Thoreau Log: A Documentary Life of Henry David Thoreau, 1817–1862* (New York: Macmillan, 1992), 93.

36. Emerson, quoted in Smith, 81.

37. Ibid., 81–82.

38. Ibid., 82.

39. Borst, 94.

40. Ibid., 93.

41. Thoreau, *Correspondence*, 113–14.

42. Fink, 92–93.

43. Emerson, *Letters*, 3: 182–84.

44. Thoreau, *Correspondence*, 130.

45. Ibid., 188.

46. Fink, 113.

47. Thoreau, *Correspondence*, 174.

48. Ibid., 169–70. Greeley was the most avid promoter of transcendental talent in the antebellum New York periodical press, employing Fuller in a powerful position as literary editor and regular contributor, and offering permanent employment, however squandered, to Ellery Channing (the younger) and Thoreau.

49. Ibid., 279–80.

50. Emerson, *Selected Letters*, 317.

51. Borst, 112.

52. Emerson, *Letters*, 3: 350–51

53. Fink, 211.

54. Thoreau, *Correspondence*, 191, 195.

55. Emerson, *Selected Letters*, 333.

56. Emerson, *Letters*, 4: 151.

57. Thoreau, quoted in Sattelmeyer, 190; William Blake, *Songs of Innocence and of Experience* (New York: Oxford University Press, 1967), 152.

58. Thoreau, *Journal*, 3: 46, 193.

59. Henry David Thoreau, *The Writings of Henry David Thoreau* (Boston: Houghton Mifflin, 1906), 3: 61–62.

60. Thoreau, quoted in Sattelmeyer, 196.

61. Sattelmeyer, 203.

62. Emerson, *Journals and Miscellaneous Notebooks*, 9: 45.

63. This judgment refers to Thoreau's stay at Walden Pond beginning in March 1845 during which he composed *A Week*. Emerson was not, however, commenting on the book, *Walden; or, Life in the Woods*, which Thoreau would not publish until 1854, when Emerson read it for the first time. Emerson noted an unevenness in the prose marked by regrettably inconsistent flashes of brilliance, "rising sometimes to very great heights," "sometimes with wonderful depth and beauty." Emerson, *Letters*, 4: 459–60; 8: 399.

64. Emerson, *Journals and Miscellaneous Notebooks*, 10: 343–45.

65. Ralph Waldo Emerson, "Experience," in *Essays: Second Series*, ed. Joseph Slater, Alfred R. Ferguson, and Jean Ferguson Carr, *The Collected Works of Ralph Waldo Emerson* (Cambridge, Mass.: Harvard University Press, 1983), 27.

66. Emerson, *Journals and Miscellaneous Notebooks*, 8:375; "Essays," 30–31.

67. Sattelmeyer, 194–95.

68. Thoreau, *Writings*, 8: 199.

69. Ralph Waldo Emerson, *The Complete Works of Ralph Waldo Emerson*, ed. Edward Waldo Emerson (Boston: Houghton Mifflin, 1904), 10: 485.

70. Emerson, *Journals and Miscellaneous Notebooks*, 9: 425.

71. Thoreau, *Correspondence*, 137.

6. SIBLING STRIFE

1. Joyce Warren's *Women, Money, and the Law: Nineteenth-Century Fiction, Gender, and the Courts* (Iowa City: University of Iowa Press, 2005) details Fern's zeal for women's economic independence: "There are three principal reasons for Fern's independent stance: her own experience with economic dependency, her change in class status, and the attack on her reputation," 283. No studies in Fern criticism have focused directly on her fame in terms of literary partnership and patronage. Linda Grasso, "Anger in the House: Fanny Fern's *Ruth Hall* and the Redrawing of Emotional Boundaries in Mid-Nineteenth-Century America," in *Studies in the American Renaissance*, ed. Joel Myerson (Charlottesville: University Press of Virginia: 1995), 251–61, offers a useful discussion of how women's public expression of anger toward family members bears relevance to my discussion of Fern's attack on Willis. Elizabeth Cady Stanton suggested that "If all tyrannical parents, husbands and brothers knew that the fantastic tricks they play at the hearthstone, would in time be judged by a discerning public, no one can estimate the restraining influence of such a fear." Quoted in Grasso, 255. As Grasso explains, "Because *Ruth Hall* reveals an intimate portrait of 'tyrannical parents, husbands and brothers in the patriarchal house of woe,' Stanton commends Fern for helping women recognize that their own anger at men is both justified and politically powerful," 255. Such anger, I argue, was also a commercially potent producer of notoriety and eventual fame.

2. George Templeton Strong, quoted in Andrew Delbanco, *Melville: His World and Work* (New York: Knopf, 2005), 98.

3. Edwin Forrest, quoted in Thomas N. Baker, *Sentiment and Celebrity: Nathaniel Parker Willis and the Trials of Literary Fame* (New York: Oxford University Press, 1999), 115.

4. The popularity of Willis's overthrow was overwhelming. Fern had started her public attack on Willis as early as July 1853 in a column entitled, "Apollo Hyacinth" for the *Musical World and Times,* two years prior to the full-scale bombardment in *Ruth Hall.* Shortly after the column appeared, the *Democratic Review* revealed that "she *is* said to be N.P. Willis's sister," and by October, the news had already reached across the Atlantic, as London's *Athenaeum* also indulged in the gossip. So by the time *Ruth Hall* appeared in December 1854, *The Home Journal,* the *New York Tribune,* and the *Boston Transcript* all acknowledged at least the family tie and in some cases commented on the nature of Fern's complaint. Thus it almost went without saying in one of the earliest reviews of the novel that "'Fanny Fern' is well known to be the sister of N.P. Willis." Quoted in Baker, 173.

5. Fanny Fern, *Ruth Hall and Other Writings,* ed. Joyce Warren (New Brunswick, N.J.: Rutgers University Press, 1986 [rpt. 1855 ed.]), 144.

6. Willis was notoriously theatrical and narcissistic. Hershel Parker, *Herman Melville: A Biography (Volume 1, 1819–1851)* (Baltimore: Johns Hopkins University Press, 1996), notes that "Willis had a knack for seeing political issues as more ephemeral than fashions," 335. Elegant, conventional, and fastidious, Willis's tastes for fashion were ever present in his writings, including *Romance of Travel,* in which a chapter is dedicated solely to men's clothes. In "Pascuali, Tailor of Venice," he lovingly describes how "four pairs of suspenders, a print of the fashions, and a motley row of the gay colored trowsers worn by the gondoliers, ornamented the window looking on the dark alley in the rear" (*Romance of Travel [*New York: S. Coleman, 1840], 139).

7. Lori Merish, *Sentimental Materialism: Gender, Commodity Culture, and Nineteenth-Century American Literature* (Durham, N.C.: Duke University Press, 2000), 5.

8. See Fern's "A Businessman's Home; or, A Story for Husbands" for another depiction of a businessman's behavior in the domestic sphere. The protagonist, Mr. Walter's opposite, learns not to be materialistic or disapproving (traits inherent in Hyacinth) in his style of parenting. The story resonates with Fern's concept of proper patronage. "I never will shut *my* door in *your* face, *no matter what you do,*" Betty proclaims. Sympathy is paramount in her speech: "as if food, and drink and clothes was all a child wanted, or wife either, for that matter; as if that was all that a husband or father was bound to furnish." Quoted in James Parton, *Fanny Fern: A Memorial Volume* (New York: Carleton, 1874), 461.

9. Merish, 4.

10. The antebellum obsession with the financial consequences of sympathy and filial love has origins that date back to Adam Smith. His 1749 *Theory of Moral Sentiments; or, An Essay Towards an Analysis of the Principles by which Men Naturally Judge Concerning the conduct and Character, First of the Neighbors and Afterwards of Themselves* (London: Cadell and Davies, 1854) interestingly anticipates Fern's willingness to break up the brother-sister friendship bond and replace it with that of ideal literary partners. Her simultaneous revision of, and adherence to, Smith is striking. Unlike women of Smith's eighteenth century, 1850s females entered the market and could find business partners to replace "the earliest

friendships" described by Smith. These "friendships, which are naturally contracted when the heart is most susceptible of that feeling, are those among brothers and sisters. Their good agreement, while they remain in the same family, is necessary for its tranquility and happiness," and thus become tokens of emotional and economic stability. Siblings "are capable of giving more pleasure and pain to one another than to the greater part of other people." Willis failed to assure that "their situation render their mutual sympathy of the utmost importance to their common happiness." By breaking the chain that "obliges them to accommodate to one another," he invited Fern's attack. Her spite is particularly venomous because he destroyed the economic and emotional sustainability that "renders sympathy more habitual, and thereby more lively, more distinct, and more determinate," 62.

11. "Review of *Ruth Hall*," quoted in Joyce Warren, "Introduction," in *Ruth Hall*, 216.

12. Cindy Weinstein, *Family, Kinship, and Sympathy in Nineteenth-Century American Literature* (New York: Cambridge University Press, 2004), 18.

13. Ibid., 9.

14. Ibid., 28.

15. Fanny Fern, "Whose Fault Is It?" in *Ruth Hall*, 327.

16. Ibid., 328.

17. Fern, *Ruth Hall*, 166.

18. Baker, 216.

19. Ibid., 163; Warren, 88; Baker, 163.

20. Fern, *Ruth Hall*, 163.

21. Ibid., 260.

22. Ibid., 318.

23. For a detailed discussion of Fern's life after the death of Eldridge, see Joyce Warren, *Fanny Fern: An Independent Woman* (New Brunswick, N.J.: Rutgers University Press, 1992), 76–82; for information on the Farrington marriage, see 83–89.

24. Fern, *Ruth Hall*, 294.

25. William Moulton, *The Life and Beauties of Fanny Fern* (New Haven, Conn.: Research Publications, 1975 [rpt. 1855 ed.]), 29–30.

26. Fanny Fern, *Rose Clark* (New York: Mason Brothers, 1856), 251.

27. Fern, *Ruth Hall*, 108–9.

28. Fern, *Ruth Hall*, 111.

29. Melissa Homestead, "'Every Body Sees the Theft': Fanny Fern and Literary Proprietorship in Antebellum America," *New England Quarterly* 74 (2001): 210–37. The culture of reprinting functioned as a promotional engine for Fern's work. "In this early periodical context," Homestead notes, "unfettered reprinting rather than proprietary control of circulation was the norm," and "a context in which Fern nevertheless thrived." *American Women Authors and Literary Property, 1822–1869* (New York: Cambridge University Press, 2005), 153. But as Susan S. Williams astutely notes, "the plagiarizing of Ruth's classmates and the local newspaper editor are initially portrayed as innocuous enough. As a widow trying to support her children, however, such a system of reprinting or exchange publication keeps Ruth in poverty while her (male) editors and publishers get her profits." *Reclaiming Authorship: Literary Women in America, 1850–1900* (Philadelphia: University of Pennsylvania Press, 2006), 50. As in Fern's own career, Ruth's short-run financial losses, which are particularly painful given her needy condition, become massive gains in public-

ity and future earnings, as the reprints circulate her work rapidly throughout the market. Exchange publication thus increases her readership and popularity by putting her writings into the hands of fans and influential agents like Mr. Walter.

30. Fern may have been trying to distance herself not only from her own sexual scandal of the Farrington divorce, an episode linking her to adultery and marital rape. She also was likely interested in keeping Ruth's pivotal relationships with characters like Mr. Walter asexual so as to not to invoke N. P. Willis's adultery trial. Already well aware of that scandal when *Ruth Hall* appeared, Fern's audience desired to read the new charges against him on the entirely separate grounds of filial neglect and abandonment. Shielding the novel from any association with sexual deviance, Fern was careful to remove erotic desire from Ruth's "love," which "is a mental love—a regard for the mind, rather than the person of the individual. You appreciate the masculine mind as such, rather than the physical form." Fern, *Ruth Hall*, 169. It would seem the Willis siblings had enough sexual scandal attached to their names when Edwin Forrest, the husband of Willis's mistress, "had beset Willis's honor (and, with it, his credibility) by advertising his younger brother's conviction for rape," according to Baker, 163. Ruth's asexual relationship with Mr. Walter is clearly a response to how all three siblings were scandalously intertwined with sexual misdeeds of adultery and rape.

31. For more on Fern's rewriting of received standards of publication practice, see David Dowling, "Capital Sentiment: Fanny Fern's Transformation of the Gentleman Publisher's Code," *American Transcendental Quarterly* 22.1 (2008): 347–64.

32. Fern, *Ruth Hall*, 211.

33. For a thorough demonstration of *Jane Eyre*'s centrality in the commercial antebellum book trade, see Cree LaFavour, "'*Jane Eyre* Fever': Deciphering the Astonishing Popular Success of Charlotte Brontë in Antebellum America," *Book History* 7 (2004): 113–41.

34. In a *New York Ledger* column, for example, Fern is astonished at "the number" of women "who are yearly added to our lunatic asylums from the ranks of the misappreciated, unhappy womanhood, narrowed by lives made up of details. Fight it! Oppose it, for your own sakes and your children's!" she cries. "Do not be *mentally* annihilated by it" and instead engage the mind through all forms of writing, she suggests. "The Women of 1867," in *Ruth Hall*, 344.

35. Corroborating this point about why Fern would pay homage to marriage, Sylvia Jenkins Cook comments that "the new self-culture and self-reliance of young, unmarried women in the workplace did not yet presuppose an equivalent shift in the domestic sphere, or indeed broad public sympathy for such a change." *Working Women, Literary Ladies: The Industrial Revolution and Female Aspiration* (New York: Oxford University Press, 2008), 154. This also explains Fern's self-effacing preface, like the scene at Harry's grave, which so glaringly contrasts with the tone of fiscal bravado etched into the bank note illustration. Cook observes that "even a highly fictionalized account of marital suffering by a wronged woman needed to be prefaced with extensive apologies and explanations in order to distance it from any suggestion that it was a personal plea for justice or an expedient to make money," 153, both of which, paradoxically, characterize *Ruth Hall*'s essential purpose.

36. Henry James, quoted in June Howard, "What is Sentimentality?" *American Literary History* 11.1 (1999): 74.

37. James Parton, *Fanny Fern: A Memorial Volume* (New York: G. W. Carleton and Co., 1873), 54.

38. Nicole Tonkovich, *Domesticity with a Difference: The Nonfiction of Catharine Beecher, Sarah J. Hale, Fanny Fern, and Margaret Fuller* (Jackson: University Press of Mississippi, 1997), 35.

39. Fern, *Ruth Hall*, 179.

40. Tonkovich, 37, 35.

41. Parton, 53, 55.

42. J. C. Derby, *Fifty Years Among Authors, Books, and Publishers* (New York: G. W. Carleton & Company, 1884), 210, 213.

43. Ibid., 209.

44. Ibid., 211.

45. Fanny Fern, *Fern Leaves from Fanny Fern's Portfolio* (Auburn: Derby and Miller, 1853), iv.

46. Susan Coultrap-McQuin argues that gentlemen publishers actively cultivated long-term relationships with their writers "like marriages, close friendships, or intimate professional associations." *Doing Literary Business: American Women Writers in the Nineteenth Century* (Chapel Hill: University of North Carolina Press, 1990), 36. Bonner, Dyer, and Derby were indeed paternalistic in the sense that they took care of their writers, much in the way Mr. Walter cares for Ruth and her children's well-being with "warmth" that personalizes their otherwise predominantly economic relationship. Yet *Ruth Hall*, with the obvious exception of Mr. Walter, does not paint a picture that uniformly matches Coultrap-McQuin's image of women writers happily playing the role of lady to their gentlemen publishers. Fern's depiction of William Moulton as the monstrous Lescom instead is more typical of the manner with which most publishers treated their women authors. The ethics of loyalty in author-publisher relations also become unstable in *Ruth Hall*. Fern insists that women authors play the market and not remain shackled by a single publisher. In her own career, she would eventually move on from Dyer to more lucrative deals. Similarly, her commitment to Mason Brothers may have appeared long-term and permanent, but her eventual signing with Robert Bonner signaled that the scale of her popularity had eclipsed outmoded concepts of loyalty to gentlemen publishers.

47. Fern, *Fern Leaves*, 376.

48. Baker notes that *Ruth Hall* was not universally lauded for precisely this reason, as many "found too much relish in the evisceration of Nat Willis's celebrity to accept the spotless character Fern had assumed herself," 179. To many, Fern's hostility appeared to transgress gender boundaries, for "on the field of honor, a lady could see her persecutors horsewhipped, but she must not seem to relish the spectacle. Because Fern so obviously did enjoy it, she must be, prima facie, no lady at all. In time, this very judgment became a common refrain in the press and parlors across the nation," but not common enough to curtail the stratospheric trajectory of her fame, 179. Those were elitist and sexist sentiments from genteel readers she might have thought of as pussycats, the opposite of her core audience.

49. Fern, [Review of] "Leaves of Grass," in *Ruth Hall*, 276.

50. For a stellar discussion of Barnum and the class bias habitually leveled against him

in the nineteenth century, see Bluford Adams, *E Pluribus Barnum: The Great Showman and the Making of U.S. Popular Culture* (Minneapolis: University of Minnesota Press, 1997).

51. Fern, *Ruth Hall,* 140–41.

52. Ibid., 147.

53. Margaret Fuller's analysis from *Woman in the Nineteenth Century* supports the interweaving of gender codes depicted in the image of a grown man crying in a nineteenth-century novel: "There is no wholly masculine man, no purely feminine woman . . . there should be no discordant collision but a ravishing harmony of the spheres." Quoted in Monica Elbert, ed., "Introduction," in *Separate Spheres No More: Gender Convergence in American Literature, 1830–1930* (Tuscaloosa: University of Alabama Press, 2000), 116. It is important to "uncover," as this scene does, "and show the commonalities . . . shared by men and women . . . thus dissolving boundaries between public and private spheres and questioning or challenging the stereotypical images of women as ineffectual or vulnerable," and men as unfeeling and cold, "in nineteenth-century society." Elbert, 2.

54. Fern, *Ruth Hall,* 162.

55. Ibid., 169, 194.

56. Ibid., 340.

57. Baker, 91.

58. Fern, "Something To Come Home To," in *Ruth Hall,* 330.

59. Fern, "What Shall We Do?" in *Ruth Hall,* 337.

60. Fern, "The Day of Rest," in *Ruth Hall,* 329.

61. From the beginning of *Ruth Hall,* Fern emphasizes the importance of production and Ruth's struggle to acculturate herself to it. Ruth confesses she does not know how to bake bread, 20. She thus made many "wonder if she would 'ever make anything,'" 14. Ruth counters with criticism of the nonproductive conventional female recreation prevalent in the culture, centered around "long forenoons spent in shopping . . . party giving, party going, primping and coquetting," 51.

62. Fern, "Editors," in Parton, 201.

63. Quoted in Parton, 65.

64. Quoted in Stanwood Cobb, *The Magnificent Partnership* (New York: Vantage Press, 1954), 37.

65. Quotation ibid.

66. N. P. Willis, *Poems of Early and After Years* (Philadelphia: Carey and Hart, 1848), 159.

CONCLUSION

1. Carlos Baker, ed., *Ernest Hemingway: Selected Letters, 1917–1961* (New York: Scribner, 1981), 61.

2. Terri A. Scandura and Belle Rose Ragins, "The Effects of Sex and Gender Role Orientation on Mentorship in Male-Dominated Occupations," *Journal of Vocational Behavior* 43.3 (1993): 251–65.

3. Kenneth S. Lynn, *Hemingway* (New York: Simon and Schuster, 1987), 169. Weininger has argued that "the woman who attracts and is attracted by other women is herself half male." Quoted in Linda Simon, *The Biography of Alice B. Toklas* (Garden City,

N.Y.: Doubleday, 1977), 50. Androgyny is thus imbued with heightened imaginative and intellectual power, a theory that influenced Virginia Woolf, who maintained that great writing transcends the limitations of gender, a concept played out particularly in her novels *Orlando* and *To the Lighthouse*.

4. Simon, 121; Hemingway, *Selected Letters*, 795. Stein also contended that the jealousy was literary, as she depicts Ford Maddox Ford cutting into her relationship with Hemingway to request her permission to dedicate his latest book to her. The image invokes both dancing and marriage. Stein, 226.

5. Old enough to be his mother, "Stein was a mother figure whom Hemingway could approve," James R. Mellow asserts. "The relationship that developed between the two in those early years of friendship might have passed for that of a son and a proud and approving mother." *Hemingway: A Life without Consequences* (Boston: Houghton Mifflin, 1992), 149, 151. Mellow allows that their friendship was intense, yet does not grapple with the sexual complexities of it as I do here.

6. Hemingway, *Selected Letters*, 650, 795.

7. Loren Glass, *Authors Inc.: Literary Celebrity in the Modern United States, 1880–1980* (New York: New York University Press, 2004). For more on the modernist literary marketplace, see Lawrence Rainey, *Institutions of Modernism: Literary Elites and Public Culture* (New Haven, Conn.: Yale University Press, 1998), and Joyce Piell Wexler, *Who Paid for Modernism? Art, Money, and the Fiction of Conrad, Joyce, and Lawrence* (Fayetteville: University of Arkansas Press, 1997).

8. Gertrude Stein, *The Autobiography of Alice B. Toklas* (London: Zephyr Books, 1947), 226. On the topic of Hemingway's physical frailty, she challenges his manhood by mentioning an incident in which a boy "who did not know how" to box accidentally "knocked Hemingway out. I believe this sometimes happens," she quips, laying waste to his image of masculine invincibility, 24. His "little story of meditations" he added to *In Our Time*, she observes, included his comment that "The Enormous Room was the greatest book he had ever read. It was then that Gertrude Stein said, Hemingway, remarks are not literature." Stein wrote under the guise of Toklas and thus referring to herself in the third person, 225. As for his courage in facing his literary rivals, she claims, "when Sherwood [Anderson] came to Paris Hemingway was naturally afraid. Sherwood as naturally was not," 222.

9. Matthew J. Bruccoli, *Hemingway and the Mechanism of Fame* (Columbia: University of South Carolina Press, 2006), 24.

10. Ernest Hemingway, *A Moveable Feast* (New York: Scribner, 1964), 15, 25.

11. Hemingway, *Selected Letters*, 79. Elsewhere Hemingway says he "learned much . . . from G. Stein" and that she was "damned smart," even in the middle of a (hetero)sexist rant of male bravado of the sort for which he was notorious, 384.

12. Ibid., 74, 75.

13. Hemingway, *Selected Letters*, 649, 650.

14. Stein, 226.

15. Hemingway, *A Moveable Feast*, 14, 17.

16. Dennis Ryan, "Dating Hemingway's Early Style/Parsing Gertrude Stein's Modernism," *Journal of American Studies* 29.2 (1995): 239. With regard to Stein's literary technique, Sheldon Grebstein also finds that "Hemingway brought experiments to fruition and made it a major resource of his style." *Hemingway's Craft* (Carbondale: Southern Illinois Univer-

sity Press, 1973), 134. "Between 1922 and 1924," Charles Fenton notes, was "the period of Miss Stein's greatest personal importance to him." *The Apprenticeship of Ernest Hemingway* (New York: Viking Press, 1954), 152.

17. James R. Mellow, *Charmed Circle: Gertrude Stein and Company* (New York: Praeger, 1974), 264.

18. Hemingway, *A Moveable Feast,* 117.

19. Stein, 176.

20. Quoted in Mellow, *Hemingway,* 151, 152.

21. Quoted in Michael Reynolds, *Hemingway: The American Homecoming* (Oxford: Blackwell, 1992), 84.

22. Hemingway, *A Moveable Feast,* 110, 118.

23. Quoted in Mellow, *Charmed Circle,* 265.

24. Quoted in Susanna Ashton, *Collaborators in Literary America, 1870–1920* (New York: Palgrave Macmillan, 2003), 170.

25. Quoted in Bruccoli, 18–19. Mellow, *Hemingway,* 152, 151.

26. T. J. Jackson Lears, "Introduction," in *The Culture of Consumption: Critical Essays in American History, 1880–1980,* ed. Richard Wightman Fox and T. J. Jackson Lears (New York: Pantheon, 1983), xi.

27. Rebecca Harding Davis, "Anne," in *Life in the Iron Mills and Other Stories,* ed. Tillie Olsen (Old Westbury, N.Y.: Feminist Press, 1985), 241.

28. Lears, xi.

29. Bette London, *Writing Double: Women's Literary Partnerships* (Ithaca, N.Y.: Cornell University Press, 1999), 211.

30. Richard Florida, *The Rise of the Creative Class: And How It's Transforming Work, Leisure, Community and Everyday Life* (New York: Basic Books, 2004), shows that places with higher gay and lesbian populations, especially urban areas, are associated with more affluence and information industry production, the functional equivalent of the print culture industry production of the nineteenth century. Further, businesses have been found to be more progressive about creating policies supporting gays and lesbians, especially in the area of partner benefits. Government, by contrast, has been resistant to the movement of gays into civil life. Brian DiSarro's research confirms that Fortune 500 companies are pioneering the institutional and social acceptance of homosexuality in the United States. "State Institutions and the Creation of Gay Rights Policy" (Ph.D. dissertation, University of Iowa, 2008).

31. Backlashes against such progress include widespread adoption of state gay marriage bans (Defense of Marriage Act) in the 2004 and 2006 elections, according to Todd Donovan, Caroline J. Tolbert, and Daniel A. Smith, "Priming Presidential Votes by Direct Democracy," *Journal of Politics* 70 (2008): 1217–31.

32. Gilbert Bailon, *American Editor* (Spring 2008): 1.

33. Henry James, "Pierre Loti," in *Essays in London and Elsewhere* (New York: Harper Brothers, 1893), 151–52.

Bibliography

Aderman, Ralph M., ed. *Critical Essays on Washington Irving.* Boston: G. K. Hill and Company, 1990.

Admari, Ralph. "Bonner and 'The Ledger.'" *American Book Collector* 6 (1935): 176–39.

Agnew, Jean-Christophe. *Worlds Apart: The Market and the Theatre in Anglo-American Thought, 1550–1750.* New York: Cambridge University Press, 1986.

Albertine, Susan, ed. *A Living of Words: American Women in Print Culture.* Knoxville: University of Tennessee Press, 1995.

Antelyes, Peter. *Tales of Adventurous Enterprise: Washington Irving and the Poetics of Western Expansion.* New York: Columbia University Press, 1990.

Ashton, Susanna. *Collaborators in Literary America, 1870–1920.* New York: Palgrave, 2003.

Bailon, Gilbert. Editor's Column. *American Editor* (Spring 2008): 1.

Baker, Thomas N. *Sentiment and Celebrity: Nathaniel Parker Willis and the Trials of Literary Fame.* New York: Oxford University Press, 1999.

Barthes, Roland. "The Death of the Author." In *Image, Music, Text.* New York: Hill and Wang, 1977.

Bell, Margaret. *Margaret Fuller.* New York: Charles Boni, 1930.

Benjamin, Walter. *The Arcades Project.* Cambridge, Mass.: Harvard University Press, 2002.

Blake, David Haven. "Reading Whitman, Growing up Rock and Roll." *Virginia Quarterly Review* 81 (2005): 34–47.

———. *Walt Whitman and the Culture of American Celebrity.* New Haven, Conn.: Yale University Press, 2006.

Blake, William. *Songs of Innocence and of Experience.* New York: Oxford University Press, 1967.

Blanchard, Paula. *Margaret Fuller: From Transcendentalism to Revolution.* New York: Dell, 1979.

Bordeau, Kristin. "'The Woman's Flesh of Me': Rebecca Harding Davis's Response to Self-Reliance." *American Transcendental Quarterly* 6.2 (June 1992): 132–40.

Borst, Raymond R., ed. *The Thoreau Log: A Documentary Life of Henry David Thoreau, 1817–1862.* New York: Macmillan, 1992.

Bowden, Mary Weatherspoon. *Washington Irving.* Boston: Twayne, 1981.

Boyd, Anne E. *Writing for Immortality: Women and the Emergence of High Literary Culture in America.* Baltimore: Johns Hopkins University Press, 2004.

Boyle, Regis. *Mrs. E. D. E. N. Southworth, Novelist.* Washington, D.C.: Catholic University Press, 1939.

Brecht, Bertolt. *Brecht on Theatre,* ed. John Willett. New York: Hill and Wang, 1964.

Brodhead, Richard. *Cultures of Letters: Scenes of Reading and Writing in Nineteenth-Century America.* Chicago: University of Chicago Press, 1993.

Brown, Herbert Ross. *The Sentimental Novel in America, 1789–1860.* Durham, N.C.: Duke University Press, 1940.

Bruccoli, Matthew J. *Hemingway and the Mechanism of Fame.* Columbia: University of South Carolina Press, 2006.

Buckley, J. F. "Living in the Iron Mills: A Tempering of Nineteenth-Century America's Orphic Poet." *Journal of American Culture* 16.1 (Spring 1993): 62–73.

Burstein, Andrew. *The Original Knickerbocker: The Life of Washington Irving.* New York: Basic Books, 2007.

Castronovo, David. *The English Gentleman: Images and Ideals in Literature and Society.* New York: Ungar, 1987.

Charvat, William. *The Profession of Authorship in America, 1800–1870,* ed. Matthew J. Bruccoli. New York: Columbia University Press, 1992 (rpt. 1968 ed.).

Cobb, Stanwood. *The Magnificent Partnership.* New York: Vantage Press, 1954.

Collins, A. S. *The Profession of Letters: A Study of the Relation of Author to Patron, Publisher, and Public, 1780–1832.* London: George Routledge and Sons, 1928.

Cook, Sylvia Jenkins. *Working Women, Literary Ladies: The Industrial Revolution and Female Aspiration.* New York: Oxford University Press, 2008.

Coultrap-McQuin, Susan. *Doing Literary Business: American Women Writers in the Nineteenth Century.* Chapel Hill: University of North Carolina Press, 1990.

Dana, R. H. "Review of *The Sketch Book.*" *North American Review* 9 (1819): 322–56.

Davis, Charles Belmont, ed. *The Adventures and Letters of Richard Harding Davis.* New York: Scribner's Sons, 1917.

Davis, L. Clarke. "A Modern Lettre de Cachet." *Atlantic Monthly Magazine* 21 (1868): 588–602.

———. *A Stranded Ship: A Story of Sea and Shore.* New York: G. P. Putnam, 1869.

Davis, Merrell R. *Melville's Mardi, a Chartless Voyage.* New Haven, Conn.: Yale University Press, 1952.

Davis, Rebecca Harding. "Life in the Iron-Mills; or, The Korl Woman." In *Life in the Iron Mills and Other Stories,* ed. Tillie Olsen. Old Westbury, N.Y.: Feminist Press, 1985. 9–65.

———. "Marcia." *Harper's Monthly* 53 (1876): 925–28.

———. *Put Out of the Way.* In *Peterson's Magazine* 57 (1870): 355–67, 431–43; 58: 30–41, 109–18.

———. "The Wife's Story." *Atlantic Monthly Magazine* 14 (July 1864): 1–19.

Delbanco, Andrew. *Melville: His World and Work.* New York: Knopf, 2006.

Denning, Michael. *Culture in the Age of Three Worlds*. London: Verso, 2004.

Derby, J. C. *Fifty Years Among Authors, Books, and Publishers*. New York: G. W. Carleton and Company, 1884.

Disarro, Brian. "State Institutions and the Creation of Gay Rights Policy." Ph.D. dissertation, University of Iowa, 2008.

Dobson, Joanne. "Introduction." In *The Hidden Hand; or, Capitola the Madcap*, ed. Joanne Dobson. New Brunswick, N.J.: Rutgers University Press, 1988. xli–xlii.

———. "Reclaiming Sentimental Literature." *American Literature* 69 (1997): 263–88.

Donovan, Todd, Caroline J. Tolbert, and Daniel A. Smith. "Priming Presidential Votes by Direct Democracy." *Journal of Politics* 70 (2008): 1217–31.

Douglas, Ann. *The Feminization of American Culture*. New York: Avon, 1977.

Eagleton, Terry. "Buried in the Life: Thomas Hardy and the Limits of Biographies." *Harper's* 315.1890 (2007): 89–94.

Elbert, Monica, ed. *Separate Spheres No More: Gender Convergence in American Literature, 1830–1930*. Tuscaloosa: University of Alabama Press, 2000.

Emerson, Ralph Waldo. *Essays: Second Series*, ed. Joseph Slater, Alfred R. Ferguson, and Jean Ferguson Carr. In *The Collected Works of Ralph Waldo Emerson*. Cambridge, Mass.: Harvard University Press, 1983.

———. *Letters of Ralph Waldo Emerson*, vols. 1–6, ed. Ralph L. Rusk; vols. 7–10, ed. Eleanor M. Tilton. New York: Columbia University Press, 1939–95.

———. *The Journals and Miscellaneous Notebooks of Ralph Waldo Emerson*, ed. William H. Gilman et al. 16 vols. Cambridge, Mass.: Harvard University Press, 1960.

———. *The Selected Letters of Ralph Waldo Emerson*, ed. Joel Meyerson. New York: Columbia University Press, 1997.

Evelev, John. *Tolerable Entertainment: Herman Melville and Professionalism in Antebellum New York*. Amherst: University of Massachusetts Press, 2006.

Fenton, Charles. *The Apprenticeship of Ernest Hemingway*. New York: Viking Press, 1954.

Fern, Fanny. *Fern Leaves from Fanny Fern's Portfolio*. Auburn: Derby and Miller, 1853.

———. *Rose Clark*. New York: Mason Brothers, 1856.

———. *Ruth Hall, and Other Writings*, ed. Joyce Warren. New Brunswick, N.J.: Rutgers University Press, 1986 (rpt. 1855 ed.).

Fink, Steven. *Prophet in the Marketplace: Thoreau's Development as a Professional Writer*. Princeton, N.J.: Princeton University Press, 1992.

Fink, Steven, and Susan S. Williams, eds. *Reciprocal Influences: Literary Production, Distribution, and Consumption in America*. Columbus: Ohio State University Press, 1999.

Florida, Richard. *The Rise of the Creative Class: And How It's Transforming Work, Leisure, Community and Everyday Life*. New York: Basic Books, 2004.

Folsom, Ed. *Whitman Making Books, Books Making Whitman: A Catalog and Commentary*. Iowa City: Obermann Center for Advanced Studies, 2005.

Fox, Richard Wightman, and T. J. Jackson Lears, eds. *The Culture of Consumption: Critical Essays in American History, 1880–1980*. New York: Pantheon, 1983.

Fuller, Margaret. *Margaret Fuller's New York Journalism: A Biographical Essay and Key Writings*, ed. Catherine C. Mitchell. Knoxville: University of Tennessee Press, 1995.

Gallup, Donald. "More Letters of American Writers." *Yale University Gazette* (July 1962): 30.

Gettmann, Royal A. *A Victorian Publisher: A Study of the Bentley Papers*. Cambridge: Cambridge University Press, 1960.

Glass, Loren. *Authors Inc.: Literary Celebrity in the Modern United States, 1880–1980*. New York: New York University Press, 2004.

Goldman-Price, Irene C., and Melissa McFarland Pennell, eds. *American Literary Mentors*. Gainesville: University Press of Florida, 1999.

Grasso, Linda. "Anger in the House: Fanny Fern's *Ruth Hall* and the Redrawing of Emotional Boundaries in Mid-Nineteenth-Century America." In *Studies in the American Renaissance, 1995*, ed. Joel Myerson. Charlottesville: University Press of Virginia, 1995. 251–61.

Greenspan, Ezra. *George Palmer Putnam: Representative American Publisher*. State College: Pennsylvania State University Press, 2000.

Harding, Walter. *The Days of Henry David Thoreau*. New York: Alfred A. Knopf, 1970.

Harris, Sharon M. *Rebecca Harding Davis and American Realism*. Philadelphia: University of Pennsylvania Press, 1991.

———. "Rebecca Harding Davis (1831–1910)."In *Kindred Hands: Letters on Writing by British and American Women Authors, 1865–1935*, ed. Jennifer Cognard-Black and Elizabeth MacLeod Walls. Iowa City: University of Iowa Press, 2006.

Haskell, Thomas L. "Capitalism and the Origins of the Humanitarian Sensibility, Part I." *American Historical Review* 90.2 (1985): 342–63.

Hedges, William L. *Washington Irving: An American Study, 1802–1832*. Baltimore: Johns Hopkins University Press, 1965.

Hemingway, Ernest. *A Moveable Feast*. New York: Scribner, 1964.

———. *Ernest Hemingway: Selected Letters, 1917–1961*, ed. Carlos Baker. New York: Scribner, 1981.

Hemphill, C. Dallett. *Bowing to Necessities: A History of Manners in America, 1620–1860*. New York: Oxford University Press, 1999.

Hesford, Walter. "Literary Contexts of *Life in the Iron-Mills*." *American Literature* 49 (1977): 70–85.

Higgins, Brian, and Hershel Parker, eds. *Herman Melville: The Contemporary Reviews*. Cambridge: Cambridge University Press, 1995.

———. *Reading Melville's Pierre; or, The Ambiguities*. Baton Rouge: Louisiana State University Press, 2006.

Higginson, Thomas Wentworth. *Margaret Fuller Ossoli*. Boston: Houghton, 1899.

Homestead, Melissa. *American Women Authors and Literary Property, 1822–1869*. New York: Cambridge University Press, 2005.

Howard, June. "What is Sentimentality?" *American Literary History* 11.1 (1999): 63–81.

Hudock, Amy E. "No Mere Mercenary: E. D. E. N. Southworth." Ph.D. dissertation, University of South Carolina, 1993.

Hulme, Peter. *Colonial Encounters: Europe and the Native Caribbean, 1492–1797*. New York: Methuen, 1986.

Ingram, Ann M. "Melodrama and the Moral Economy of E. D. E. N. Southworth's *The Deserted Wife*." *American Transcendental Quarterly* 13.4 (1999): 263–80.

Irving, Pierre M. *The Life and Letters of Washington Irving, Vol. I*. New York: Oxford University Press, 1935.

Irving, Washington. *Letters I*, ed. Ralph M. Aderman, Herbert L. Kleinfield, and Jennifer S. Banks. Boston: Twayne, 1978.

———. *Journals and Notebooks, Vol. II, 1807–1822*, ed. Walter A. Reichart and Lillian Schlissel. Boston: Twayne, 1981.

———. *Journals and Notebooks, Vol. III, 1819–1827*, ed. Walter A. Reichart. Madison: University of Wisconsin Press, 1970.

———. *Journals and Notebooks: Vol. V, 1832–1859*, ed. Walter A. Reichart and Lilian Schlissel. Boston: Twayne, 1981.

———. *The Sketch Book*, ed. Haskell Springer. Boston: Twayne, 1978.

Jackson, Leon. *The Business of Letters: Authorial Economies in Antebellum America*. Stanford: Stanford University Press, 2008.

James, Henry. *Hawthorne*. London: Macmillan, 1967.

———. "Pierre Loti." In *Essays in London and Elsewhere*. New York: Harper Brothers, 1893. 151–85.

———. Review of *Waiting for the Verdict*, by Rebecca Harding Davis. *The Nation*, November 21, 1867, rpt. in *Literary Criticism: Essays on Literature, American Writers; English Writers*, ed. Leon Edel. New York: Library of America, 1984.

Kasson, John F. *Rudeness and Civility: Manners in Nineteenth-Century Urban America*. New York: Hill and Wang, 1990.

Kay, Donald. "Herman Melville's Literary Relationship with Evert Duyckinck." *College Language Association Journal* 18 (1975): 339–53.

Kelley, Mary. *Private Woman, Public Stage: Literary Domesticity in Nineteenth-Century America*. Oxford: Oxford University Press, 1984.

Kleinfield, Herbert L. "Irving: As Seen Through His Letters." In *Washington Irving: A Tribute,* ed. Andrew B. Myers. Tarrytown, N.Y.: Sleepy Hollow Restorations, 1972. 61–75.

LaFavour, Cree. "'*Jane Eyre* Fever': Deciphering the Astonishing Popular Success of Charlotte Brontë in Antebellum America." *Book History* 7 (2004): 113–41.

Langford, Gerald. *The Richard Harding Davis Years: A Biography of a Mother and Son.* New York: Holt, Rinehart, and Winston, 1961.

Laskin, David. *A Common Life: Four Generations of American Literary Friendship and Influence.* New York: Simon and Schuster, 1994.

Lazar, David. "On Mentorship." *Ohio Review* 5 (1994): 25–33.

Leslie, C. R. *Autobiographical Recollections, Vol. II,* ed. Tom Taylor. London: John Murray, 1860.

Leyda, Jay, ed. *The Melville Log, vols. I–II.* New York: Gordian Press, 1969.

London, Bette. *Writing Double: Women's Literary Partnerships.* Ithaca, N.Y.: Cornell University Press, 1999.

Long, Lisa A. "The Postbellum Reform Writings of Rebecca Harding Davis and Elizabeth Stuart Phelps." In *The Cambridge Companion to Nineteenth-Century Women's Writing,* ed. Dale M. Bauer and Philip Gould. New York: Cambridge University Press, 2001.

Looby, Christopher. "Southworth and Seriality: *The Hidden Hand* in the *New York Ledger.*" *Nineteenth-Century Literature* 59.2 (2004): 179–211.

Lynn, Kenneth S. *Hemingway.* New York: Simon and Schuster, 1987.

Lyons, Paul. "Melville and His Precursors: Style as Metastyle and Allusion." *American Literature* 62 (1990): 450–62.

Lysaker, John T., and William Rossi, eds. *Emerson and Thoreau: Figures of Friendship.* Bloomington: University of Indiana Press, 2010.

Marchalonis, Shirley, ed. *Patrons and Protégées: Gender, Friendship, and Writing in Nineteenth-Century America.* New Brunswick, N.J.: Rutgers University Press, 1988.

McClary, Ben Harris, ed. *Washington Irving and the House of Murray: Geoffrey Crayon Charms the British, 1817–1856.* Knoxville: University of Tennessee Press, 1969.

———. "Irving's Literary Pimpery." *American Notes and Queries* 10 (1972): 150–51.

Mellow, James R. *Hemingway: A Life without Consequences.* Boston: Houghton Mifflin, 1992.

Melville, Herman. *Correspondence,* ed. Lynn Horth. Evanston, Ill.: Northwestern University Press, 1993.

———. "Hawthorne and His Mosses." In *The Piazza Tales and Other Prose Pieces,* ed. Harrison Hayford, Alma A. MacDougall, and G. Thomas Tanselle. Evanston, Ill.: Northwestern University Press, 1987. 239–53.

———. *Moby-Dick; or, The Whale,* ed. Harrison Hayford, Hershel Parker, and G. Thomas Tanselle. Evanston, Ill.: Northwestern University Press, 1988.

———. *Pierre; or The Ambiguities,* ed. Harrison Hayford, Hershel Parker, and G. Thomas Tanselle. Evanston, Ill.: Chicago: Northwestern University Press, 1971.

———. "Rip Van Winkle's Lilac." In *A Century of Commentary on the Works of Washington Irving, 1860–1974,* ed. Andrew B. Myers. Tarrytown, N.Y.: Sleepy Hollow Restorations, 1976.

———. *White Jacket,* ed. Harrison Hayford, Hershel Parker, and G. Thomas Tanselle. Evanston, Ill.: Northwestern University Press, 1970.

Menand, Louis. "The Lives of Others: The Biography Business." *New Yorker,* August 6, 2007, 64–66.

Merish, Lori. *Sentimental Materialism: Gender, Commodity Culture, and Nineteenth-Century American Literature.* Durham, N.C.: Duke University Press, 2000.

Merton, Thomas. *Sierra* 93.1 (January–February 2008): 24.

Metzler, Milton, and Walter Harding. *A Thoreau Profile.* New York: Thomas Y. Crowell Co., 1962.

Milder, Robert. *Exiled Royalties: Melville and the Life We Imagine.* Oxford: Oxford University Press, 2007.

Miller, Perry. *The Raven and the Whale: Poe, Melville, and the New York Literary Scene.* Baltimore: Johns Hopkins University Press, 1997.

Mock, Michele L. "'An Ardor That Was Human, and a Power That Was Art': Rebecca Harding Davis and the Art of the Periodical." In *The Only Efficient Instrument: American Women Writers and the Periodical, 1837–1916,* ed. Aleta Feinsod Cane and Susan Alves. Iowa City: University of Iowa Press, 2001.

Moore, Arlene. "The Letters of Harriet and Leon Lewis to Robert Bonner." *Dime Novel Roundup* 61.1 (1992): 2–7.

Moss, William. "'So Many Promising Youths': Emerson's Disappointing Discoveries of New England Poet-Seers." *New England Quarterly* 49.1 (1976): 46–64.

Mott, Frank Luther. *A History of American Magazines, Vol. II: 1850–1865.* Cambridge, Mass.: Harvard University Press, 1938.

Moulton, William. *The Life and Beauties of Fanny Fern.* New Haven, Conn.: Research Publications, 1975 (rpt. 1855 ed.).

Noble, Marianne. *The Masochistic Pleasures of Sentimental Literature.* Princeton, N.J.: Princeton University Press, 2000.

Noel, Mary. *Villains Galore: The Hey-Day of the Popular Story Weekly.* New York: Macmillan, 1954.

Okker, Patricia. *Social Stories: The Magazine Novel in Nineteenth-Century America.* Charlottesville: University of Virginia Press, 2003.

Olsen, Tillie. "A Biographical Interpretation." In *Life in the Iron Mills and Other Stories,* ed. Tillie Olsen. Old Westbury, N.Y.: Feminist Press, 1985. 69–174.

Ozick, Cynthia. "A Youthful Intoxication." *New York Times Book Review*, December 10, 2006, 35.

Pancost, David. "How Washington Irving Published *The Sketch Book* in England." *Studies in American Fiction* 14.1 (1986): 81.

Papashvily, Helen Waite. *All the Happy Endings: A Study of the Domestic Novel in America, the Women Who Wrote It, the Women Who Read It, in the Nineteenth Century*. New York: Harper Brothers, 1956.

Parker, Hershel. *Herman Melville: A Biography (Volume 1, 1819–1851)*. Baltimore: Johns Hopkins University Press, 1996.

———. "*The Isle of the Cross* and *Poems:* Lost Melville Books and the Indefinite Afterlife of Error." *Nineteenth-Century Literature* 62.1 (2007): 29–47.

Parton, James. *Fanny Fern: A Memorial Volume*. New York: Carleton, 1874.

Peterson, Charles J. Editorial. *Ladies' National Magazine* 3 (April 1843): 128.

Pfaelzer, Jean. *Parlor Radical: Rebecca Harding Davis and the Origins of American Social Realism*. Pittsburgh: University of Pittsburgh Press, 1997.

Pochman, Henry A. "Washington Irving: Amateur or Professional?" In *A Century of Commentary on the Works of Washington Irving*, ed. Andrew B. Meyers. Tarrytown, N.Y.: Sleepy Hollow Restorations, 1976. 425–35.

Porte, Joel. *Emerson and Thoreau: Transcendentalists in Conflict*. Middletown, Conn.: Wesleyan University Press, 1965.

Post-Lauria, Sheila. *Correspondent Colorings: Melville in the Marketplace*. Amherst: University of Massachusetts Press, 1996.

Pratt, Mary Louise. *Travel Writing and Transculturation*. New York: Routledge, 1992.

Putnam, Robert D. *Bowling Alone: The Collapse and Revival of American Community*. New York: Simon and Schuster, 2000.

Rainey, Lawrence. *Institutions of Modernism: Literary Elites and Public Culture*. New Haven, Conn.: Yale University Press, 1998.

Remer, Rosalind. *Printers and Men of Capital: Philadelphia Book Publishers in the New Republic*. Philadelphia: University of Pennsylvania Press, 1996.

Review of "A Modern Lettre de Cachet." *Medical and Surgical Reporter* (May 30, 1868): 18–22.

Review of *The Sketch Book*. In *British Critic* 14 (1820): 514–25.

Reynolds, David S. *Beneath the American Renaissance: The Subversive Imagination in the Age of Emerson and Melville*. Cambridge, Mass.: Harvard University Press, 1989.

Reynolds, Michael. *Hemingway: The American Homecoming*. Oxford: Blackwell, 1992.

Rice, S. Grantland. *The Transformation of Authorship in America*. Chicago: University of Chicago Press, 1997.

Robbins, Sarah. "Gendering Gilded Age Periodical Professionalism: Reading

Harriet Beecher Stowe's *Hearth and Home* Prescriptions for Women's Writing." In *The Only Efficient Instrument: American Women Writers and the Periodical, 1837–1916*, ed. Aleta Feinsod Cane and Susan Alves. Iowa City: University of Iowa Press, 2001. 45–65.

Robertson-Lorant, Laurie. *Melville: A Biography.* Amherst: University of Massachusetts Press, 1996.

Roiphe, Katie. *Uncommon Arrangements: Seven Portraits of Married Life in London Literary Circles, 1910–1939.* New York: Dial Press, 2007.

Rose, Jane Atteridge. "The Artist Manque in the Fiction of Rebecca Harding Davis." In *Writing the Woman Artist*, ed. Suzanne W. Jones. Philadelphia: University of Pennsylvania Press, 1991.

Rubin-Dorsky, Jeffrey. "Washington Irving and the Genesis of the Fictional Sketch." *Early American Literature* 21 (1987): 226–47.

Ryan, Dennis. "Dating Hemingway's Early Style/Parsing Gertrude Stein's Modernism." *Journal of American Studies* 29.2 (1995): 239.

Sattelmeyer, Robert. "'When He Became My Enemy': Emerson and Thoreau, 1848–49." *New England Quarterly* 62.2 (1989): 187–204.

Scandura, Terri A., and Belle Rose Ragins. "The Effects of Sex and Gender Role Orientation on Mentorship in Male-Dominated Occupations." *Journal of Vocational Behavior* 43.3 (1993): 251–65.

Sellers, Charles. *The Market Revolution: Jacksonian America, 1815–1846.* Oxford: Oxford University Press, 1996.

Shaffer, Helen Woodward. "Rebecca Harding Davis: Pioneer Realist." Ph.D. dissertation, University of Pennsylvania, 1947.

Sharp, Michael D. *Contemporary Popular Writers.* Tarrytown, N.Y.: Marshall Cavendish, 2005.

Simon, Linda. *The Biography of Alice B. Toklas.* Garden City, N.Y.: Doubleday, 1977.

Smith, Adam. *Theory of Moral Sentiments.* London: Cadell and Davies, 1854.

Smith, Harmon. *My Friend, My Friend: The Story of Thoreau's Relationship with Emerson.* Amherst: University of Massachusetts Press, 1999.

Sondey, Walter. "From Nation of Virtue to Virtual Nation: Washington Irving and American Nationalism." In *Narratives of Nostalgia, Gender, and Nationalism*, ed. Jean Pickering and Suzanne Kehde. Washington Square: New York University Press, 1997. 54–65.

Southworth, E. D. E. N. *The Artist's Love.* Philadelphia: T. B. Peterson, 1872.

———. *The Deserted Wife.* Philadelphia: T. B. Peterson and Brothers, 1855.

———. *The Hidden Hand; or, Capitola the Madcap.* New York: G. W. Dillingham, 1888 (rpt. 1859 ed.).

———. *The Lost Heiress.* Philadelphia: T. B. Peterson, 1854.

Stadler, Gustavus. *Troubling Minds: The Cultural Politics of Genius in the United States, 1840–1890.* Minneapolis: University of Minnesota Press, 2006.

Steele, Jeffrey. "Transcendental Friendship: Emerson, Fuller, and Thoreau." In *The Cambridge Companion to Ralph Waldo Emerson*, ed. Joel Porte and Saundra Morris. New York: Cambridge University Press, 1999. 121–36.

Stein, Gertrude. *The Autobiography of Alice B. Toklas*. London: Zephyr Books, 1947.

Stiller, Jack. *Multiple Authorship and the Myth of the Solitary Genius*. Oxford: Oxford University Press, 1991.

Stoner, Ruth. "Rebecca Harding Davis's 'Second Life'; or 'Her Hands could be Trained as Well as His.'" *Legacy* 19.1 (2002): 44–52.

Sundquist, Eric. "Introduction." In *American Realism: New Essays*, ed. Eric Sundquist. Baltimore: Johns Hopkins University Press, 1982. 1–14.

Tebbel, John. *Between Covers: The Rise and Transformation of Book Publishing in America*. New York: Oxford University Press, 1987.

Thoreau, Henry David. *A Week on the Concord and Merrimack Rivers*, ed. Carl F. Hovde Princeton, N.J.: Princeton University Press, 1980.

———. *Huckleberries*, ed. Leo Stoller. Iowa City: Windover Press, 1970.

———. *Journal*, vols. 1–6, ed. John C. Broderick et al. Princeton, N.J.: Princeton University Press, 1981–2000.

———. *The Correspondence of Henry David Thoreau*, ed. Carl Bode. Baltimore: Johns Hopkins University Press, 1958.

———. *The Writings of Henry David Thoreau*. Boston: Houghton Mifflin, 1906.

———. *Walden*, ed. J. Lyndon Shanley. Princeton, N.J.: Princeton University Press, 1971.

Tonkovich, Nicole. *Domesticity with a Difference: The Nonfiction of Catharine Beecher, Sarah J. Hale, Fanny Fern, and Margaret Fuller*. Jackson: University Press of Mississippi, 1997.

Traubel, Horace. *With Walt Whitman in Camden*. Boston: Small, Maynard, 1906.

Urbanski, Marie. "Henry David Thoreau and Margaret Fuller." *Thoreau Journal Quarterly* 8.4 (1976): 24–29.

Wagenknecht, Edward. *Washington Irving: Moderation Displayed*. New York: Oxford University Press, 1962.

Warren, Joyce. *Fanny Fern: An Independent Woman*. New Brunswick, N.J.: Rutgers University Press, 1994.

———. *Women, Money, and the Law: Nineteenth-Century Fiction, Gender, and the Courts*. Iowa City: University of Iowa Press, 2005.

Weinstein, Cindy. *Family, Kinship, and Sympathy in Nineteenth-Century American Literature*. New York: Cambridge University Press, 2004.

Weisbuch, Robert. *Atlantic Doublecross: American Literature and British Influence in the Age of Emerson*. Chicago: University of Chicago Press, 1986.

Wells, Daniel A. "'Bartleby the Scrivener,' Poe, and the Duyckinck Circle." *ESQ: A Journal of the American Renaissance* 21 (1975): 33–50.

Welty, Eudora. "The House of Willa Cather." In *The Eye of the Story: Selected Essays and Reviews.* New York: Vintage, 1979.

Wexler, Joyce Piell. *Who Paid for Modernism? Art, Money, and the Fiction of Conrad, Joyce, and Lawrence.* Fayetteville: University of Arkansas Press, 1997.

Widmer, Edward L. *Young America: The Flowering of Democracy in New York City.* Oxford: Oxford University Press, 1999.

Williams, Stanley T. *The Life of Washington Irving.* Vol. 1. New York: Oxford University Press, 1935.

Williams, Susan S. "Authors and Literary Authorship." In *A History of the Book in America, Vol. 3, The Industrial Book, 1840–1880.* Chapel Hill: University of North Carolina Press, 2007. 91–116.

———. *Reclaiming Authorship: Literary Women in America, 1850–1900.* Philadelphia: University of Pennsylvania Press, 2006.

Willis, Nathaniel Parker. *Poems of Early and After Years.* Philadelphia: Carey and Hart, 1848.

———. *The Romance of Travel.* New York: S. Coleman, 1840.

Wilson, R. Jackson. *Figures of Speech: American Writers and the Literary Marketplace from Benjamin Franklin to Emily Dickinson.* Baltimore: Johns Hopkins University Press, 1990.

Yanella, Donald, and Kathleen Malone Yanella. "Evert A. Duyckinck's Diary: May 29–November 8, 1847." In *Studies in the American Renaissance, 1978,* ed. Joel Myerson. Boston: Twayne Publishers, 1978. 230–48.

Zboray, Ronald J. *A Fictive People: Antebellum Economic Development and the American Reading Public.* New York: Oxford University Press, 1993.

Zboray, Ronald J., and Mary Saracino Zboray. *Literary Dollars and Social Sense: A People's History of the Mass Market Book.* New York: Routledge, 2005.

Index